DATE DUE

Walking, Literature, and English Culture

The Origins and
Uses of Peripatetic
in the Nineteenth Century

ANNE D. WALLACE

CLARENDON PRESS · OXFORD

Oxford University Press, Walton Street, Oxford OX2 6DP
Oxford   New York   Toronto
Delhi   Bombay   Calcutta   Madras   Karachi
Kuala Lumpur   Singapore   Hong Kong   Tokyo
Nairobi   Dar es Salaam   Cape Town
Melbourne   Auckland   Madrid
and associated companies in
Berlin   Ibadan

Oxford is a trade mark of Oxford University Press

Published in the United States
by Oxford University Press Inc., New York

First published 1993
First published in Clarendon Paperback 1994

British Library Cataloguing in Publication Data
Data available

Library of Congress Cataloging in Publication Data
Wallace, Anne D.
Walking, literature, and English culture : the origins and uses of
peripatetic in the nineteenth century / Anne D. Wallace.
Includes bibliographical references and index.
1. English literature—19th century—History and criticism.
2. Walking—England—History—19th century.   3. England—
Civilization—19th century.   4. Walking in literature.   I. Title.
PR468.W35W34   1993
820.9'355—dc20   92-32637
ISBN 0–19–818328–3

Printed in Great Britain
on acid-free paper by
Biddles Ltd.
Guildford and King's Lynn

for Sarah

Acknowledgements

THE first version of this book was my dissertation, and so my first thanks must be to the University of Texas at Austin for its sustained intellectual and financial support during my doctoral programme. The libraries of both the University of Texas and the University of Kansas, with their superb collections and unfailingly helpful staffs, provided that indispensable aid and comfort available only in great university libraries.

Parts of chapters 2 and 3 appeared in *Texas Studies in Literature and Language* 34:4 (Winter 1992), 509–540, and are reprinted by permission of the University of Texas Press. Excerpts from 'Setting Out' and 'Returning' from *Collected Poems* copyright © 1982, 1984 by Wendell Berry, published by North Point Press and reprinted by permission of Farrar, Straus & Giroux, Inc.

I deeply appreciate my teachers' time and thought and care. Kurt Heinzelman not only taught me about georgic but showed me how to read my own prose. The steady, encouraging pressure of his analysis and his fine eye/ear for language have helped transform my thinking and writing about literature. Carol MacKay, so quick to apprehend context, helped situate peripatetic in Victorian literature; Joseph Moldenhauer's precise attention to textual history kept the particulars of Wordsworth's and Thoreau's work in view; and Lee Fontanella and Juan Lopez-Morillas will hear the work we did in their seminars, kept fresh in talks over the years, resonating in these pages.

Of the many others who helped me find both words and heart to write, I am especially indebted to Terry Moore, George Worth, Daryl Palmer, Cindy Patton, and Richard Sha. To Rod Runyan, for all he gave, unutterable thanks.

My parents, Douglass Stuart Wallace and Virginia Vogel Wallace, did everything in their power to make me financially and emotionally free. Absent and present, they anchor my life by their labour and love.

A.D.W.

Hattiesburg, Mississippi
1992

Contents

Standard References

A L L quotations from Virgil's *Georgics* are taken from L. P. Wilkinson's translation (Harmondsworth: Penguin, 1982) and are indicated in the text by book and line numbers.

Quotations from William Wordsworth's poetry are drawn from the following sources, and are also indicated by book and/or line numbers. Wherever possible, I have chosen early versions of the poems so that I can read them as they were during the crucial period between the 1780s and 1830s when attitudes toward and practice of walking began to change.

For *The Excursion, The Poetical Works of William Wordsworth*, ed. Ernest de Selincourt and Helen Darbishire, vol. v (Oxford: Clarendon Press, 1949). (Occasional references to this edition are indicated by *PW* followed by volume and page number.)

For *The Prelude*, the 1805 text in *The Prelude, 1799, 1805, 1850*, ed. Jonathan Wordsworth, M. H. Abrams, and Stephen Gill (New York and London: Norton, 1979).

For all other poems, unless otherwise indicated, *William Wordsworth*, ed. Stephen Gill (Oxford and New York: Oxford University Press, 1984).

Quotations from John Clare's poetry and prose are drawn from *John Clare*, ed. Eric Robinson and David Powell (Oxford and New York: Oxford University Press, 1984), with poetry cited by line number and prose by page number.

In all quotations I have retained the source's spelling and punctuation, even where that would now be considered irregular.

Introduction

ON the evening of 4 July 1983, my friend and I stood at the top of Silver How, looking out over the vale of Grasmere toward Windermere in the distant south-east and Churn-milk Force nearer on the west, watching the setting sun ignite the grey clouds with faint, quickly flaring and fading pink. Our small adventure exhilarated us to sleeplessness that night: it was our first long walk together, our first time in the Lakes, our first time in England. She climbed the fell because she was my friend, I because I was 're-searching' (how I laughed at that then!) the paper required by our enrolment in the University of Kansas Summer Institute in Great Britain. I regarded my topic, 'Walking in Wordsworth's Poetry', mostly as an excuse to read Wordsworth, to see Grasmere, and to walk to Rydal and to Easedale Tarn, and I anticipated writing a somewhat impressionistic paper that would help me sort out some things about Wordsworth.

But, being a conscientious student, despite my summery lapses, I did try to research the topic and discovered a disturbing inter-pretative gap. There were books that talked about where Words-worth walked and what poems were connected with what walks, but none that considered walking as a crucial metaphorical or narrative structure in his poetry. There seemed to be no general commentary on walking in literature either; I had at that time found just one historical account of literary walkers, Morris Marples's *Shanks's Pony* (1959), and no histories of walking itself that might shed some peripheral light on the subject. Yet as I read on, I became convinced by the number and quality of Wordsworth's walking poems that they were indeed somehow significant: his first two published poems, both of the completed portions of his projected philosophical masterpiece *The Recluse*, and dozens of shorter poems including 'Michael', 'Resolution and Independence', 'The Solitary Reaper', 'The Old Cumberland Beggar', and the Salisbury Plain poems, have pedestrian narrators or characters and/or walking 'plots'. Even if walking's initial importance in his texts was 'merely' biographical, the represented action plainly took on further importance as he wrote. And the more I thought over what I knew of nineteenth-century British literature, the more walking episodes I could think of, in Austen, in Dickens, in Coleridge, in the Brontës. Frustrated, I wondered why no one was reading the walking in Wordsworth, or the rest of nineteenth-century literature, and began to try to read it myself. In the course of this reading I have discovered more companions than in my first limited search. Kim Taplin's brief but rich literary and historical study of *The English Path* (1979) points to crucial sources of information and to writings about walking I might not otherwise have discovered. Jeffrey Robinson's *The Walk: Notes on a Romantic Image* (1989) catalogues an even broader spectrum of texts and offers helpful interpretations of pedestrian activity in several, including Dickens's essay 'Night Walks' and John Clare's poetry, that I will consider at some length. A number of readers, including John Elder, Ellen Moers, Laurie Langbauer, Raymond Williams, Meena Alexander, and Sandra Gilbert and Susan Gubar, focus more briefly on pedestrian action in literature, and their comments and interpretations have stimulated and often redirected my own project. And, since the completion of this manuscript, Roger Gilbert's *Walks in the World* has contributed an articulation of 'the walk poem as a genre' which contends that 'the walk uniquely answers the various and often incompatible impulses to redefine and remake poetic representation that have guided American poets over the last century'.[1] There may be others with whose work I simply have not connected: the fact that walking has not been an important object of scrutiny means that it has generated no scholarly indexes, very few references in individual book indexes, and few library subject entries.

For the most part, however, walking in literature remains unread. Even those interpreters who identify walking as an important metaphorical and narrative structure tend to produce partial readings that attribute remarkable effects to pedestrian action—intimate knowledge of the walker's environment, the recovery of memory and past values, enhanced creative expression—but leave us unsure as to why walking, the specific physical process, should be able to produce those effects. These varieties of non-reading became particularly disturbing to me when I realized that they

[1] Roger Gilbert, *Walks in the World: Representation and Experience in Modern American Poetry* (Princeton, NJ: Princeton University Press, 1991), 4.

represented unexplored layers of historical attitudes that are still invoked, in various odd combinations, in popular contemporary writings about walking.

Readers overlook walking in literature for several reasons. The most common difficulty is something I call 'falling up', moving immediately from the material terms of the text into the immaterial, the ideological or psychological or whatever, and then staying in abstraction without closely examining the image or plot movement or other material representation which generated that extended meaning. In the case of interpreting walking, 'falling up' has two related causes (beyond the rage for grand interpretation which fosters the more general problem). The first appears to be simple not-seeing: walking vanishes because it is too common to notice. The extended meanings of 'pedestrian'—boring, commonplace, unimportant—express the famous contempt bred of familiarity, which in literary interpretation simply effaces the text's statement that walking is going on. Raymond Williams, for instance, devotes an entire chapter of *The Country and the City* to 'The Figure in the City' from whose perspective we see the urban landscape and says that 'from the beginning' this figure has been 'a man walking, as if alone, in its streets'.[2] Despite the fact that this person is positively walking and only seemingly alone, Williams's subsequent discussion never considers 'walking', focusing instead on 'alone', taking us immediately away from the physical to the psychological terms of perception.

To read walking as travel compounds this tendency by permitting direct access to the extensive life-as-journey motif, which the reader then moves into without considering the implications of any specific mode of travel. That is, seeing 'walking', the person reads 'travel'. M. H. Abrams tells us that Wordsworth's 'literal journeys' in *The Prelude* 'modulate easily into symbolic landscapes traversed by a metaphorical wayfarer'.[3] Abrams himself finds this modulation so easy that, despite his recognition that these journeys are not only many and symmetrically disposed, but specifically pedestrian, he pays no attention to the repetition of walking itself (or, for the most part, to the physical terms of travel

[2] Raymond Williams, *The Country and the City* (London: Chatto & Windus, 1973), 231.
[3] M. H. Abrams, *Natural Supernaturalism: Tradition and Revolution in Romantic Literature* (New York: Norton, 1971), 285.

in general), but flies directly into the extended meanings of the journeys as education, self-discovery, and so forth. Similarly, Simon Gatrell, whose essay on Hardy as a 'Travelling Man' handles a goodly amount of Hardy's poetry in an otherwise very satisfying fashion, identifies walking as 'the most usual form of [Hardy's] journeying' in his second paragraph, praising it as a mode which 'leads to an active and intimate contact with the environment and so can serve as the frame of his observations'.[4] Despite this comment, and despite the fact that the travel in his opening and closing examples (and most of those in between) is decidedly pedestrian, Gatrell then treats travel metaphorically without any further attempt to explain why walking should be the usual form of travel in Hardy, or how it 'leads to' this remarkable 'contact with the environment'.

Gatrell's brief characterization of walking exemplifies another variety of not-reading in which the interpreter reads walking as walking but reads it formulaically, simply restating, usually quite briefly, some portion of this assumed principle: because walking is natural, slow, successive yet continuous movement, it stimulates/ represents superior perception, cognition, and narration. Most often the reader names this superiority, as Gatrell does, as intimacy with (usually natural) environment, claiming its physical source in direct contact with the earth and its literary extension in the representation of particularized or localized detail. Very often (Gatrell does this too) the reader pulls textual walking back into authorial walking, so that consideration of a figure in the text merges insensibly into consideration of the process of composition.

In straightforward biography the problem becomes clearer. Michael Millgate talks about the young Hardy becoming 'familiar with the occupants of every cottage, the name of every field and every gate, the profile of every tree, the depth and temperament of every pond and stream' because Hardy travelled mostly on foot, and describes Hardy's series of walks in south-west England before the composition of *Tess of the D'Urbervilles* as 'part of a deliberate process of thinking himself into the social as well as the emotional texture of his new story, of invoking that sense of historical time and visitable place which provided the essential

---

[4] Simon Gatrell, 'Travelling Man', in Patricia Clements and Juliet Grindle (ed.), *The Poetry of Thomas Hardy* (n.p.: Vision, 1980), 155.

underpinning for his most ambitious imaginative enterprises'.[5] A number of questions occur: if walking does indeed operate on the author in this marvellous educative fashion and affects his expression so powerfully, how does it function in his texts? How do we know that this intimate knowledge is in fact the effect of Hardy *walking*? Why should we regard pedestrian perception and knowledge as superior?

John Elder's *Imagining the Earth: Poetry and the Vision of Nature* (1985) includes a chapter on Wordsworth and Basho called 'The Footpath of Tradition' which, by attempting to 'focus . . . on those passages [in *The Prelude*] referring directly to the poet's physical path over the earth', produces an unusually lucid account of walking as 'a process of reconciliation' between past and present, body and earth, life and death, linearity and cycle, which 'provides the dynamic unity of [Wordsworth's] life'.[6] If my own readings are accurate, Wordsworth's poetry does indeed show walking accomplishing just such reconciliation, and in more areas than Elder identifies. But Elder does more than argue that walking performs this way in Wordsworth's texts. Like Gatrell and Millgate, he implies that walking actually functions this way for the poet, not just for Wordsworth but for Basho and Ammons and others.

The opening paragraph of Elder's chapter demonstrates what I mean:

Just as the wasteland and the wilderness are reconciled through earth's circuit of soil-building decay, the landscape and the imagination may be united through the process of walking. The mind's flicker of attention from the earth to its own associations seems on one level to have an inescapably binary quality. But mental sunlight and clouds are also borne out under a larger sky in the meandering circuit of the poet's walk. Walking becomes an emblem of wholeness, comprehending both the person's conscious steps and pauses and the path beneath his rising and falling feet.[7]

The wording of the last point—'walking becomes an emblem'— seems to indicate something that happens in a text, which is what Elder then declares he will demonstrate happening in Wordsworth

[5] Michael Millgate, *Thomas Hardy* (Oxford and New York: Oxford University Press, 1985), 293.

[6] John Elder, *Imagining the Earth: Poetry and the Vision of Nature* (Urbana and Chicago: University of Illinois Press, 1985), 93, 97.

[7] Ibid. 93.

and Basho. But what walking becomes an emblem of is 'whole-ness', the wholeness of the person walking with the land he walks on. Where does this emblem become? In 'the poet's walk'. And why does it become? Because 'the landscape and the imagination may be united through the process of walking'—that is, Words-worth can make walking into an emblem of wholeness because that's how walking works for 'the poet', as a connective mecha-nism between all of these various states of being. Notice, too, that Elder rhetorically equates this connective mechanism with the natural process of vegetation decaying toward soil, so that walking's uniting of landscape and imagination appears (despite the tenta-tive intervention of 'may') as an inevitable, natural result of the action. This seems to draw textual walking back not just into an individual author's practice but into a hypothetical general authorial practice of walking, the positive effects of which appear to be assumed a priori.

Elder's appeal to some generally understood practice is not in error: the popular understanding of walking's function in experi-ence ranges along just the lines described by literary interpreta-tion. The negative assumption of ordinariness—ordinariness as fault—appears in the absence of histories of walking, in the cult of the car, and in the attitudes of some non-walkers toward walkers (I speak here from personal experience). Certainly the positive assumptions about pedestrian perception and expression, deriving in part from seeing walking as educative travel, were my assump-tions when I went to the Lakes that summer: by walking I would get to 'know' Wordsworth's home ground, become a better reader of and writer about Wordsworth, and even (the thought did lurk there, I admit), maybe, a better poet myself. I didn't think much about those assumptions at the time, nor, apparently, do most people. Magazines from *Modern Maturity* to *Kansas Wildlife* offer advice on where and how to walk without bothering to talk much about why we might want to walk, while Patricia Edwards Bleyle tells us in the July 1988 issue of *Ms.* that she regards walking as a possible form of psychotherapy because it can help 'give you a better perception of reality, shore up your courage, and awaken your senses'. Although differently directed, Bleyle's account of the origin of these changes closely resembles Elder's: she defines her 'walking cure' as 'the sustained and regular rhythm of solitary movement through the countryside', and talks about the importance

of sensation, particularly the sense of the feet on the ground—
'grounded cultivation', as Elder calls such projects in his book's
introduction. The results of this sensational continuity, too, are
familiar. When we walk 'In the unspoiled solitude' of beaches or
fields, Bleyle tells us,

we gain a sense of oneness with nature. . . . we restore our sanity, and
serenity seeps in. Our perspective changes as the self, such a cosmic speck
in comparison with our surroundings, is more easily transcended. In
silent, open spaces, our unproductive thinking becomes apparent. And
[quoting Thoreau's 'Walking'] 'there will be so much more air and sunshine in our thoughts . . .' (pp. 24, 25)

In this popular guide to psychotherapeutic walking, as in Elder's
description of walking in Wordsworth's poetry, pedestrian action
produces intimacy with nature, fosters a 'better perception of
reality', makes us think better, allows us to transcend ourselves
but also, clearly, to be more fully ourselves.

An article by Noel Grove on the Appalachian Trail, in the
February 1987 issue of the *National Geographic*, comes even
closer to Elder's description of reconciliative walking:

Except for the propane, cameras, and Gore-tex fabrics, the scene [at a
trail-side shelter] could have been cut from this nation's infancy. Foot
travelers meeting, sharing shelter, exchanging food, information, and
nicknames. In an era of office highrises they had walked back in time
through a tunnel of green . . . [quoting a former Duke University chaplain
now living near the Trail:] 'Most are people at some transitional point in
their lives—divorce, job change, or just self-discovery . . . It's a pilgrimage
not unlike those made in the Middle Ages. Thru-hikers emphasize self-
reliance and simplicity—basic pioneer virtues rarely practiced in this country
any more.' (pp. 234–5)

Here we see walkers not only re-creating themselves but going
back in time—and to what an astonishing temporal location! They
return simultaneously to a world filled with the green of wild
vegetation, to 'this nation's infancy' when 'basic pioneer virtues'—
not just 'self-reliance and simplicity' but communality and generosity too—were the norm, and to a time somehow also like the
Middle Ages (we assume in piety). When/where was this? More to
the point, can we get there too? Of course, descriptions like this
assert: anyone who goes walking, preferably over a long stretch of
relatively natural ground, will reconnect with his own past and his

nation's past, indeed with the human race's ideal past as he imagines and longs for it.

My point is not that these walkers are daft, or even that this
account of walking is fantastic (although 'walking as time machine'
is amazing, when you think about it). I am a walker myself, and
have also felt that lifting of daily cares, that recentring in myself
and yet extension into outer world, that flood of memory, even
that sense of participation in some past time. So I felt when I
walked up Silver How. But I have read Wordsworth and the
National Geographic and Tolkien (remember the Nine Walkers
set against the Nine Black Riders?); I am part of a culture—
English-speaking, technologically developed—in which received
opinion about walking includes the expectation of such benefits.
My question is not whether walking 'actually works' this way but
why we believe it does, what factors those beliefs are based on,
and how they are bound to our understanding of time, memory,
change, self and world, past and present, nature and technology,
and to the values generated by such understandings. I wish to
focus on how the figure of walking operates in literature, not only
because literature is my own special passion but because our most
optimistic expectations of walking derive from very particular
literary sources: Wordsworth's extension of the georgic mode into
a previously unrecognized literary mode that I name 'peripatetic',
and a body of essays about walking written throughout the
nineteenth century that work to explicate Wordsworthian peripatetic as ideology. But I also wish to ground the development of
those literary and ideological expectations in the material history
of the time, a project which will indicate the importance of reading
peripatetic to an understanding of our past and present attitudes
toward technological development.

I have not worked toward this grounding by generating intensely particularized histories of relatively small temporal spaces
and/or single texts. Instead, my approach is deliberately broad,
aimed at representing the long flow of several histories that
converged in peripatetic and the range of texts that make use of
the mode, to the end of making its aesthetic and ideological
functions visible. One might imagine a retelling of Wordsworth's
walk to Easedale Tarn on the day he composed 'My Heart Leaps
Up', or a rereading of the poem as peripatetic, re-encompassing
the walk's/poem's domestic, economic, and political implications.

But such an approach seems premature to me. The current significance of peripatetic lies in its simultaneous widespread use and
critical invisibility as literary mode/material practice: it remains a
functional but unrecognized mediation of our continuing encounters
with technology, speed, and change, contributing to the unwitting
perpetuation of Romantic ideology. The first order of business,
it seems to me, is a general survey of the material and literary
conditions long obscured by traditional contempt for the practice
of walking and by the nineteenth-century dehistoricization of
Wordsworthian peripatetic's origins. For the same reason, my eye
remains on peripatetic as a mode, rather than on the plenitude of
other possibilities in individual texts that use peripatetic, and my
readings of those texts are directed by my concern for the explication of the mode itself.

Readers of this study should also be aware that although I value
Marxist, specifically cultural materialist critiques, as must be
evident from my engagement with readings by Raymond Williams
and John Barrell, I am not performing such a critique myself. I
understand the politics of peripatetic as becoming manifest through
(not as prior to but as congruent with) its aesthetic claims, claims
which do indeed obscure or rewrite class conflicts in ways that
must draw our attentive concern and questioning. I say very little,
however, of the political revolutions of the late eighteenth and
nineteenth centuries, and speak generally, with the exception of
my attention to the mechanization of transport, of the other much-
analysed revolution of the period, industrialization. Instead, as the
following summary indicates, I focus on the articulation of peripatetic as a solution to the aesthetic problems connected with—
both generating and generated by—the transport revolution and
enclosure. As we shall see, such an articulation does indeed inter-
rogate peripatetic's political agendas. Its primary purpose in this
study, however, remains the explication of the less overtly political
manifestations of these pressures on representations and practices
of travel, walking, farming, and everyday rural life.

The varieties of non-reading discussed above describe a genea-
logy of writings about walking, with a significant shift from negative
representations to positive: walking not written; 'walking' written
as 'travel', suppressing its specific material mode; walking written
as travel in the positive educative sense, and as a reconciliative
or connective activity of remarkable range, capable of positively

affecting communities as well as single individuals. This shift takes place in England in the first few decades of the nineteenth century in congruence with ongoing material changes that caused or permitted changes in the material and ideological shape of walking. One of these was the transport revolution beginning in the mid-eighteenth century, which, by the early nineteenth century, affected walking in several ways. First, it altered the socio-economic content of walking by making fast, cheap travel available to the labouring classes, thus increasing the attractiveness of travel in general and removing walking's long-standing implication of necessity and so of poverty and vagrancy. Second, by making the attainment of distant destinations relatively easy, and by multiplying the variety of speeds (and so perceptual frameworks) available to the traveller, the transport revolution fostered a shift in the traveller's attention from destination to process. These changes made it possible to regard walking as a deliberately selected mode of travel, and to compare its highly legible process with other travel processes. They also undermined the prevailing pictorial aesthetic in art and poetry, which, like destination-oriented travel, preferred perceptions rendered from selected discrete viewpoints or from the unbounded, processless 'flight of fancy'.

In the mid-eighteenth century, too, the enclosures which had been slowly overtaking open-field agriculture since the sixteenth century accelerated, appropriating almost all of the remaining agricultural land—about 50 per cent of England's total cultivated area—by the mid-nineteenth century. This rapidly altered local landscapes, paralleling the effect of transport's multiplying frames of reference by multiplying changes in the physical environment so that even those who lived in one place were subject to constantly shifting perceptions. More specifically, enclosure often closed the public footpaths which marked the necessary everyday passage of people through a locality, from home to field, from field to village or market, from home to church, thus altering traditional economies and, in the most fundamental sense, traditional perspectives. But, in the controversy over public rights of way through private lands that ensued, walking emerged as a possible mitigation of these ills, for English common law provides that public use itself creates public right of way. Thus walkers on a public footpath were, by means of walking itself, unenclosing that path, reappropriating it to common use and preserving a portion of the old landscape against change.

This action takes on further significance when we consider that enclosure was widely perceived as a principal contributor to the economic decline of the rural labourer and freeholding farmer, which in turn was perceived as indicative of the end of an ideal agrarian way of life. Locating this English golden age of yeomen and communal hospitality in actual time proves, as Raymond Williams demonstrates in the second chapter of *The Country and the City*, a task for the Tantalus of historians, who finds his goal receding ever farther into the past. But the growing impoverishment of countrymen and ascendancy of industrial, and agro-industrial, wealth on into our own time seem real enough, and the perception of alienation from traditional rural life was emotionally real, as John Clare's life and poetry indicate. Although pedestrian reappropriation of footpaths could not reverse the first of these trends, it could preserve an important topographical expression of the older economy (in which everyday walking played a significant part) and so establish a formal site for the cultural values ideally associated with self-sustaining rural labour.

Western literature classically embodies the value of agricultural labour in georgic, and the decline of the English freeholder was accompanied by what is widely regarded as the disappearance of georgic in English, a logical accompaniment to the disappearance of what were understood as the mode's material, realistic referents. What actually happened, it seems to me, was that pastoral and georgic merged under the name 'pastoral', a term now very broadly conceived as virtually anything having to do with rural life, so that 'georgic' disappeared, while its specific concerns with labour and cultivation continued in things now called by the other rural mode's name. Over the last decade, scholars have debated the benefits of reviving the term 'georgic'. I join Anthony Low and Kurt Heinzelman in advocating that revival for the very particular reason that in Wordsworth's walking poetry I see an extension of Virgilian georgic accomplished by placing the walker in the ideological space vacated by the farmer. The result, which I call 'peripatetic', represents excursive walking as a cultivating labour capable of renovating both the individual and his society by recollecting and expressing past value.

Clearly the success of this move depends upon the related effects of the transport revolution and enclosure, both in the sense that it relies upon their alteration of the possible meanings of walking and in the sense that it resolves some of the aesthetic and economic problems they generate. As a deliberate mode of travel, walking accomplishes material and metaphorical educations, explorations of world and self that can be regarded as a cultivation of both the individual and his society. At the same time, local walking, the repetitive everyday tracing of footpaths, not only suggests agriculture by its formal and its economic relations to farming, but materially reappropriates common land, a crucial element of the open-field system and an economic stay for small freeholders. Such walking also preserves some portion of local topographies against widespread, nationalizing physical changes and, by extension, partially preserves the sites in which the ideal values of agrarian England were supposed to have flourished.

Wordsworth elaborates upon these possibilities in several ways. Consistent with the play between outward-bound travel and the local repetitive footpath walking, and with the sense of expansion and contraction internal to each—the travel being both exterior and interior, taking the traveler into other cultures and returning him to his own, and the footpath walking localizing the landscape but opening it to public and national use—he defines cultivating walking as excursive, moving out into the world but continually returning to recover familiar ground. By reshaping walking in this way, Wordsworth engages the pedestrian narrators and characters of poems like 'The Old Cumberland Beggar' and 'When first I journeyed hither' in the recollective actions and perspectives he distinguishes as poetic, thus identifying pedestrian action with poetic labour. Wordsworth also juxtaposes Virgilian cultivation and excursive walking, suggesting certain similarities but finally showing peripatetic succeeding where georgic fails. Nowhere is this more evident than in Book I of *The Excursion*, as the Wanderer redeems the failed cultivating labours of Margaret and her husband through poetic recollection enabled by pedestrian action and perspective. The *Excursion* as a whole attempts to effect this kind of redemption for society at large, striving to bring the best of old agrarian values into consonance with the industrialization of the nation, and continually embodying that effort as excursive walking.

The result is a literary mode that asserts the possibility of idyll in Schiller's difficult sense of motion and change comprehended in a stable cultural vision. Peripatetic suggests that the motion of excursive walkers stabilizes culture because their recollective perspective enables them to transform even sorrowful alterations like Margaret's death into moral understandings that preserve the essential value of what is lost. The proposal of a moving yet continuous perspective for citizens and poets also appears to solve the aesthetic problems generated by the increasing awareness of change and process in a travelling, industrializing world, giving the common person a material labour which can be performed to recover and preserve the good of the past, and the poet a mimetic alternative to the increasingly unsatisfactory perception and representation of natural scenes as discrete 'views'.

As the nineteenth century progresses, English and American essays discussing the effect and meaning of walking establish the basic tenets of what I designate 'peripatetic theory', which attempts an explicit and coherent account of how walking actually works in experience. Essays by William Hazlitt, Henry David Thoreau, John Burroughs, Robert Louis Stevenson, and Leslie Stephen, although differing in detail, all argue that the natural, primitive quality of the physical act of walking restores the natural proportions of our perceptions, reconnecting us with both the physical world and the moral order inherent in it, and enabling us to recollect both our personal past and our national and/or racial past—that is, human life before mechanization. As a result, the walker may expect an enhanced sense of self, clearer thinking, more acute moral apprehension, and higher powers of expression.

The formal debt of this account to Wordsworthian peripatetic is obvious, and allusions to Wordsworth in these essays implicitly acknowledge that debt. Interestingly enough, however, they tend to speak of the virtues of walking as if these had been known from time immemorial, citing the accomplishments of past great pedestrians like Ben Jonson and Shakespeare (I suppose as a strolling player) in a way that implies that these men thought of walking in the same way the essayists themselves do. The uniformity of walking's meaning and effect across time thus comes to constitute part of their argument for walking. Moreover, the peripatetic theorists do not talk about walking as narrative and metaphor in literary texts, but only as authorial activity, so that the effects of walking appear only as effects in the 'real' world and not as expectations generated by textual constructs or as 'mere' figures of speech.

These universalizations of peripatetic potential—extending the nineteenth-century interpretation of walking back in time and isolating it from its literary antecedents—harden the literary mode into an ideology of walking which finds nearly unaltered expression in twentieth-century popular and literary interpretative writings. By obscuring the origins of that ideology in the specific conditions of the early nineteenth century and in Wordsworth's poetry, peripatetic theory prevents us from directly reading its more disturbing implications—namely, that conceiving of walking as a cultivating labour involves the walker in socio-economic action, and requires a belief in a continuous Wordsworthian cosmos in which perceptual and memorial continuity translate into continuities between individual and society, rich and poor, human and natural, natural and divine, self and other, past and present. The durability of peripatetic theory lies in this combination of explication and obfuscation: by explicitly stating the expectations of walking implicit in Wordsworthian peripatetic and then decontextualizing those expectations, peripatetic theory defines a conventional cultural response to walking that accurately but uncritically recognizes a particular interpretation of that action.

Our common use of that response obscures not only its own historical origins but the actual range of interpretations of Wordsworthian peripatetic in Victorian literature. These vary from brief conventional appeals to the mode, to sustained peripatetics, all displaying fluent understanding of its uses but expressing varying degrees of discomfort with its mediative claims, particularly in those areas peripatetic theory manages to suppress. Thus Eliot and Gaskell appeal to pedestrian perspectives of industrializing countryside to set up their discussions of that change, but do not resolve their novels' conflicts in those terms. Arnold presses hard for peripatetic resolution, yet the bifurcation and eventual disappearance of his Scholar-Gipsy reveals considerable strain on Wordsworth's fusion of poet and wanderer. Dickens, too, tries to use excursive walking to recollect the past and reform the future, in his practice as well as in his writings, but despite his anxious reassertion of such expectations, a pattern of failure and destruction contains and disrupts the occasional successes of pedestrian action. And Hardy, abandoning advocacy of peripatetic cultivation, deliberately contrasts the expectations his characters have of walking with its ineffectual or destructive results, withdrawing pedestrian recollection into a very small, entirely personal sphere.

Twentieth-century writers as diverse as E. M. Forster, Edward Thomas, Robert Frost, Ursula Le Guin, A. R. Ammons, and Wendell Berry continue to use peripatetic as an index of our potential for achieving those continuities Wordsworth posited among the natural and the human, the past and the present, the rich and the poor, the material and the spiritual, the urban and the rural, the public and the private. Despite the nuances of their peripatetics, however, critical responses to representations of walking and to walking as authorial practice (when such responses occur at all) unquestioningly perpetuate the ideology of walking derived from Wordsworthian peripatetic. Even Roger Gilbert, whose *Walks in the World* works to articulate 'the walk poem' as a genre enabling various representations of experience, describes the genre as deriving from a universal human understanding of the walk as creative act and potential aesthetic object (his account actually goes back to Genesis and God walking in the garden). Typically, Wordsworth's peripatetics disappear from view. Gilbert assesses 'An Evening Walk' as the summit of Wordsworth's achievements in the walk poem and argues that the genre essentially dies out in England at that point, 'migrating' to America and reappearing in the works of Thoreau and Whitman. And although Gilbert thoroughly explicates what he regards as the inherent formal similarities between a walk and a poem—sequentiality, the possibility of continued outward movement and thought contained and intensified within a definite frame, and so forth—he assumes a Wordsworthian contiguous universe in which walking's physical continuities translate directly into temporal, spatial, and spiritual (or intellectual) continuities, and *so* generate text: 'The walk transcends its own contingent, occasional character by disclosing a totality that extends beyond the walker's perceptual limits. It is this nonphenomenal apprehension of the world that ultimately allows the walk to assume the permanence of a poem'.[8]

Gilbert's project differs from mine in its concern with contemporary poetics, and his focus on the aesthetics of walking is understandable in that context. Yet I cannot help but think that this kind of universalizing, aestheticizing account of walking and its

[8] Gilbert, *Walks in the World*, 252.

representations restricts not only our reading of literary texts but the conduct of our own lives, our understanding of our perceptions under conditions of mutable speed, and our estimations of the efficacy of the actions by which we may hope to resist or alter those conditions. Beginning to read peripatetic will, I believe, provide yet another increment of clarity in the reading and writing of our lives.

I

The Results of Destination

INTERPRETERS of *The Prelude* and *The Excursion*, to take two particularly obvious and important cases, have traditionally read right past the specific terms of these poems' metaphors into the more general 'life-as-journey' motif, thus making the selection of walking as the mode of these journeys seem arbitrary or inessential. The portion of the poems these interpreters have read they have read aright, for clearly peripatetic derives in part from the older metaphor of life as travel. Richard Sommer describes that metaphor as being composed of two interlacing 'archetypal sensibilities' represented by the *Odyssey* and the *Aeneid*:

The first of these stems from an impulse toward renewal, restoration, rejuvenation. . . . The journey toward God is here regarded in terms of the renovation of self, life renewed, salvation and immortality granted. The journey away from God, in so far as it is undertaken for the expiation of guilt, is of this type, since what is sought is the renewal of a former state of innocence. . . . The second type of sensibility . . . is [in part] an impulse after unity of knowledge, or understanding; in this respect it is, very simply, the product of man's desire to make sense out of his world, to make the disparate elements of spirit and experience cohere. . . .

Another related aspect is what we may call an impulse toward social, rather than intellectual order. In its more salient forms, this impulse tends to equate with the ethical manifestations of society and religion.[1]

The satisfaction of these very impulses—toward the re-creation of the self, reconnection with nature and so with the divine, continuity of sense, mind and spirit, community and connection with a communal past—is what peripatetic claims for walking. Peripatetic differs, however, from the more general life-as-journey motif in specifying a particular mode of travel as the source of these benefits, and in insisting on physical process as fundamental to, literally of one piece with, the journey's metaphorical goals. Peripatetic theory, indeed, goes on to argue that other modes of

---

[1] Georg Roppen and Richard Sommer, *Strangers and Pilgrims: An Essay on the Metaphor of Journey* (New York: Humanities Press, 1964), 17–18.

travel, particularly the railroad and the motor car, actually work against the fulfilment of the traditional life-journey because of the quality of their physical movement and how that affects the traveller's perceptions.

Both peripatetic's link with the life-as-journey tradition and its new assertions are possible because of changes in the practice of and attitudes toward travel in general, and walking in particular, which accompany the transport revolution beginning in the mid-eighteenth century. Before the transport revolution the process of travel was so physically and psychologically difficult that it was avoided both in practice and in text. The positive representations of travel during this time, including life-as-journey texts and theories of 'good' travel practice, elide process and emphasize destination, so that any benefits experienced by the traveler appear to be the result of destination rather than of movement. Because walking was not only especially physical but also carried quite specific negative socio-economic meanings—necessity, poverty, homelessness, even criminality—it tended to disrupt this avoidance of process, drawing the traveller/reader's attention to its material content and to the continuity of change between destinations. Thus walking was excluded altogether from the positive traditions of travel practice and representation, or was admitted only with special precautions designed to further distance its physical process from the ideal, process-less travel which presumably generated the desirable results. Only as the transport revolution shifted travellers' attention toward the process of travel and altered the socio-economic content of walking did people begin to think of walking as a desirable way of travel, practically or metaphorically.

For those of us who live in the developed countries it is hard to comprehend how difficult and restricted travel was, even over 'short' (by our standards) distances, just two and a half centuries ago, and even harder to form any clear picture of what it was like before that time (or still is for many people). A good deal of this problem is linguistic. When we say 'travel', we as often as not mean 'travel for fun', as in, 'I'm going to travel this summer'. Despite the continuing necessity of travel for business and other non-recreational purposes, we tend to regard even these necessary jaunts as potential recreation. A trip to some less than exciting place may be viewed as a chance to 'get out of town', with the implication that such a change will do the traveller good. But our word 'travel' originally—and recently—derives from 'travail', which not only connotes but denotes suffering or labour or both (as in the travail of childbirth). The entry in the *Oxford English Dictionary* for 'travel' suggests that the seventeenth century was the period of transition when both terms were widely used to mean roughly what we mean by 'travel', with 'travail' persisting into the early eighteenth century and 'travel' rarely appearing before the seventeenth. The separation of the two forms, which occurred over the same period during which the positive theories of 'true travel' developed and the practice of the Grand Tour began, reflected and permitted a connotative shift away from 'travail', with the result that we can now speak of 'travel' without necessarily uttering 'pain' and 'labour'. That linguistic gap constitutes a huge psychological gap between early eighteenth-century and late twentieth-century travellers.

We must also struggle with a significant informational gap caused by the paucity of historical and statistical records on travel conditions before the eighteenth century. Sidney and Beatrice Webb, for instance, admit that their historical study of English road administration must 'pass rapidly over the first thirteen or fourteen hundred years of historical knowledge about England', about which, with respect to their own topic, 'there is next to nothing known. Of the fifteenth, sixteenth, and seventeenth centuries we can form some imperfect vision; whilst from the beginning of the eighteenth the records are abundant.'[2] Philip Bagwell's comprehensive history of *The Transport Revolution from 1770* likewise rarely reaches back further than fifty years before its titular date for comparative data, not merely because of its chosen scope, I think, but because until travel conditions began to change and diversify there was no reason to keep any comparative records. Thus, as in our later examination of the suppression of process in representations of travel, we must often consider what the absence of certain kinds of information means, particularly when that kind of information appears at a later time.

For instance, although there are no statistical histories of walking as transport before the highly specialized studies now done for urban planning and the like, what we know about other kinds of

---

[2] Sidney and Beatrice Webb, *The Story of the King's Highway* (1913; repr. London: Frank Cass & Co., 1963), 1.

land transport indicates that walking must once have been the only mode of such travel available to the mass of humanity. Until the mid to late eighteenth century, there were only two alternatives, the riding horse and the animal-drawn wheeled vehicle. Sidney and Beatrice Webb stress the importance of the horse as a swift and flexible form of transport for a wide range of purposes. Listing fictional and historical riders from Chaucer's Canterbury pilgrims to James Watt and William Cobbett, they note that 'Right down to the nineteenth century . . . every increase of travel meant, for the most part, an increase in the number of well-mounted horsemen, with their saddle bags behind them, that were a constant feature of the roads'.[3] In her study of *Travellers in Eighteenth-Century England*, however, Rosamond Bayne-Powell comments on the limitations which accompanied the advantages of travelling on horseback. Despite his freedom to leave the road, avoiding delays caused by difficult road conditions, and his savings in coach hire,

a man riding alone was liable to be attacked by highwaymen. He must know the language and the roads or he might go far out of his way and find himself benighted in a bog. He would be obliged to send all the property, which he could not cram into two saddlebags, by the stage waggon or by sea, with the risk of never seeing it again.[4]

Bayne-Powell is thinking here of foreigners travelling in England, but, even given an Englishman with little baggage, it seems clear that this mode of travel would best suit an active man of some financial means. Whatever the rider 'saved' on coach fare, he must have incurred the expense of buying and keeping, or renting, a horse, and that too was considerable. *Emma*'s Mr Knightley, for instance, although he owns a carriage and is certainly a gentleman, keeps no horses, 'having little spare money'.[5] Another alternative, posting on horseback, was 'more exclusive still and very much more expensive' than traveling by coach.[6] Despite the advantages

    [3] Ibid. 63–4.
    [4] Rosamond Bayne-Powell, *Travellers in Eighteenth-Century England* (London: John Murray, 1951), 9.
    [5] Jane Austen, *Emma*, ed. Ronald Blythe (Harmondsworth: Penguin, 1966), 223. Emma, it is true, does not think this a necessary frugality, and chides him for 'get[ting] about as he could'—in short, for walking a lot (ibid.).
    [6] D. H. Aldcroft and H. J. Dyos, *British Transport* (Leicester: Leicester University Press, 1969), 76.

of riding, then, and the ubiquity of riders among travellers, it seems clear that in absolute numbers those who travelled by horseback must have been few.

Still, for those who could afford it physically and economically, riding on horseback must have been an attractive alternative to riding in carriages and carts. The wheeled vehicles available to even the wealthiest classes were extremely uncomfortable and not particularly fast. Carriages for the nobility were introduced into England after the Crusades, and for some time thereafter were simply enlarged and elaborately decorated versions of a peasant's cart. In fact, until Obadiah Eliot's invention of the elliptical spring in 1804, all wheeled vehicles, no matter how elaborate, were springless. At best they were equipped, in latter eras, with leather strap 'shocks' that let the coach swing like a pendulum in response to the inevitably bumpy roads. The results of this particular innovation were not entirely salutary: 'In the 1790s to be "coached" meant getting used to the nausea, akin to sea-sickness, which travelling in these vehicles induced'.[7] None the less, this sensation may have been an improvement over the trials of carriage riders in earlier times: 'With the admirable candour characteristic of her family, Queen Elizabeth once informed the French Ambassador that after a coach-journey when she had been obliged for some reason to travel unusually fast, she had been so severely jolted that she had been unable to sit down with comfort for several days.'[8]

'Unusually fast' probably meant five or six miles an hour at the most, assuming good weather and good roads. The fastest coaches of the 1820s and 1830s, the peak era of coach travel in England, averaged about ten miles an hour, while at the beginning of the nineteenth century, Thomas De Quincey tells us, the usual coach-pace was 'never so much as six miles an hour, except upon a very great road; and then only by extra payment to the driver'.[9] Even

---

[7] Philip S. Bagwell, *The Transport Revolution from 1770* (London: B. T. Batsford, 1974), 48.

[8] Cyril Huches Hartmann, *The Story of the Roads* (London: George Routledge & Sons, 1927), 37.

[9] Bagwell, *Transport Revolution*, 42–3; Thomas De Quincey, 'Travelling in England in the Old Days', in *The Collected Writings of Thomas De Quincey*, ed. David Masson (London: A. & C. Black, 1896), 279. Masson has altered De Quincey's original title, which was simply 'Travelling', because he felt the original insufficiently descriptive. Although De Quincey collected this essay into his 'Autobiographic Sketches' (1853), Masson says it comes 'mainly from an article of De Quincey's in an extra number of Tait's for December 1834'.

these modest speeds—about three and two times average walking speed respectively—were 'within the reach of a tiny fraction only of the total population, as a comparison of the [1830s coach] seating capacity available to the inhabitants of any sizeable town shows'.[10]

In fact, most of the population travelled at walking pace or less, even when they paid for vehicles to help them over long distances:

For the poor [in the early nineteenth century], travel with a stage waggon moving at no more than three miles an hour was often the only alternative to walking, for the fare by waggon might be as low as 1/2 d. a mile whereas the outside seat on a coach would cost at least four times as much. In the case of the carriers Russell and Co. of Falmouth it was understood that traveller's luggage would be carried and sleeping space would be provided within the vehicle at night, but that when the party was on the move passengers would be expected to walk alongside the waggon except in inclement weather.[11]

Travellers by coach, as well as by wagon, routinely got out and walked to lighten the load on hills or over muddy stretches. Nor were coaches always faster than their cheaper cousins.[12] Bayne-Powell tells the story of one eighteenth-century woman who, being 'fond of taking country walks, had on one occasion resolved to meet a coach at an inn and take it part of the way home. When she reached the inn she found it had already passed; but by walking quickly she was able to catch it up.'[13] Even those few able to afford coach travel, then, although relieved of the burden of luggage and enjoying certain comforts, frequently travelled no faster than if they had been walking.

The slowness, discomfort, and expense of road travel right into the nineteenth century were not, of course, results of primitive vehicular technology alone. Bayne-Powell offers a collection of travellers' complaints about the paucity of decent accommodation, service, and food and the depredations of highwaymen that now

[10] Aldcroft and Dyos, British Transport, 76.
[11] Bagwell, Transport Revolution, 55.
[12] Malcolm Letts reports similar conditions on the Continent. Although a weekly coach ran from Venice to Augsburg in the late 17th cent., 'the roads were bad and passengers were expected to alight and walk whenever the way was steep' ('Germany and The Rhineland', in R. S. Lambert, Grand Tour: A Journey in the Tracks of the Age of Aristocracy (London: Faber & Faber, 1935), 120).
[13] Bayne-Powell, Travellers, 19.

seems entertaining but reflects serious obstacles to travel in earlier times.[14] In what Bayne-Powell calls 'the palmy days of the highwaymen'[15] in the seventeenth century, fear of their attacks literally closed roads and determined the character of localities:

[Grand Tourists] were glad to traverse the first path of the Dover Road in the clear morning light, for it was no place to go through at night, when you were setting out for a long foreign tour with a good deal of ready money on you. . . . John Evelyn was pleased to drink the waters of Shooter's Hill, but it was as the haunt of footpads and highwaymen that the place was more generally known, and it never managed to flourish as a spa. The bodies of highwaymen could often be seen on the gibbets by the road.[16]

This level of fear persisted well into the middle of the eighteenth century, when improved roads and policing began to reduce the vulnerability of travellers to criminal attack.

What set the scene for all kinds of mercantile and criminal highway robbery was undoubtedly the roads themselves, which were so poorly marked, badly built, and irregularly maintained that they often reduced the pace of already slow vehicles to a crawl, making the passengers easy targets for poor innkeepers and desperate highwaymen alike. Parish maintenance of the roads came into existence in 1555 through the Highways Act, the first general road legislation in England, and these localized and generally inadequate provisions (which involved impressed labor and elected Parish Surveyors) continued in existence with no significant change until the Highway Act of 1835 created a nationally maintained highway system.[17] The quality of even the best-maintained roads was extremely poor until the innovations of the road builders John Metcalfe, Thomas Telford, and John MacAdam in the late eighteenth century began to make stable, smooth-surfaced roads possible. De Quincey dates the great improvement of English roads to 'after the year 1815' and credits MacAdam with remodelling them 'upon principles of Roman science. From mere beds of torrents and systems of ruts, they were raised universally to the condition and appearance of gravel walks in private parks or shrubberies.'[18]

[14] Ibid. 25–54.   [15] Ibid. 34.
[16] Douglas Woodruff, 'From London to Paris', in Lambert, *Grand Tour*, 36–7.
[17] Aldcroft and Dyos, *British Transport*, 35, 63.
[18] De Quincey, 'Travelling', 283.

Describing what these earlier road conditions meant for travellers, De Quincey remembers what he saw when, as a child, he stood at the front windows of his mother's carriage:

The postilion (for so were all carriages then driven) was employed not by fits and starts, but always and eternally, in *quartering*—i.e., in crossing from side to side—according to the casualties of the ground. Before you stretched a wintry length of lane, with ruts deep enough to fracture the leg of a horse, filled to the brim with standing pools of rain water; and the collateral chambers of these ruts kept from becoming confluent by thin ridges . . . Go to sleep at the beginning of a stage, and the last thing you saw—wake up, and the first thing you saw—was the line of wintry pools, the poor off-horse planting his steps with care, and the cautious postilion gently applying his spur, whilst manœuvring across this system of grooves with some sort of science that looked like a gipsy's palmistry.[19]

Even allowing some latitude for De Quincey's ability to dramatize a situation, it is little wonder, with roads like this, that a coach journey from London to Edinburgh in the 1750s was two days longer in winter than in summer—or that in summer the same journey still took ten days.[20] Great wonder, on the other hand, that foreign visitors from Cesar de Saussure to Casanova regularly praised the condition of English roads.[21] Continental roads must have been horrible to contemplate, much less to traverse.

These physical barriers created a situation in which travel was, in one sense, an exclusive 'privilege', and yet was actively feared and avoided, not only because of the personal physical and psychological discomfort involved, but because of the cultural insularities normal to a non-travelling society. When Bagwell comments on Jonathan Swift's preference for beginning journeys on Sunday, when all the appropriate prayers for the protection of travellers would have just been said, he also notes that

[Swift] was one of a very select company of people who could afford the luxury or time to travel. The vast majority of his contemporaries were villagers who rarely, in a lifetime, travelled further than a day's walking distance from home. Even in 1817 Hazlitt considered that country dwellers were 'out of the world', so different was their way of life from that of townsmen.[22]

---

[19] Ibid. 274–5.   [20] Bagwell, *Transport Revolution*, 42.
[21] Bayne-Powell, *Travellers*, 28.   [22] Bagwell, *Transport Revolution*, 11.

That is, given such confinement of movement, human society took shape as small, idiosyncratic cultural islands, far more insular and less communicative with the outside world—that is, the world more than one day's walk away—than any country in a time of main roads and interstates, or even railroads, could be. What we would term 'culture shock' was not something experienced over great distances but the regular experience of travellers over even 'short' distances as they passed through circle after circle of local movement and knowledge in which they, as people from more than a day's walk away, were disoriented and essentially lost. The parish road maintenance Acts legally described this situation: roads were fundamentally local, and remained so until the combined effects of the transport revolution and enclosure reduced the isolation of locality from locality.

John Barrell discusses at some length the insularity of local transport systems and travellers' perceptions of the pre-enclosure landscape as 'mysterious and hostile':

The system of roads in an open-field parish . . . is in the first place for the circulation of men and cattle within the parish, and often, if a way exists through several parishes from one town to another, it is not a direct route but the result of various such internal road-systems meeting at the parish boundaries and thus interlacing. And so there will often be no particular distinction between a road that will in fact lead the traveller, however indirectly, out of the parish, and one which leads the farmer to his land and the labourer to his work but takes the traveller nowhere. . . . For [the Revd St John] Priest [and other agricultural writers] the road-system of an open-field village is a labyrinth, whose secret cannot be learned without a guide, and which it is positively dangerous to enter without one.[23]

Two things must be noted here. One is that the desire of Priest and his compatriots—William Pitt, Arthur Young, James Tyley, and others—'to *explain* the countryside, open it out, and to make each particular place more available to those outside it' speaks of the difficulty travellers faced in finding a passage through localities (and, of course, of the growing eighteenth-century desire for certain kinds of travel).[24] The second, if we may return to Bagwell's terms, is that, in the ordinary context of the vast majority of the population,

[23] John Barrell, *The Idea of Landscape and the Sense of Place, 1730–1840* (Cambridge: Cambridge University Press, 1972), 87.
[24] Ibid. 84.

the non-travellers, walking was an insular and confining act. Each individual's day's-walk-circle defined his 'particular place'; as his surest regular transport, walking took him to labour, to church, to market, to courting, but in so doing it kept him, both literally and figuratively, in his place.[25] Walking set boundaries and did not break them, it moved in its own circles and did not move through, it remained at home and did not travel, and the walker, although he might be the guide within the labyrinth, did not ordinarily leave it. Peripatetic eventually perceives this placing function as a virtue, but that revision involves seeing walking as a kind of travel with positive associations. Before the transport revolution, walking ordinarily was the localizing movement opposed to travel.

The difficulties arising from travelling through the day's-walk-circles were not, of course, all on the traveller's side as he attempted to find a way through the unfamiliar locality. The locality itself was changed by his movement through it, the residents confronted with 'foreign' ways and knowledge and ignorance that altered them in passing, and not always in salutary ways. Considering the physical and intellectual opening of the Highlands after late eighteenth-century improvements of the roads, A. J. Youngson muses unhappily over the resulting dilution of Highland culture and depopulation:

In the 1720s [Edward] Burt seems to have been unable to move more than a mile or two out of Inverness without a guide; but fifty years later it was a simple matter at least to ride over scores of miles of road even north of the Great Glen. Commercially the roads were not of much importance. But men and ideas travelled along them, bringing the Highlanders into increasing contact with a world other than their own, further weakening their local attachments to old ways and old superiors. Easier travel, instead of improving matters, tended to intensify dissatisfaction and unsettlement in the Highlands. And as time passed, people left in increasing numbers.[26]

The Highlands, of course, are a highly visible case, a large, relatively remote, obviously culturally distinct area. But the same observations apply on a much finer scale to the changes in the innumerable

---

[25] For convincing reconstructions of traditional patterns of local footpath use, see Kim Taplin's *The English Path* (Woodbridge, Suffolk: The Boydell Press, 1979), particularly ch. 3, 'The Beaten Path'.

[26] A. J. Youngson, *Beyond the Highland Line: Three Journals of Travel in Eighteenth Century Scotland* (London: Collins, 1974), 34–5.

circles of local knowledge throughout Great Britain. As enclosure accelerated and the open-field system disappeared, the 'hostile and mysterious [local] road system was tamed and made unmysterious by being destroyed', at first on paper and then in the countryside itself.[27] Enclosure award maps ignored old paths and roads and wrote in straight new roads whose primary purpose was connection with the outside world, with the big market towns and, in time, with railroads; and since the new roads were in actuality new, stable and broad and well-maintained, all of those same enlargements suffered and enjoyed in the Highlands occurred in the heartlands of agricultural England—an altered landscape, the arrival of new people and thoughts, and the departure of many whose families had been bound for centuries to the circle of a single day's walk on the land.

From the vantage point of a thoroughly travelled era, we often imagine the untravelled world in unrealistically nostalgic terms. Barrell and Youngson obviously, and justifiably, regret the loss of the pocket cultures, the regional diversity that flavoured even a small island nation. But what they really want, I think, is what we all want: to simultaneously have and enjoy these cultures, to be able to experience their diversity by means of the very ease of travel that diminished that diversity. If this is so, then clearly what we mourn never was nor will be, for travel by its nature alters the places travelled through and opens it to the world through the traveller and the road. The majority of English people before the transport revolution had no chance of ever experiencing more than one of these delightfully individualized places. The upper echelons of English society, in fact, seemed intent upon preserving this situation, for to the already great material and psychological difficulties inherent to travel they added legislative barriers which controlled and/or stigmatized the traveller and increased the natural fear of strangers in essentially closed localities.

These legal barriers indicate that the expenses and dangers of travel were perceived as not only individual but societal, and in fact it was in the fourteenth century, when feudal bonds weakened and unhappy rural labourers took to the roads in relatively large numbers, further threatening the stability of the economic and social system, that the new restrictions began to appear:

[27] Barrell, *Idea of Landscape*, 94.

No one might leave his village if he did not bring a 'letter patent containing the cause of his going and the date of his return, if he were to return'.... These letters would be sealed by a 'good man' (*prod homme*), assigned in each hundred, city, or borough, by the justices of the peace, and special seals were to be expressly made, said the statute, bearing in the middle the king's arms, the name of the county around, and that of the hundred, city or borough across. The case even of fabricating false letters was forseen, which shows what a burning wish to quit their neighbourhoods was felt to be in persons of this class. Every individual surprised without regular papers was put into prison provisionally.[28]

One might travel legitimately for a number of reasons and under a number of authorities—as a messenger for one's lord, as a true pilgrim, as a licensed minstrel, pedlar, or other working stroller, or as a student. Even these travellers, however, were viewed with suspicion and might be summarily jailed. Students, for instance, were 'comprised in the same category ... as beggars, and were put into irons if they had not the regulation letter'. A 1388 statute likewise set pilgrims under 'the same statutes as the beggars and the wandering workmen. Henceforward ... they also must have, like these, letters of passage with a special seal entrusted to certain law-worth[y] men.'[29]

As the frequent legal comparison of other classes of travellers to beggars indicates, these travel restrictions also acted as economic restrictions intended to prevent freelancing by granting better control of economic power to the 'good men' who issued the necessary permits. In 1572, for instance, an 'Acte for the punishment of Vacabondes' stated:

All and everye persone and persones beynge whole and mightye in Body and able to labour, havinge not Land or Maister, nor using any lawfull Marchaundize Crafte or Mysterye whereby hee or shee might get his or her Lyvinge; & all Fencers Bearewardes Comon Players in Enterludes & Minstrels, not belonging to any Baron of this Realme or towardes any other honorable Personage of greater Degree; all Juglers Pedlars Tynkers and Petye-Chapmen; whiche ... shall wander abroade and have not Lycense of two Justices of the Peace at the leaste, whereof one to be of the Quorum, when and in what Shier they shall happen to

[28] J. J. Jusserand, *English Wayfaring Life in the Middle Ages* (London: T. Fisher Unwin, 1888), 269.

[29] Ibid. 270–1, 361.

wander ... shalbee taken adjudged and deemed Roges Vacaboundes and Sturdy Beggars.[30]

Clearly the underlying principle here is that unrestricted travel leads to unrestricted work, and that people's labour should be directed toward specific and known ends controlled by the authorities. Clearly, too, wandering itself—what we would think of as genuine wandering, moving about without bounds or permission or (necessarily) explicit purpose—was traditionally criminal, and English laws fostered the perception of travellers as potential wanderers whose character and motives should properly fall under suspicion.

The greatest suspicion of all fell on pedestrians, whose mode of travel proclaimed their poverty and therefore the greater probability of their being wanderers with some illicit or economically disruptive motive. Walking was the cheapest kind of travel, but also the slowest, most physically gruelling, and most dangerous. Jusserand says simply that, in avoiding the uncomfortable passage of springless coaches over terrible roads, 'People of any worth journeyed on horseback. As to those who travelled on foot, they were used to all sorts of misery'.[31] That is, walkers on the road were likely to be among the economically discontented and disenfranchised who had little or no choice as to their modes of travel —beggars, fleeing serfs, unscrupulous pedlars, or thieves already accustomed to hunger, exposure, and fear. Right through the eighteenth century, as Bayne-Powell notes,

It was supposed that no man of substance would ever walk, except with a gun over his shoulder, and that everyone who tramped the roads was either a footpad or a pauper. The roads were generally in such a bad state that walking could not have been pleasant and there was always the danger of attacks from footpads. It was not till the early nineteenth century when the highways were improved and robbers were less numerous, that walking became the pleasure and pastime of all classes.[32]

Special difficulties faced women walkers, especially if they walked alone, because their peripateia translated as sexual wandering. This

---

[30] Quoted in Andrew Gurr, *The Shakespearean Stage, 1574–1642* (Cambridge: Cambridge University Press, 1980), 28.
[31] Jusserand, *English Wayfaring Life*, 83.
[32] Bayne-Powell, *Travellers*, 22.

interpretation derives in part from traditional rural lower-class courtship patterns, in which 'walking out' with someone was the equivalent of steady dating or engagement today. Often, as Jocelyn Pierpont in Hardy's *The Well-Beloved* is aware, walking out was understood to include sexual intercourse, and even where complete consummation of a pre-marital relationship was frowned upon, the lovers' walk provided the perfect opportunity for such activity. This, I think, is one of the unrecognized reasons Gabriel is so hard hit by Gretta's admissions at the end of Joyce's 'The Dead': when he asks if she loved Michael Furey, she says that she 'used to go out walking with him', a phrase which in a country-bred woman's mouth might well indicate a full-scale sexual relationship as well as serious emotional involvement.[33]

Most 'walking out', of course, was regarded as perfectly respectable. But the latent sexual content of the activity combined with its class content and standard prejudices about women's 'nature' and proper roles in society to make women's walking, even on local footpaths, unusually perilous to their reputations. As we shall see, that sexual content seems to preserve fearful reactions to women's walking even when favourable interpretations of men's walking have become standard, not only in literary texts but in experience. In the still-current term 'streetwalker', we hear the most extreme implications of the old rural custom translated into urban criminal usage: a streetwalker is the poorest, least prestigious, most dangerous of prostitutes, who signals her willingness to stray sexually by walking.

Among the robbers so feared by early travelers, too, 'footpads' were understood to be of a lower class and were thus viewed with greater suspicion and fear. Carl Philip Moritz, a German clergyman travelling in England in 1782, contrasts 'the highwaymen, who ride on horseback, and often, in their desire to relieve the traveller of his purse, put him in terror with an unloaded pistol', with pedestrian thieves. Highwaymen, Moritz notes, 'have been known to return part of their plunder to a victim gravely distressed, and in any event they do not murder lightly'. Not so 'the lowest and vilest class of criminal—the footpads':

---

[33] James Joyce, *Dubliners* (Harmondsworth: Penguin, 1967), 219. Ch. 4 of Taplin's *English Path*, 'Between the Acres of the Rye', describes the custom of 'walking out' and its rich implications in detail.

Tragic examples may be read almost daily in English newspapers of poor people met on the road who have been brutally murdered for a few shillings. These thieves probably murder because they are unable to take flight like the highwayman on his horse, and so, should anyone live to give information concerning them, they can be pretty easily overtaken by a hue-and-cry.[34]

The shape of a footpad's life, indeed, is simply another version of that circle of a day's walk confining the more respectable poor. Because the footpads walk, they cannot easily detain or overtake a rider or a coach; their likeliest victims are walkers, probably poor themselves, and so the footpads remain poor, desperate, and *pedestrian*, unable to obtain the horses that might let them rise in their own society. As Moritz notes, this ensures their moral as well as their economic desperation, since the possibility of swift and effective escape is sealed off by their lack of transport. And, completing the circles of confinement for walkers as a class, the honest pedestrian traveller is thus the type of traveler most often faced with the worst criminal threats to body and purse, while being simultaneously regarded with the greatest suspicion by settled folk and fellow travellers alike.

Moritz, who toured England mostly on foot, provides a firsthand account of late eighteenth-century attitudes toward pedestrians. As he tells his adventures through letters to Friedrich Gedike, a friend with whom he had taken walking excursions in Germany, Moritz initially comments very little on the mode of travel he has chosen. By the time he reaches Windsor, however, he has 'already undergone so many hardships as a pedestrian that [he is] undecided whether to continue in this manner or not':

A pedestrian seems in this country to be a sort of beast of passage—stared at, pitied, suspected and shunned by everybody who meets him. . . . [After crossing the Thames] I went to a house and asked a man standing at the door if I was on the right road for Oxford.

'Yes,' he said, 'But you'll want a carriage to get you there.'

I answered that I intended to go there on foot, whereupon he gave me a look full of meaning, shook his head and went in the house. . . . As I went on again every passing coachman called out to me: 'Do you want to ride on the outside?' If I met only a farm worker on a horse he would

[34] Carl Philip Moritz, *Journeys of a German in England*, trans. Reginald Nettel (London: Eland, 1983), 104–5.

say to me companionably: 'Warm walking, sir,' and when I passed through a village the old women in their bewilderment would let out a 'God Almighty!'[35]

Again and again Moritz finds his moral and economic character interpreted—and thus, in this case, misinterpreted—through his mode of travel. A waiter at an inn in Windsor behaves so badly that Moritz 'honestly believe[s] the fellow thought it not proper for him to wait on a miserable mortal who went afoot'; two German travellers whom Moritz approaches in Richmond 'don't consider me fit to talk to because I'm a walker'; and although the landlord's family at the Mitre 'approved' his plan to walk on, 'it set them wondering a great deal, and in the end they told me quite frankly that they would not have put me up had I not arrived there under special circumstances'.[36] Moritz himself regards the rare fellow pedestrian with trepidation, and with some reason. He does actually meet a footpad who, he says, 'From the first . . . struck me as suspicious', and is saved from robbery and probable violence only by the approach of a coach which frightens the demanding man away. Even when accosted in friendly fashion by an Oxford clergyman who happens to be on foot, Moritz at first 'did not know if [his] fellow-traveller was to be trusted' and so presents himself as 'a poor wanderer' until his companion's status becomes clear.[37]

It is possible at times to hear a certain paranoia in Moritz's account of such slights and mistaken identities. We do not really know, for instance, why the German travellers ignored him, but must rely on his account of their attitude. Reginald Nettel, from whose translation of Moritz I have been quoting, argues that Moritz is too ready to advance his mode of travel as an explanation for poor treatment, and cites the universally bad conditions of travel that we have already discussed. As Bayne-Powell notes, however, Moritz's experience was not singular, nor was it 'merely because he was a foreigner. Richard Warner, an English clergyman, who was so eccentric as to go on walking tours, met with gross rudeness from inn-keepers and jeers and missiles from small boys.'[38] On at least one occasion, moreover, Moritz has the opportunity

---

[35] Ibid. 110–11.   [36] Ibid. 113, 118, 139.
[37] Ibid. 120–1, 132–3.   [38] Bayne-Powell, Travellers, 21–2.

directly to compare the treatment of pedestrian travellers with that of those who travelled by other means. Having arrived at an inn where he had to seek out the staff, he is relegated to the kitchen for his supper:

While I was eating, a post-chaise drove up to the inn, and immediately the whole household started into motion to receive the distinguished guests they heard approaching. But the gentlemen got out for only a moment, called for nothing more than a couple of pots of beer and then drove on again. But if you come in a post chaise you are treated with all possible respect![39]

Whatever the difficulties faced by travellers in general, pedestrian travel and vehicular travel were obviously interpreted very differently by people along the way whose livelihood depended upon knowing which travellers were most likely to enrich them. At yet another inn Moritz is denied a bed and finally plants himself in the kitchen, saying that he will sleep there. From this vantage point he hears the servants discussing his probable status:

A woman took my part, saying: 'I dare say he is a well-bred gentleman.' Another contradicted her because I had come on foot, and said: 'He is a poor travelling creature.'
My ears still tingle when I think of the way she said 'Poor travelling creature.' In a few short words it forced upon me the disdain they had for an outcast—all the tragedy of a man with no native place.

When they find that Moritz won't leave, they finally give him a bed. But it is not until the next morning, when the 'poor' pedestrian, asked for a shilling tip, gives them a half-crown, that they begin to treat him 'very politely and apologetically'.[40]

Unless we are to discredit Moritz completely, anecdotes like these confirm what our other historical evidence suggests: before the transport revolution, the specific socio-economic content of walking intensified the usual interpretations of travel in general. To walkers and non-walkers alike, walking as travel meant poverty, alienation from society whether for legal or extra-legal reasons, possible moral turpitude, and probable danger to the individuals and communities touched by the act. The distinctive element in this field of meaning is clearly poverty, for this is the

[39] Moritz, *Journeys*, 124.   [40] Ibid. 174.

circumstance which suggests the extremities of alienation and of moral, material, and psychic danger legally embodied as 'Roges Vacaboundes and Sturdy Beggars'. Thus, when Moritz feels people's reaction to him as pedestrian traveller as 'disdain . . . for an outcast—all the tragedy of a man with no native place', he is feeling a reaction intensified by the socio-economic content of his mode of travel: his walking is read as a sign of the extreme level of alienation and possible threat to others which would be produced by involuntary, poverty-induced homelessness, a perversion of the usual localizing function of walking.

Indeed, if we may return to the broader point at hand, while the laws against wandering primarily address the materially destabilizing force of travel by trying to keep countrymen on the land and robbers off the roads, other texts work to confront and partially counter the threat of cultural destabilization. Advice written for legitimate travellers who sought the kind of education eventually institutionalized as the Grand Tour stresses the necessity of maintaining the traveller's stable cultural identity, both for his own sake and for the sake of the society to which he would eventually return. Francis Bacon's essay 'Of Travaile' (1625) advises

That Young Men travaile under some Tutor, or grave Servant . . . So that he be such a one, that hath the Language, and hath been in the Country before; whereby he may be able to tell them, what Things are worthy to be seene in the Country where they goe, what Acquaintances they are to seeke; What Exercises or discipline the Place yeeldeth.[41]

All this is meant to open the eyes of the young men who would otherwise 'looke abroad little', but clearly Bacon also feels that the experience should be carefully controlled and guided. He requires that the returned traveller maintain correspondence with his foreign acquaintances, but show few outward signs of change:

let his Travaile appear rather in his Discourse, then in his Apparrell, or Gesture: And in his Discourse, let him be rather advised in his Answers, then forwards to tell Stories: And let it appeare, that he doth not change his Country Manners, for those of Forraigne Parts; But onely, prick in some flowers, of that he hath Learned abroad, into the Customes of his owne Country.[42]

---

[41] Francis Bacon, 'Of Travaile', in The Essayes or Counsels, Civill and Morall, ed. Michael Kiernan (Cambridge, Mass.: Harvard University Press, 1985), 56.
[42] Ibid. 58.

Travel à la Bacon should—will, one gathers—change the traveller's mind but should never change his manner. That is, individual
change is desirable only when properly guided and externally
suppressed—when the culture the traveller came from is kept safe
from change by his unchanged manner.

James Howell's *Instructions and Directions for Forren Travell*
(1650) similarly advises that the potential traveller have taken a
University degree, be 'well grounded and setle [*sic*] in his *Religion*,
the *beginning* and *basis* of all wisdom', and know the topography,
government, and history of his home country well enough 'to
satisfy a stranger by exchange of discours, in any thing touching
the State of [the traveller's] owne Country'.[43] A traveller should,
in short, take every precaution that his own cultural biases be
settled and firm. Even in this case additional exposure to other
lands and ways should not be deliberately sought:

if business and the quality of his life will permit, he may make one flying
journey over againe, and in one Summer review all those Countreys,
which hee had been forty Months a seeing before ... But being *his Redux*,
being returned the second time, let him think no more of forren Journeys,
unlesse it be by command, and upon publique service.[44]

Thus Howell's argument, like Bacon's, although explicitly in favour
of travel as a mode of education, implies, none the less, that travel
is dangerous to both the individual traveller and his society, and
must be carefully designed and restricted.

Eighteenth-century fictional travel accounts explore the fears
implied in these early preparations for travel. Defoe's *Robinson
Crusoe* and *Farther Adventures of Robinson Crusoe* (1719) and
Swift's *Gulliver's Travels* (1726) weigh the terrors of uncontrolled
travel, and in particular its threat to the cultural identity of the
individual and his society, against the potential for adventure and
novelty that clearly seduced the books' readers as readily as their
protagonists. Crusoe's exploits abroad, which provide the substance of the narrative and the focus of the reader's interest, none
the less are framed and inlaid with warnings from his parents, his
wife, and his own experience against the 'chronical Distemper' of
a wanderlust which takes him into slavery, the acquisition and

[43] James Howell, *Instructions and Directions for Forren Travell* ... (London:
Humphrey Mosley, 1650), 9, 12.
[44] Ibid. 124–5.

loss of fortunes, various shipwrecks and rescues, and other threats to his life and reason.[45] Crusoe learns about other places and people in the sense of learning facts about them, but his survival and prosperity depend upon his determination not to let foreign ways and knowledge corrupt his Englishness. Indeed, as the well-known story of his shipwreck on an island shows, Crusoe crowns his physical taming of the island by imposing his own culture on other people: he clothes and Christianizes Friday, breaking him of the cannibalism which not only violates one of the most fundamental prejudices of European culture but also suggests Crusoe's own fear of being consumed by savagery, and finally styles himself king of the island, which he has made as English as possible. Yet even this missionary vigilance does not provide the traveller with complete protection against naturalization to the foreign. Crusoe finds it hard to adjust to English clothes after his rescue, and returns to England to discover few friends and family left alive and himself 'as perfect a Stranger to all the World, as if I had never been known there'.[46]

In *Gulliver's Travels* the cultural differences which Crusoe holds at bay with at least some success engulf the traveller and invade his home country. Like Crusoe, Gulliver perceives his desire to travel as an unreasonable passion which, although at first gratified as a corollary to economic necessity, must soon be satisfied despite good sense, 'the Thirst I had of seeing the World, notwithstanding my past Misfortunes, continuing as violent as ever'.[47] Gulliver's conversion to Houyhnhnmism is of course a satirical indictment of English xenophobia, but it also gives palpable shape to the worst nightmares of Bacon and Howell and, one suspects, of Swift's less perspicacious readers: that a traveller may become so alienated that, even when rescued by good Englishmen, he never comes home psychologically and so becomes an internal threat to the coherence of his home culture.

Given all these negative aspects of travel before the transport revolution, the physical and socio-economic and psychic and

[45] Daniel Defoe, *The Life and Strange Surprizing Adventures of Robinson Crusoe of York, Mariner, and The Farther Adventures of Robinson Crusoe*, 3 vols. (Oxford: Basil Blackwell, 1927), i. 44.

[46] Ibid. ii. 74.

[47] Jonathan Swift, *Gulliver's Travels*, ed. Robert A. Greenberg (New York: Norton, 1970), 127.

cultural dangers, it is really rather amazing that there is any positive tradition associated with travel at all. Yet we have not only the life-as-journey metaphor, which associates travel with spiritual renewal, intellectual growth, and the various other benefits Sommer outlines, but the institutions of pilgrimage and Grand Touring, travel practices which were accepted for reasons corresponding very neatly to Sommer's two 'sensibilities'. Pilgrimage, one of the licensed forms of travel after Richard II's edicts, plainly fits the requirements of the first sensibility: set as a task of penance, or undertaken by personal choice either as penance or as holy works, the journey to a shrine theoretically renewed one's spiritual life. The Grand Tour, first encouraged by the Elizabethan government 'in order to increase the usefulness of likely young men' and becoming virtually expected of such promising young (male) subjects by the eighteenth century, has rather less spiritual content than Sommer's search after unity of knowledge but is certainly of the same mould, being intended as an educational experience and involving an impulse toward social order. Like pilgrimage, Grand Touring was at first under close legal control, in this case through 'permits of absence, which were generally for a year, but sometimes for as much as three, [specifying] places which were not to be visited'.[48] Eventually, of course, the Grand Tour was thought of as a series of places which should be visited, and in this was very like pilgrimage: instead of forming a new spiritual man by visiting particular holy sites, the Grand Tourist hoped to form a new civic man, better able to participate in his government and culture, by visiting prescribed sites in France and Italy and so forth.

This common emphasis upon destination is a crucial element in the advocacies of certain kinds of travel which appear with increasing frequency and fervour from the early seventeenth century on. Bacon and his brief recognition of travel as 'a Part of Education' is followed by Howell and William Bromley (*Remarks made in Travels through France and Italy*, 1693) and their detailed descriptions of what the young man abroad should see and do. By 1778, when Thomas Nugent publishes his four volumes on *The Grand Tour*, the implicit fears of earlier writers about the stability of travellers and their home countries have given way to positive

[48] Woodruff in Lambert, *Grand Tour*, 40.

enthusiasm. Nugent does warn against slow and inconvenient conveyances, offering tables of boat and carriage and post departure times and advice as to which mode of travel is best, and suggests the equivalent of a sleeping bag to those likely to encounter dirty and bug-ridden beds. But he opens his text with a celebration of travelling and travellers which prefigures similar arguments by the peripatetic theorists. As Leslie Stephen later cites great literary and philosophic walkers as part of his proof of the intellectual benefits of walking, so Nugent trots out a long list of mythical and historical travellers of renown that includes Caesar's Druids, the Argonauts, Bacchus, Hercules, Ulysses, Pythagoras, Herodotus' Homer, the emperor Hadrian, Columbus, Amerigo Vespucci, Drake, and Raleigh to support his claims for the salutary effects of travel:

Travelling, even in the remotest ages, was reckoned so useful a custom, as to be judged the only means of improving the understanding, and of acquiring a high degree of reputation ... those who first distinguished themselves in the republic of letters, were all travellers, who owed their learning, name and reputation to different peregrinations.... I should be glad to find that I have been able to contribute to the improvement of that noble and ancient custom of travelling, a custom so visibly tending to enrich the mind with knowledge, to rectify the judgment, to remove the prejudices of education, to compose the outward manners, and in a word to form the complete gentleman.[49]

Certainly the benefits Nugent assigns to travel, although translated into more determinedly secular terms, match those proposed in metaphors of life as a journey: acquisition of knowledge, rectification of judgement, the making of the self, the stabilization of the social order. But his assertion that actual material travel has always been regarded in such supremely favourable terms is as specious as Stephen's assertions about 'the good old walking tour', which at the time was less than a century old. The tone and implicit fears of earlier advocates of travel, the difficulty and rarity of travel itself, the centuries of legislation restricting and discouraging both domestic and foreign travel, and even the fact that Nugent sets forth a ten-page argument on the subject, all suggest

---

[49] Thomas Nugent, *The Grand Tour; Or, A Journey through the Netherlands, Germany, Italy and France*, 3rd edn., vol i. (London: J. Rivington & Sons *et al.*, 1778), pp. i–ii, xi.

that his assessment of 'the noble and ancient custom of travel' is both fairly new and fairly limited. Nugent's dehistoricizing tactics, like Stephen's, obscure critical rhetorical and practical restrictions. When Stephen and the peripatetic theorists praise the virtues of walking, they are not talking about all walking but about a carefully defined 'true walking', the authenticity of which is measured by its conformity to selected aspects of Wordsworthian excursive walking, and the practice of which, despite its new popularity, is a distinctly middle- to upper-class activity. In the same way, Nugent and his like are advocating what I call 'true travel', travel undertaken by a very limited class of people to a prescribed (although, by Nugent's time, a fairly extensive) set of places. 'True travel', a term I will continue to use to indicate this destination-oriented travel, ideally excludes the process of travel, the travail of moving from place to place, and its advocates and practitioners seek to make that process as nearly transparent and unnoticeable as possible.

Textually this means making the process of travel literally unreadable. Accounts of and guides to the Grand Tour, and to other sorts of travelling for education and pleasure as these began to be more widely practised, avoid describing actual travel, the movement between places or the mode of movement, as assiduously as Swift and many others avoided travel itself. This passage from Bromley's *Remarks made in Travels through France and Italy,* for instance, omits any commentary on the movement of the traveller, or how he moves, or the duration or quality of the movement, or the environment surrounding the selected sites upon which he does comment:

I passed through *St. Denis;* in the great Church of the Abbey are reposed the Bodies of the Kings of *France,* as with us in *Westminster;* and here is kept the Treasure, so well known by the name of the *Treasure of St. Denis;* which I could not see, all the Priests being then officiating in the Choire. Betwixt *St. Denis* and *Paris* are erected seven Crosses at those Places where *St. Denis* rested himself in coming hither after he was beheaded at *Paris.*[50]

The road which we presume runs between St Denis and Paris, and along which we presume the seven crosses stand, does not appear

⁵⁰ William Bromley, *Remarks made in Travels through France and Italy* (London: Thomas Basset, 1693), 6.

in the text, nor is there any palpable distance between the two cities: their names transport us instantly from one to the other, from the treasure to the beheading. We do not feel the good saint's need to rest.

In the same way, Bacon suggests a list of 'Things to be seene and observed' in 'On Travaile'—'The Churches, and Monasteries, with the Monuments which are therein extant: The Wals and Fortifications of Cities and Townes; and so the Havens and Harbours: Antiquities, and Ruines' and so forth—and Nugent's subtitle for *The Grand Tour* announces that he will provide:

I. A Description of the principal Cities and Towns, their Situation, Origin, and antient Monuments. II. The public Edifices, the Seats and Palaces of the Princes and Nobility, their Libraries, Cabinets, Paintings, and Statues. III. The Produce of the Countries, the Customs and Manners of the People, the different Coins, their Commerce, Manufactures, Learning, and present Government. IV. An exact List of the Postroutes, and of the different Carriages by Water and Land, with their settled Prices.

Clearly the benefits Bromley and Bacon and Nugent expect from 'travel' do not derive from the process of travelling itself, or from any particular way of travelling (although Nugent speaks of such things practically—and last), or even from the totality of the traveller's observations, but from particular observations of particular, essentially isolated things or places, the destinations of travel.

Sommer tells us, in fact, that the life-as-journey metaphor, from which optimism like Nugent's plainly gathers support, has little or nothing to do with representations of travel itself. Citing the episodic structure of pre-nineteenth-century narratives of fictional travel from *The Odyssey* to Smollett's *Roderick Random*, he warns his readers that they

may find that we say relatively little about travelling in itself, and that what might be regarded as an inordinate amount of time is spent upon wayside episodes, people, and human struggles apparently unrelated to the dreary process of plodding down a road or rowing a ship. . . . the nineteenth-century attention to the journey for its own sake and in itself has few earlier counterparts. . . . until close to the nineteenth century, most of the time, the journey was treated less as an experience in itself, and more as a formal arrangement of adventures in literature.[51]

[51] Roppen and Sommer, *Strangers and Pilgrims*, 19–20.

Sommer explains that 'This leap of attention from episode to episode occurs because ancient man, like the modern primitive, did not conceive of space or time as homogeneous or continuous; he understood the space and time through which he travelled always in terms of destination-points and particular adventures which had emotional or religious importance for him.'[52] As we shall see, this perceptual difference does indeed define the difference between the aesthetic of true travel and that of peripatetic. But I would locate the source of that difference not in some primitive 'misunderstanding', but in a highly functional response to the enormous material and psychological barriers to movement through time and space. The process of travel itself was such a gruelling experience, so fraught with dangers to individual and society, that in art as in life it was avoided whenever possible. Indeed, it may well be that some unconscious recognition of continuity, of the fact that travel is not only dangerous and uncomfortable in itself but is the means by which life-altering destinations and episodes are reached, forced a compromise in which change is confronted but a crucial portion of the means of change is suppressed. Observing only destinations contains and 'places' travel, apparently resolving its potential for change into discrete, manageable increments and separating it from both the traveller and his culture.

Interestingly enough, even representations of travel as destructive or useless conform to this pattern of suppression. Crusoe and Gulliver tell us surprisingly little of travel itself but explain all their sufferings and troubles as if these were the results of destination alone. Voltaire's *Candide* (1758) and Johnson's *Rasselas* (1759), both of which speak directly against the doctrine of 'true travel' in their concluding retreats, are as episodic as Bromley's descriptions of France and Italy. In *Rasselas*, Imlac talks about pilgrimage not in terms of movement versus stasis, but in terms of the efficacy of particular places:

Long journies in search of truth are not commanded. Truth, such as is necessary to the regulation of life, is always found where it is honestly sought. Change of place is no natural cause of the increase of piety, for it inevitably produces dissipation of mind. . . . but that some places may

[52] Ibid. 19.

operate upon our own minds in an uncommon manner, is an opinion which hourly experience will justify.[53]

Here, as in works that view the effects of travel more favourably, journeys are not considered useful in themselves, but particular destinations are understood to produce particular effects, perhaps even salutary ones. This representation of travel produces the illusion of the continuing, stabilizing isolation of place from place that legislation against travel and the implied definition of true travel also attempt to maintain.

The aesthetic of true travel, then, necessarily values isolated views and atomized perceptions that will not disturb local isolations, points of view that can display difference without permitting it to spread past its original boundaries. R. W. Frantz's study of *The English Traveller and the Movement of Ideas* suggests that in the Restoration and early eighteenth century this aesthetic took the shape of a growing concern for scientific accuracy and objectivity in travel accounts. Frantz demonstrates that English travellers of this period 'strove to adhere to certain ideals, voiced from time to time by the members of the Royal Society, which were intended to guide the serious promoters of the New Science. Of these, three were outstanding: objectivity, skepticism, and precision'. Thus, 'the normal in Restoration and early eighteenth-century travel-book prose style [was] the express concern for brief, precise statement and the penchant for detailed description of observable phenomena'.[54] This scientific strain remains a force in travel accounts of our own time—one may think of articles in the *National Geographic*, for instance—and was certainly still a powerful influence in the middle and late eighteenth century. Paul Fussell tells us that the 'primary orientation' of Captain Patrick Brydone, whose account of a tour of Sicily was among the most popular books of its day, is that of 'scientific observer and reporter. He wants to "account" for things . . . He is devoted to thermometer and barometer readings.'[55] Samuel Johnson, too, believes that 'No man

[53] Samuel Johnson, *Rasselas*, in *Rasselas, Poems, and Selected Prose*, 3rd edn. enlarged, ed. Bertrand H. Bronson (New York: Holt, Rinehart & Winston, 1958), 631.

[54] R. W. Frantz, *The English Traveller and the Movement of Ideas*, University Studies, vol. 32 (Lincoln: University of Nebraska Press, 1934), 30, 65.

[55] Paul Fussell, Jr., 'Patrick Brydone: The Eighteenth-Century Traveler as Representative Man', in Warner G. Rice (ed.), *Literature as a Mode of Travel* (New York: New York Public Library, 1963), 60.

should travel unprovided with instruments for taking heights and distances', and advocates extensive on-the-spot notes of one's observations:

He who has not made the experiment, or who is not accustomed to require rigorous accuracy from himself, will scarcely believe how much a few hours take from certainty of knowledge, and distinctness of imagery; how the succession of objects will be broken, how separate parts will be confused, and how many particular features and discriminations will be compressed and conglobated into one gross and general idea.[56]

As Johnson's comment suggests, a scientific perspective is particularly suitable to the practitioners of true travel. The theory behind such analysis and objectification, after all, is that the separation of parts from a whole and from other parts of that whole produces the best—the most accurate, most complete, and most useful—understanding both of the separated parts and of the whole field of observation. Clearly this theory concurs with that of true travel, in which the greatest value derives from viewing discrete destinations as if they were separated from each other and from the trip as a whole, thus compartmentalizing their differences and reducing the chance that one's observations will adversely affect oneself or one's own country. Johnson rigorously requires not only the rhetorical construction of spatial separation but an attempt at a similar temporal separation by which original distinct, 'separate', 'particular' observations may be held apart from the passage of time and so kept from coalescing into memory's 'gross and general idea[s]'. (One notices here the opposition between this theory of perception and Wordsworth's insistence upon recollection as the necessary arbiter of poetic vision—a direct conflict between the aesthetic of true travel and that of peripatetic.)

Adopting such a perspective produces a distinctive style of description, already exemplified to a certain extent in Bromley, but perhaps represented at its most developed by passages like these from Johnson's *Journey to the Western Islands of Scotland* (1775), in which he describes the small island Inch Kenneth and its even smaller neighbour:

[56] Samuel Johnson, *Journey to the Western Islands of Scotland*, in Johnson and James Boswell, *Journey to the Western Islands of Scotland and Journal of a Tour to the Hebrides with Samuel Johnson, L.L.D.*, ed. R. W. Chapman (Oxford: Oxford University Press, 1924), 133.

In the morning we went again into the boat, and were landed on Inch Kenneth, an island about a mile long, and perhaps half a mile broad, remarkable for pleasantness and fertility. It is verdant and grassy, and fit both for pasture and tillage; but it has no trees. Its only inhabitants were Sir Allan Maclean and two young ladies, his daughters, with their servants. . . .

Even Inch Kenneth has a subordinate island, named Sandiland . . . where we landed, and found a rock, with a surface of perhaps four acres, of which one is naked stone, another spread with sand and shells, some of which I picked up for their glossy beauty, and two covered with a little earth and grass, on which Sir Allan has a few sheep. . . .

Having wandered over those extensive plains, we committed ourselves again to the winds and waters; and after a voyage of about ten minutes, in which we met with nothing very observable, were again safe upon dry ground.[57]

If Johnson pays more attention to natural features than Bromley, he still contains our perceptions by focusing on the measurable qualities of numerical extent and human usage. The four acres of Sandiland are separated each from the other, as if stone, shell, and grass ended abruptly at some magical boundary; Sir Allan and his daughters rise like Easter Island stones from the verdant ground of Inch Kenneth, figures mysteriously without their landscape, unhoused and unmet. Most telling of all, journeys are literally 'unobservable': nothing can be read between entering a boat and landing on an island except, occasionally, one's watch.

When a journey is observable, in fact, it becomes an impediment, as when Johnson investigates the sea caves on Ulinish: 'We then walked through a natural arch in the rock, which might have pleased us by its novelty, had the stones, which incumbered our feet, given us leisure to consider it. We were shown the gummy seed of the kelp, that fastens itself to a stone, from which it grows into a strong stalk.'[58] Johnson's aesthetic appreciation of the arch is spoiled by his awareness of walking. He does not notice that this movement also creates the opportunity for possible appreciation, only that his awareness of his feet, of the physical process of walking, breaks up his attempt to isolate the cave's arch into some realm of pure observation and objective reaction. He turns quickly from this unpleasant consciousness to the kelp seeds which,

[57] Ibid. 129, 131.   [58] Ibid. 67.

with their adhesive stability, seem to steady him in his customary mode of analysis.

This is not an unconscious or unexamined reaction for Johnson, who is aware of how and why admitting the process of travel disrupts the aesthetic of true travel. When he and his party stop in a mountain valley to let their horses rest and feed, Johnson is able to enjoy a wild scene

such as a writer of Romance might have delighted to feign. I had indeed no trees to whisper over my head, but a clear rivulet streamed at my feet. The day was calm, the air soft, and all was rudeness, silence, and solitude. Before me, and on either side, were high hills, which by hindering the eye from ranging, forced the mind to find entertainment for itself. Whether I spent the hour well I know not; for here I first conceived the thought of this narration.[59]

Within this lovely view, framed by the hills and by Johnson's own stillness, true travel seems to be operating just as it should, the traveller's experience of renewal remaining contained in a particular destination which also moves him to unify his knowledge, 'to make the disparate elements of spirit and experience cohere', as Sommer puts it, in the form of a representation of his journey's ends. On the other hand, this passage does not have that tight analytic focus that we have so far associated with the aesthetic of true travel. Indeed, because the scene is natural, and the expressive impulse so simply stated, we might be tempted to read this as a Romantic travel experience if Johnson did not immediately assert that the process of travel actually threatens the scene's beneficial effects:

We were in this place at ease and by choice, and had no evils to suffer or to fear; yet the imaginations excited by the view of an unknown and untravelled wilderness are not such as arise in the artificial solitude of parks and gardens. . . . The phantoms which haunt a desert are want, and misery, and danger; the evils of dereliction rush upon the thoughts; man is made unwillingly acquainted with his own weakness, and meditation shows him only how little he can perform. . . . Whoever had been in the place where I then sat, unprovided with provisions and ignorant of the country, might, at least before the roads were made, have wandered among the rocks, till he had perished with hardship, before he could have found either food or shelter.[60]

[59] Ibid. 35.   [60] Ibid. 35–6.

At ease, by choice, with accessible roads at hand—these are the conditions of travel which help render its travail transparent and permit Johnson to reap the intellectual and emotional benefits of his destinations. Even under these ideal conditions, the spectres of wandering—poverty, aimlessness, hardship, mortality—afflict the imagination, casting shadows which distract Johnson from his appreciation of the scene at hand. He is painfully conscious that to become aware of the process of travel is to lose sight of destinations, to depart from them, in a sense, so that accurate, contained observation cannot be continued, and the aesthetic and intellectual advantage of true travel is lost.

Certainly Johnson's insertion of this argument immediately after his representation of a wild landscape suggests some kind of slip toward the uncontainable that his scientific perspective does not completely offset. In fact, as eighteenth-century travellers' observations shift toward appreciations of nature, the still dominant aesthetic of true travel finds a useful new manifestation in William Gilpin's advocacy of picturesque travel and sketching. Gilpin, a schoolmaster who travelled extensively during his vacations, described his search for picturesque views in a series of guides beginning in 1782 with *Observations of the Wye River*. In three 1792 essays, 'On Picturesque Beauty', 'On Picturesque Travel', and 'On the Art of Sketching Landscape', Gilpin articulates and popularizes an already extant practice of observing and representing landscape in terms of the artistic principles of sketching and painting, a practice which frames and controls one's perceptions. At least as early as 1769, when Thomas Gray made his historic tour of the Lake District, some travellers carried a Claude glass, an optical instrument that had been standard equipment in artists' studios since the seventeenth century.[61] The traveller happening upon a good view could, by turning his back and looking into the varnish-tinted, slightly convex mirror of the Claude glass, see the landscape as if it were a framed picture washed with the golden-brown glow of a painting by Claude Lorrain. William Wilberforce, who followed

---

[61] The primary source for my account of the Claude glass's construction and use is the entry for 'Claude glass' in *The Oxford Companion to Art*, ed. Harold Osborne (Oxford: Clarendon Press, 1970). The provenance of the glass remains unclear, but the use of the glass by artists dates from, or slightly before, Claude's work. Interestingly, the *OED*'s first usage citation is to Gilpin's 'On Picturesque Beauty' (1792), suggesting an entrance into English popular discourse and practice through Gilpin's essays.

Gray's example in his use of the glass as well as in his choice of locales, describes his delight in one particularly successful view taken during his tour of the Lakes in the summer of 1779: 'On the Right, from behind a piece of Rock which projected, breasted forth a Torrent of Water which I caught in my Glass (through a tree romantically fix'd in the Bare Rock & twisted) shining like diamonds, a Picture the finest my eyes ever beheld.'[62]

Looking at a natural landscape like this must have been something like walking through one of those English gardens in which follies and lakes are strategically placed so as to create 'views'. One thinks particularly of the eighteenth-century Rievaulx Terrace, which is constructed to allow successive but unconnected views of a landscape. The visitor to this garden walks along a winding grassy terrace bordered by trees which are cut away in strategic spots to afford brief views of the ruins of Rievaulx Abbey in the valley below. One might as well fly as walk, however: since even a step or two out of each leafy frame will destroy its effect, the impact of the design depends not upon movement but upon standing still at just the right point to see each view.

But the user of a Claude glass manipulates his view into something more literally 'picturesque' than any gardener could achieve. The coloured convex lens of the glass miniaturizes, colours, and simplifies the chosen image so that it becomes a study in light and shade—hence artists' common use of the glass, which abstracted compositional elements from a complex mass of perceptions. Moreover, in order to look through the glass, the viewer has to turn his back on the view, so that he actually cannot see it unmediated by the framing, colouring, proportioning glass.

Gilpin's essays make it clear that the pictorial aesthetic embodied in the Claude glass, although certainly not applicable only to the perceptions of travellers, descends in part from the doctrines of true travel. The 'picturesque traveller', engaged in 'amusing [himself] with *searching after effects*', may seem a rather dissolute version of the true-travelling pilgrim or Grand Tourist but, as Gilpin indicates, their basic principles are the same: 'as many travel without any end at all, amusing themselves without being able to give a reason why they are amused, we offer an end, which

---

[62] William Wilberforce, *Journey to the Lake District from Cambridge*, 1779 (Stocksfield: Oriel Press, 1983), 53.

may possibly engage some vacant minds; and may indeed afford a rational amusement to such as travel for more important purposes'.[63] To have an end, any end—to avoid wandering, in short—is as important to picturesque travelling as it is to the older forms of true travelling. Moreover, as the scientific traveller perceptually and rhetorically isolates his observations, the picturesque traveller seeks to separate his 'effects' from the process of travel and from each other. Arguing that 'The *art of sketching* is to the picturesque traveller [as] the art of writing is to the scholar . . . necessary to fix and communicate its respective ideas', Gilpin offers this advice:

when you meet with a scene you wish to sketch, your first consideration is to get it in the best point of view. A few paces to the right, or left, make a great difference. The ground, which folds awkwardly here, appears to fold more easily there; and that long blank curtain of the cattle, which is so unpleasing a circumstance, as you stand on one side, is agreeably broken by a buttress on another.[64]

Like the visitor to Rievaulx Terrace, Gilpin's sketcher moves about to find his view. But it is finally stillness and not movement that 'creates' the view, setting it in its frame; once the frame is found, the same movement '[a] few paces to the right or left' that established the view will destroy it.

As his recommendation of the Claude glass in 'On Picturesque Beauty' suggests, Gilpin not only urges finding and framing 'best' views but also isolating parts of views so that these parts can be detached from their original context and used to improve lesser views:

Sometimes we examine [natural scenes] under the idea of a *whole*: we admire the composition, the colouring, and the light, in one *comprehensive view*. . . . [but] we are more commonly employed in analyzing the *parts of scenes*; which may be exquisitely beautiful, tho unable to produce a whole. We examine what would amend the composition; how little is wanting to reduce it to the rules of our art; what a trifling circumstance sometimes forms the limit between beauty, and deformity.[65]

[63] William Gilpin, *Three Essays: On Picturesque Beauty; on Picturesque Travel; and on Sketching Landscape: To which is added a poem, On Landscape Painting* (London: R. Blamire, 1792), 41.

[64] Ibid. 61, 63.

[65] Ibid. 48–9. When James Plumptre wrote to Gilpin, apologizing for his satire of picturesque travel in *The Lakers* (1798), Gilpin's response included the claim

Thus, to some otherwise interesting scene occurring in barren surroundings Gilpin suggests adding hills observed elsewhere; where 'the lines of the country . . . run false', the sketching traveller 'must contrive to hide the offensive parts with woods; to cover such as are too bald, with bushes', and so forth.[66] Whether with or without a Claude glass, the picturesque sketcher abstracts forms from the landscape he sees, regarding them as compositional elements which may be rearranged at will.

Although Samuel Johnson might deplore the 'inaccuracy' of Gilpin's method, it is clearly a logical extension of Johnson's own analytic mode of observation and representation. Gilpin simply extends objectification to a complete detachment of parts from contexts so that, by reassembling the parts into more desirable configurations, fidelity to artistic (rather than scientific) principles can be achieved. To an even greater extent than the scientific traveller, in fact, the picturesque traveller avoids dangerous psychological engagement in movement, process, and change, for he need not perceive or represent his destinations as they are, but may immediately reshape them to fit his already settled ideas of beauty. Exotic shapes or combinations pose no problem: the picturesque traveller calmly makes them familiar.

In this sense, too, the picturesque solution to the problem of travel radically extends the scientific: not only is the process of travel, which embodies the movement and change feared (and desired) by the traveller, suppressed but the destinations of travel are effaced. The picturesque traveller need not 'go' anywhere, not even to the destinations sought by pilgrims, Grand Tourists, and scientific travellers, because he can displace his own experienced movement, moving and changing his destinations rather than himself. The picturesque taste for the sublime, for scenes inspiring terror and awe, is possible precisely because this displacement distances the viewer from what he sees and places the scene under his control. Like the audience of an Aristotelian tragedy, seekers

---

that he 'had [the use of the Claude glass] from Mr. Gray. I thought it a pleasing, as a novel mode of exhibiting nature; but I never esteemed it farther.' Gilpin's readers, it seems clear, thought otherwise. See the quotation from Gilpin's letter to Plumptre of 3 Feb. 1801 in Peter Bicknell and Robert Woof, *The Discovery of the Lake District, 1750–1810: A Context for Wordsworth* (Grasmere: Trustees of Dove Cottage, 1982), 40.

[66] Gilpin, *Three Essays*, 56, 70.

after the picturesque experience what might be overwhelmingly
negative emotions primarily as catharsis. What they see they see,
to some extent at least, as art, not as implacable or personally
threatening reality, and so some part of them remains unmoved,
capable of enjoying the distanced emotion from the viewpoint of
'not feeling'. In the same way the picturesque traveller, by keeping
both the process and the destinations of his travel essentially
invisible, can theoretically reap the aesthetic and intellectual
advantages of true travel from some still vantage point of 'not
travelling.'

Like Johnson's direct commentary, the implications of picturesque travel theory remind us that the high visibility of travel
practice before the transport revolution not only generates the
aesthetic of true travel but continually threatens it. This in turn
suggests that walking would be a particularly poor mode of travel
for one who pursues the ideal benefits of true travel. Certainly no
mode of travel during this period is so insistently legible as walking,
both because of its intense and often unpleasant physicality and
because of its socio-economic content. Unlike riding on a horse or
in some vehicle, modes which, despite their respective discomforts,
permit a certain illusion of passivity and 'stillness', walking demands muscular exertion, constantly pressing the traveller toward
direct, personal awareness of movement and so, as Johnson discovered, disrupting attempts to observe things in still isolation.
Walking is also read by others (and, where read correctly, by the
walker himself as well) as an announcement of a traveller's low
social and economic status, and hence his probable lack of both
the fitness and the means to achieve the desirable goals of true
travel. The demands of true travel aside, indeed, the negative
connotations of walking were so universally and clearly legible
that legal authorities sometimes specified public walking in their
sentences. In 1313, for instance, the penance required of Nicholas
the Porter, who had assisted civil authorities in breaching sanctuary, -
included (between whippings) a barefooted walk from the church
of St Nicholas to the cathedral in Durham on three successive days
of Whitsuntide.[67] The requirement that Nicholas be barefoot makes
it clear that the act of walking itself, not just the ordeal of public
exhibition, is meant as punishment, for bare feet enhance both the

[67] Jusserand, *English Wayfaring Life*, 157–8.

physical exertion and the implications of low social status associated with walking.

When walking is practised and/or represented as true travel,
then, its extraordinary degree of legibility resists the usual suppression of process with far more vigour and success than other
modes of travel. As a result, not only is such practice and representation rare, but it is designed to contain the legibility of walking
in extraneous or allegorical positions where the mode need be
only partially read, thus preserving the destination-oriented character of true travel mostly undisturbed. In the case of pilgrimage,
for instance, despite the traditional iconographic association between pilgrims and walking staffs, most licensed pilgrims were
well-to-do folk who eschewed the hardship and low prestige of
walking unless their extreme gratitude or penance required visible
personal humiliation. For these pilgrims, as for Nicholas the Porter, walking functioned as a lowering of personal prestige, a kind
of social bending of the knee, that was not a fundamental or
important part of pilgrimage itself but an embellishment appropriate to special cases. Henry Littlehales's *Some Notes on the Road
from London to Canterbury in the Middle Ages*, for instance,
includes this offhand remark on pilgrimages to Becket's shrine:
'The whole journey was sometimes performed on foot... The
Countess of Clare, in gratitude for the recovery of her son, made
the pilgrimage barefooted.'[68] Like the Porter, the Countess goes
barefoot, increasing her physical hardship and making herself look
(at least from her ankles down) poor, and so expresses her extraordinary gratitude by personal pain and humiliation. Pilgrims
in general, however, made no such sacrifices, being much better
represented by the fourteenth-century royal pilgrim for whom
carriages, as swifter and safer means of attaining important destinations, were classified with 'other necessaries'.[69]

In the same way, literary representations of pilgrimage specify
walking only when religious penance must be emphasized, and
even then work to distance the spiritual terms of the metaphor
from the physical. In Chaucer's *Canterbury Tales*, for instance, in
which the religious function of the pilgrimage has been reduced to
a bare minimum and the pilgrims' destinations appear to be the

[68] Henry Littlehales (ed.), *Some Notes on the Road from London to Canterbury
in the Middle Ages* (London: N. Trubner & Co., 1898), 52.
[69] Ibid. 53.

often secular and bawdy stories told along the way, horses are as indispensable as cloaks and boots, and the riding styles of their owners serve as natural parts of the pilgrims' portraits. On the other hand, the pilgrims of *Everyman*, *Piers Plowman*, and Bunyan's *The Pilgrim's Progress* do walk, for the same reason that they are named 'Everyman' or 'Christian', to signal the simultaneous commonness and difficulty of the life-journey toward salvation. The highly legible signs of 'the walker', the common, poor, sinful man, and 'walking', a universal yet difficult process, serve these allegories so well because we are constantly reminded that they are allegorical signs and so may be comfortably read. *Piers Plowman* and *Pilgrim's Progress*, in fact, make sure we read walking as a type rather than a material process by framing the 'action' as dream. We see not walking but dreams of walking, thus suggesting that walking can function as true pilgrimage only when it is abstracted from its powerfully annoying physical origins.

Even when such an allegory seems to mimic pedestrian process, as *Pilgrim's Progress* does to an astonishing extent for a pre-Romantic representation of walking, the fact that it is allegory prevents the reader from reading the physical process of walking itself as a necessary component of the journey toward salvation. At the foot of the Hill of Difficulty, for instance, Bunyan describes three ways leading on, one going straight up the hill and one on either side leading into woods and mountains respectively, and shows travellers on each way. When Christian climbs the hill he '[falls] from running to going, and from going to clambering upon his hands and his knees, because of the steepness of the place'.[70] This apparently intense physicality and recognition of process is mitigated, however, by its confinement between determinedly allegorical destinations: the Hill of Difficulty, the tempting byways Danger and Destruction, the Arbour of grace and rest, the meeting with Timorous and Mistrust at the top of the Hill. These repeated abstractions which demand our recognition of walking as allegory press us to read Christian's four-limbed clambering as spiritual rather than physical effort.

Moreover, the simple fact that walking as often takes a pilgrim off the true path as advances him along it shifts the emphasis of

---

[70] John Bunyan, *The Pilgrim's Progress*, ed. Roger Sharrock (Harmondsworth: Penguin, 1965), 74.

the narrative away from the mode of travel on to its destinations, all of which must be passed through in proper order by the traveller seeking salvation. It does not avail Ignorance, for instance, that he finally walks along the road to the Celestial City with Christian. Because he has come to the road by 'a little crooked lane' rather than by the Wicket Gate at the beginning of the way, not passing through the same sequence of trials, Christian tells Ignorance that he is liable to be charged as 'a thief and a robber instead of getting admittance into the City'.[71] Nathaniel Hawthorne's 'The Celestial Rail-road' presents an illuminating contrast, for in this satiric revision of Pilgrim's Progress whether one walks or not appears to be *the* factor which determines one's eligibility to enter the Celestial City. The way remains difficult for the foot-traveller, but all the walkers arrive at last at their salvation, while those who ride the Celestial Rail-road quite literally never touch upon the true way. To a much greater extent than Bunyan, clearly, Hawthorne connects the attainment of salvation with the selection of a mode of travel rather than with the selection of destinations.

Of course, secular true travelers such as Grand Tourists had little need to increase their degree of penitential humiliation. In one sense this meant the legibility of walking presented less threat to the benefits of true travel, since there was no reason to choose walking other than economic necessity—a rare condition among those of a class likely to undertake a Grand Tour, and so a rare phenomenon until that crucial period around the turn of the nineteenth century when Wordsworth took his pedestrian tour. Thus Richard Pyke, describing the Italian leg of the Grand Tour, asserts that there was 'One thing the traveller never did—walk. Only outlaws and madmen walked; it was considered neither safe nor a pleasure.'[72] More specifically, the absence of information on pedestrian routes and special requirements of foot travel in pre-nineteenth-century tour guides as comprehensive as Nugent's, with its otherwise detailed listings of transport routes, departure times,

---

[71] Ibid. 162.

[72] Richard Pyke, 'Round Italy', in Lambert, *Grand Tour*, 97. Two exceptions are William Coxe, whose walks through Switzerland Janet Adam Smith thinks may have been taken 'from pleasure rather than necessity', and William Beckford, who was 'in advance of his age in exploring some of the Rhine country on foot' ('Switzerland and the Alps', in ibid. 89; Letts, 'Germany and the Rhineland', in ibid., 130).

prices, and so forth, contrasts sharply with the enthusiasm for pedestrian touring evident in later guides. Janet Adam Smith sites this shift within the remarkably small range of thirty years: although 'by 1818 the "pedestrian tour" was being commended in the English edition of Ebel's [Swiss] Guide, both for reasons of health and economy', 'The 1788 Tour through Swisserland [Martyn] did not envisage foot-travel, except where no other kind was possible'.[73] Clearly, until this crucial period, walking was even more thoroughly excluded from the usual practice of Grand Touring than it was from that of pilgrimage.

When a Grand Tourist or other respectable traveller did go on foot, however, suppressing the mode of travel and keeping the subversive connotations of walking illegible evidently became quite difficult. Accounts of such pedestrian journeys tend, in the absence of religious allegory as a ready distancing device, to turn to humour. Thomas Coryate, perhaps the original Grand Tourist and 'foremost among . . . early literary pedestrians', spent May to September of 1608 travelling from his home near Odcombe in Somerset to Venice and back, accomplishing most of his return trip on foot.[74] His account of this journey, Coryat's Crudities: Hastily gobled up in five Moneths travells in France, Italy, etc. (1611), was 'the first, and for a long time remained the only handbook for continental travel', providing a quantity of information arguably unsurpassed until Nugent's Guide appeared.[75] Yet Coryate could not find a bookseller willing to print his book until he got a number of important people, including Ben Jonson, John Donne, Thomas Campion, and Inigo Jones, to make fun of his tour in mock panegyrics, and added these as a preface.

Some of Coryate's difficulty in finding a printer and some of the potential for parody in his adventures was unquestionably due to the oddity of touring in general in the early seventeenth century. As we might expect, Coryate avoids writing about the process of travel in general and pedestrianism in particular, and argues as a classic true-travel theorist that a traveller 'whose feete doe only move from place to place' is far inferior to one 'who moveth more

[73] Smith, in Lambert, Grand Tour, 89.
[74] Morris Marples, Shanks's Pony: A Study of Walking (London: J. M. Dent & Sons, 1959), 1.
[75] Edward Godfrey Cox, A Reference Guide to the Literature of Travel, vol. i (Seattle: University of Washington Press, 1935), 97.

in minde then body'.[76] Again as we might expect, what walking he did was probably motivated by economic necessity rather than by preference or bravado: 'On the outward journey, perhaps because [Coryate] still had money in his pocket, he used normal methods of transport whenever he could, travelling generally on horseback or by coach, sometimes by boat, and, when crossing the Alps . . . by *chaise-a-porteurs*.'[77]

But the aftermath of Coryate's publishing woes makes me suspect that his pedestrianism may have been the particular element of his travels which required the special distancing effects of parody. In the early summer of 1618 Ben Jonson, who edited Coryate's 'panegyrics' as well as contributing to them, set out to walk from London to Edinburgh. No one really knows why a man of his sedentary habits, age (he was 46), and weight (280 pounds) undertook such a journey, partly because Jonson never acted upon his reported intention 'to writt his foot pilgrimage hither, and to call it a Discoverie'.[78] Still, we do have a version of this journey, because John Taylor followed Jonson about a month later and recounted his own travels, including a brief meeting with Jonson, in *The Pennyles Pilgrimage, or The Money-lesse Perambulation of John Taylor, Alias The Kings Majesties Water-Poet* (1623).

Taylor's walk was perceived by his contemporaries as a physical parody of Jonson, and the *Pennyles* was expected to be another textual parody like Taylor's send-up of *Coryate's Crudities, Three Weekes, three daies, and three houres Observation and Travel, from London to Hamburgh in Germanie* (1617). The textual link between Jonson and Coryate, together with Jonson's decision to walk, makes a comparison of the two men and their travels seem natural, and parody evidently seemed a natural mode for such a comparison. Jonson himself jokes about the similarity, commenting to Drummond that the shoes he wore from Darnton to Leith were 'appearing like Coriats: the first two dayes he was all excoriate'.[79] When Taylor writes his book, he denies 'that I did undergoe this project, either in malice, or mockage of Maister

[76] Thomas Coryat[e], *Coryat's Crudities: Hastily gobled up in five Moneths travells in France, Italy, etc.*, 2 vols. (Glasgow: James MacLehose & Sons, 1905), 73, 74.
[77] Marples, *Shanks's Pony*, 3.
[78] William Drummond, *Ben Jonson's Conversations with William Drummond of Hawthornden*, ed. R. F. Patterson (London: Blackie & Son, 1924), 36.
[79] Ibid. 53.

Beniamin Jonson', whom Taylor met with on amiable terms while the two were in Scotland.[80] Instead, Taylor says, his intention was to test the hospitality of various places and people by travelling without money, relying on freely offered 'entertainment', as he calls it, to sustain him on his journey.

Still, one feels lurking in this endeavour a backhanded shot at Jonson by way of Coryate and pedestrianism. Despite Taylor's protestations that 'all is true', his earlier claim in the subtitle that 'he travailed on foot from London to Edenborough in Scotland, not carrying any Money to or fro, neither Begging, Borrowing, or Asking Meate, drink or Lodging' bears little resemblance to fact. Although Taylor sets out on foot and without ready cash, he takes with him both a servant and a 'guelded Nagge, | That with good understanding bore my bagge'. That 'bagge' includes a supply of food and drink for those times when hospitality fails him—and, as Marples points out, his reputation and acquaintance were extensive enough for Taylor to rely upon those failures being rare.[81] By the time the 'pedestrian' turns south again he rides a horse lent by a particularly generous friend (perhaps he only meant he would not *ask* for loans). Little wonder that Taylor, unlike a genuine vagrant, can get to Edinburgh without begging. Taylor's text, too, is traditionally episodic and destination-oriented. As Marples remarks, 'Although the road must have been crowded with all sorts of humble pedestrians—pedlars, tinkers, entertainers of all sorts . . . Taylor tells us nothing about them, and one might have supposed that he met no one on the journey other than his various hosts.'[82] But the *figure* of a penniless pilgrim, besides obviously being intended as an oddity and a selling-point, also immediately suggests to contemporary readers Jonson and Coryate's variously linked travels and the irony of such men—particularly Jonson— travelling in such a way. What did they do along the way, the reader wonders? If they had money, why walk? And if penniless, then did they beg their 'entertainment'? One way lies daftness, the

---

[80] Jonson's friendliness at this meeting may have been compounded with expedience. Drummond records Jonson's awareness that 'Tailor was sent along here to scorn him', and Jonson's kind reception of his fellow pedestrian included giving Taylor 'a piece of gold of two and twenty shillings to drink his health in England', circumstances suggesting a certain anxiety on Jonson's part, expressed, perhaps, with a bit of bribery (Drummond, *Ben Jonson's Conversations*, 50; Taylor quoted in ibid., p. xix).

[81] Marples, *Shanks's Pony*, 12.   [82] Ibid. 14.

other disgrace, and on neither road a way out for Jonson. Taylor's disclaimer becomes ironic itself: little need for direct mockery when Jonson's own actions proclaim themselves faintly ridiculous.

This trio of walkers and their texts show something of the complex forces working on secular representations of walking. On one hand such a mode of travel should be, and to a certain extent can be, disregarded: no one cares about 'pure' pedestrianism because all travel process is textually elided. On the other hand, the intense legibility of even partial pedestrianism draws the curious stare of the respectable, a selling-point perhaps, but one which must be handled with care. If the walker is not a genuine beggar or criminal, the reader confronts an uncomfortable incongruity between the walker's actual social identity and the apparent material and socio-economic content of his actions. In the case of religious pilgrimage, penitential intent offers a serious and acceptable explanation of the difference. In the case of these secular walks, however, in which even the term 'pilgrimage' takes on an ironic tint, no serious explanation seems up to the task, and the incongruity tends to resolve into laughter.

The specific origin of this laughter in walking can be seen in texts which are not travel accounts but which deliberately exploit the same reading of walkers. The rather scurrilous *A Walk to Islington* (1701), for instance, relies on the association between walking and promiscuity still evident in our phrase 'streetwalker', deriving partially from the old country custom of 'walking out', to play with 'commonness' in its sexual and social senses: 'when the Ladies of London | Walk out with their Spouses', they become rhetorically equivalent to 'Whores [who] have a more than an ord'nary Itching | To visit the Fields, and so Ramble a Bitching'.[83] Although in a much less bawdy vein, and with far greater skill, John Gay's georgic parody *Trivia; or, the Art of Walking the Streets of London* (1715) also depends upon the commonness of walking to contrast with the rarity of art. Even James Plumptre's *The Lakers* (1798), which contrasts two moral and gentlemanly pedestrians with a scoundrel true-traveller and a ridiculous female picturesque traveller, is written as 'A Comic Opera'. Taylor

---

[83] *A Walk to Islington. With a Description of New Tunbridge-Wells and Sadler's Music House. By the Author of the Poet's Rambles after Riches* (London, 1701). No page or signature numbers appear in this edition. The quotation is from the opening lines of the poem.

obviously recognizes and exploits this tendency to laugh at the discomfort generated by the spectacle of respectable walkers, and I believe Coryate's additions to his *Crudities* worked so well partly because they further defused the particular unfamiliarity of pedestrian travel by a respectable man. As for Jonson's 'Discoverie', I suspect it remained unwritten partly because of the discomfort inherent in 'writing a foot pilgrimage', a discomfort enhanced by Taylor's subtle parody of his journey.

The nearest things we have to serious literary representations of walking as secular true travel are derived from the traditional belief that the classical Greek philosophers called 'Peripatetics' were so called because they walked as they talked, taught, and meditated. Although this tradition is now considered spurious, walkers and peripatetic theorists from Thelwall to Stephen trot it out as an argument by exemplification, and it does in fact generate texts which seriously associate walking with philosophy. In a sense this tradition, although not overtly concerned with travel nor representing walking as travel *per se*, does seem to show walking as a vehicle by which Sommer's 'impulse after unity of knowledge, or understanding', one of the goals of secular true travel, may be attained. This positive connection is possible, however, precisely because (*a*) the usual connotations of walking as travel are not evoked and (*b*) walking remains a mere analogue of thought, rather than a genuine instrument or agent of it.

The first stanza of Thomas Traherne's 'Walking', for instance, characterizes its subject in this way:

> To *walk* abroad is, not with Eys,
> But Thoughts, the Fields to see & prize;
> Els may the silent Feet,
> Like Logs of Wood
> Mov up & down, & see no Good,
> Nor Joy nor Glory meet.[84]

In later stanzas Traherne utilizes natural and agricultural imagery that, in its association with walking, prefigures Romantic peri-

---

[84] Thomas Traherne, *Poems of Felicity*, ed. H. I. Bell (Oxford: Clarendon Press, 1910), 111. Traherne's 'Walking' was not published until the early 20th cent. and its specific date remains problematic. For an account of the manuscript of *Poems of Felicity*, of which 'Walking' is one, and of the probable parameters of these poems' dates of composition, see H. I. Bell's introduction. Traherne lived from 1637 to 1674.

patetic. But the poem as a whole valorizes the process of thought, not that of walking, and actually works to disconnect the two. As in the first stanza, the mind, not the eyes and feet, accomplishes the important labour. The body's action appears, in the poem's terms, merely as a physical analogue of an immaterial and higher process: 'To *walk* is by a Thought to go; | To mov in Spirit to & fro' (111). Thus the poem concludes:

> While in those pleasant Paths we talk
> 'Tis *that* tow'rds wch at last we walk;
> For we may by degrees
> Wisely proceed
> Pleasures of Lov & Prais to heed,
> From viewing Herbs & Trees.[85]

'*That*' is 'perfect Manhood . . . to which we shall be brought' by elevating ourselves from physical views to intellectual and spiritual ones, from viewing herbs and trees to viewing 'Lov & Prais'. Once again the crucial results of the journey are the results of its destination, an ideal perspective in the most extended sense which depends particularly on transcending physical processes. Thus walking, although offering a convenient analogy, is so utterly separated from the perfection of thought as to be devalued by it.

Similarly, in Samuel Johnson's 'To Spring' (*Rambler*, No. 5), his argument for reading 'the volume of nature' in order to 'multipl[y] the inlets to happiness' includes this curiously unintegrated remark: 'A French author has advanced this seeming paradox, that *very few men know how to take a walk*; and, indeed, it is true, that few know how to take a walk with a prospect of any other pleasure, than the same company would have afforded them at home.'[86] Within the context of his other comments, Johnson seems to mean that walking attentively, with 'Thoughts, the Fields to see & prize', is a good way to gather new observations for reflection and so improve one's disposition. Johnson does not make this connection explicit, however, and he rhetorically isolates the sentence on walking, giving it its own paragraph and not naming or alluding to 'walking' at any other point in the essay. The reader may forge the link to account logically for the presence of this odd paragraph, but the very act of that linking emphasizes the rhetorical

[85] Ibid. 112–13.
[86] Samuel Johnson, 'To Spring', in *Rasselas, Poems, and Selected Prose*, 75.

and cognitive gaps Johnson leaves between walking and the contemplation of nature: walking remains an inessential analogy to the important process of philosophical thought.

Although technically not a part of the English tradition, Rousseau's *Reveries of the Solitary Walker* (1782) deserves mention as perhaps the clearest case of the distancing of material walking from the intellectual and spiritual benefits of philosophy in this older 'peripatetic' tradition.[87] Rousseau presents this late 'appendix to [the] *Confessions*' as a record of 'The leisurely moments of my daily walks [which] have often been filled with charming periods of contemplation.'[88] But Rousseau's definition of 'reverie' identifies reverie with wandering, and disassociates both from purposeful philosophy:

> Reverie relaxes and amuses me; reflection tires and saddens me; thinking always was a painful and charmless occupation for me. Sometimes my reveries end in meditation, but more often my meditations end in reverie; and during these wanderings my soul rambles and glides through the universe on the wings of imagination ... [When depressed] I would wander at random through the woods and mountains, not daring to think for fear of stirring up my sufferings ... My eyes incessantly strayed from one object to another ... [and] I delighted in this ocular recreation which in misfortune relaxes, amuses, distracts the mind and suspends the troubled feeling.[89]

Walking as Rousseauan reverie, then, functions as leisurely, aimless wandering that releases the mind from both the labour of thought and the material bounds of the body so that it can achieve the disembodied flight of fancy. These benefits, moreover, are obtained by a solitary walker who has left the distractions and demands of human community behind. This solitary wandering does foster a 'return to nature' which nourishes the walker, but Rousseau's comments on the unfortunate distraction of physical existence from the spiritual make it clear that even the virtues of wandering are best disconnected from their material context. Within a page of

---

[87] Wordsworth's knowledge and use of Rousseau is much discussed, but there is no indication that he specifically knew *Reveries*. See esp. James K. Chandler's 'Rousseau and the Politics of Education', a chapter in Chandler's *Wordsworth's Second Nature: A Study of the Poetry and Politics* (Chicago and London: University of Chicago Press, 1989), 93–119.

[88] Jean-Jacques Rousseau, *The Reveries of the Solitary Walker*, trans. Charles E. Butterworth (New York: Harper Colophon, 1979), 6.

[89] 'Seventh Walk', ibid. 91–2.

his resolution to write about his walks he says that, despite the
ageing of his body, his 'soul is still active . . . [while] my body is
no longer anything to me but an encumbrance, an obstacle, and
I disengage myself from it beforehand as much as I can'. Again,
in the 'Seventh Walk', commenting on how knowledge of the
medicinal uses of plants rather spoils one's pleasure in them,
Rousseau argues that 'my soul could not rise up and glide through
nature as long as I felt it holding to the bonds of my body . . . No,
nothing personal, nothing which concerns my body can truly occupy
my soul.'[90] In such a context there can be little question that
'walking' has been dephysicalized into analogy and its material
components separated from the intellectual and spiritual growth it
'stands for'.

Before the transport revolution, then, the rare practice or representation of walking as true travel takes special measures to
elide walking's material character so that its subversive content—
poverty, necessity, wandering, and physical exertion and awareness—becomes less legible. Only through this careful suppression,
it appears, does it become possible to associate 'walking', now
well distanced from the material act, with the intellectual and
spiritual renovations which validate true travel. Clearly, Wordsworthian peripatetic and peripatetic theory, which emphasize
walking's process and describe it as the most effective mode in
which to pursue the life-journey impulses toward renewal and
knowledge, demonstrate a significant shift in interpretation that
nonetheless builds upon traditional apprehensions of walking and
upon the theory of true travel. Although the commonness of walking
still associates the walker with poverty and the labouring classes,
as in 'The Old Cumberland Beggar' or 'Michael', peripatetic now
also writes that commonness as 'common humanity', 'common
sense', 'compassion', 'economic sufficiency', even 'poetic labour'
and so 'artistic choice'. Similarly, although aimless wandering (like
Margaret's after her husband's enlistment in Book I of *The Excursion*) still threatens individual and community, the Wanderer
who returns averts the full force of this blow. His excursive perspective defines an aesthetic as carefully restricted, although restricted in particular movement rather than in particular stillness,
as true travel's pictorial aesthetic.

[90] 'First Walk', ibid. 6–7; 'Seventh Walk', ibid. 94–5.

The transport revolution's realization of the goals of true travel clearly contributes to this interpretative shift. As travel in general becomes physically easier, faster, and less expensive, more people want and are able to arrive at more destinations with less unpleasant awareness of their travel process. At the same time the availability of an increasing range of options in conveyance, speed, price, and so forth actually encouraged comparisons of these different modes—hence the explosion of statistics on travel toward the close of the eighteenth century—and so an increasingly positive awareness of process that even permitted semi-nostalgic glances back at the bad old days like De Quincey's. Then, too, although local insularity was more and more threatened, and localities did indeed begin to 'lose their character' in the ways Youngson and Barrell note, people also quite literally became more accustomed to travel and travellers, less fearful of 'foreign' ways, so that they gradually became able to regard travel as an acceptable recreation. Finally, as speeds increased and costs decreased, it simply ceased to be true that the mass of people were confined to that circle of a day's walk: they could afford both the time and the money to travel by various means and for purely recreational purpose—'at ease, by choice', with roads nearby, as Samuel Johnson puts it. And as walking became a matter of choice, it became a possible positive choice: since the common person need not travel by walking, so walking travellers need not necessarily be poor. Thus, as awareness of process became regarded as advantageous, 'economic necessity' became only one possible reading (although still sometimes a correct one) in a field of peripatetic meanings that included 'aesthetic choice'.

As the discussion above indicates, the first great surge of these transformations was accomplished by the 1820s or 1830s. The generalized marker—'the end of the eighteenth century' or 'the beginning of the nineteenth', often used by Bagwell, the Webbs, and Youngson for the change in travel conditions, by Marples and Bayne-Powell for the change in attitudes toward walking, and by Sommer for the change in representations of travel—may be specified to a surprising extent. De Quincey cites MacAdam's influence, which by February 1818 had extended from the latter's appointment in 1816 as surveyor for a Bristol turnpike trust to eleven other trusts, encompassing more than 700 miles of road in fifteen counties. Telford's ideas, upon which MacAdam's were considered an improvement, had only been in official use in some areas since around 1810.[91] Changes in the practice and representation of walking seem to have been almost simultaneous. In the early 1790s pedestrian tours like Wordsworth's in Europe and Joseph Budworth's in the Lakes are still isolated affairs, and the walkers' representations of their experience still celebrate the picturesque aesthetic. When James Plumptre, himself a vigorous pedestrian tourist in the Lake District, publishes his send-up of 'Lakers' in 1798, he represents pedestrians as heroic but uncommon, looked upon with contempt or astonishment by other travellers.[92] Yet within less than twenty years, Wordsworthian peripatetic finds its fullest single expression in *The Excursion* (1814), and the inclusion of pedestrian touring advice in the 1818 Ebel's *Guide* marks the practical acceptance of walking as a positive educative mode of travel.

This cluster of dates represents the first 'dramatic climax' of the transport revolution, when travel by fast new carriages on stable roads entered its period of dominance, and differences from past modes of travel became dramatically apparent. 'By about 1820', Bagwell tells us, 'it was quicker to travel by fast coach than on horseback.'[93] By this time, too, the turnpikes, 'now serv[ing] national rather than predominantly local purposes', 'made it possible for the roads to accommodate a greatly increased number of vehicles which could travel with relative safety at speeds two, or even three, times those of the pre-turnpike era. . . . Comparing the 1750s with the 1830s journey times on the main routes linking the principal cities were reduced by four-fifths; comparing the 1770s with the 1830s the times were halved.'[94] That the turnpikes were in fact designed with 'national' purposes in mind only increased the natural effect of increased speed and safety: the number of people travelling the roads appears to have increased dramatically, further reducing local isolation and, evidently, fear of travel. The

[91] Bagwell, *Transport Revolution*, 40.
[92] Peter Bicknell and Robert Woof identify Budworth's *A Fortnight's Ramble in the Lakes* (1792) as 'the first recorded Lake District walking tour. Budworth walked upwards of 240 miles besides boat and chaise conveyance' (p. 36). For a thorough and interesting account of the beginning and progress of Lake District tourism, including pedestrian touring, see Bicknell and Woof's *The Discovery of the Lake District, 1750–1810: A Context for Wordsworth* (Grasmere: Trustees of Dove Cottage, 1982).
[93] Bagwell, *Transport Revolution*, 49.   [94] Ibid. 41.

statistics are impressive. Bagwell calculates that ten million coach journeys were made in 1835, so that '15 times as many people were travelling by stage coach in the mid 1830s as were doing so 40 years earlier'.[95]

Even this increase seems small, however, when Bagwell goes on to compare it with the change between '30 million journeys a year by rail in 1845 and 336½ million journeys by the same means in 1870'.[96] The rise of railway construction from the 1830s, peaking in the astonishing year of 1846 (the transport revolution's second 'dramatic climax'), when 4,540 miles of railway were sanctioned by Parliament, produced an explosion of travel that thoroughly eclipsed the increases in coach travel.[97] Much of this travel, too, was holiday travel undertaken by people who could not have afforded the time or money to take such a holiday by road. Bagwell cites the specific case of the Newcastle and Carlisle line, upon which, after the opening of

its entire length on 18 June 1838 eleven times as many persons travelled by train as had previously gone by coach. Before the railway enabled the weavers and the mechanics of Dundee to reach the seaside resort called the Ferry very few of them made the effort to reach it as the only means of travel was on foot or by one of the carriers' slow moving carts. In seven months of 1839, however, not less than 61,876 third-class tickets were sold on this short line.[98]

In 1839 the price of a third-class ticket might still be relatively high, depending on the railway. In 1844, however, Gladstone's Railway Act was passed, ensuring that third-class accommodations would be available 'on at least one train a day in each direction through each company's network', providing the labouring classes with 'penny-a-mile travel under the minimum conditions of comfort'. Improvements in third-class coaches followed, and, for some time after that, third-class travel on railways increased even more rapidly than first- and second-class, until by 1890 72.5 per cent of the Midland Railway's annual revenue was from third-class travel.[99]

Parliament eventually pressed for even cheaper fares that would permit labourers to live outside of city centres—that is, to live more

[95] Ibid. 43.   [96] Ibid.   [97] Ibid. 94.
[98] Ibid. 107.   [99] Ibid. 109, 109–10.

than walking distance away from their work. At first this was done by constraining individual corporations, as in the Great Eastern Railway Act of 1864, which required Great Eastern 'to provide at least one workmen's train up to town before 7 a.m. and from town after 6 p.m. from Edmonton, Walthamstow and other specified stations to Liverpool Street at no more than one penny for the whole journey'. In 1883 the Cheap Trains Act traded exemption from paying Passenger Duty on third-class tickets on workmen's trains for the right of the Board of Trade to determine schedules for those trains, with the result that three decades later workmen's tickets accounted for about one-quarter of suburban rail travellers. The final link in this transportation chain was the London Underground, which took workers from rail stations on into the city, thus reducing the congestion of the roads and, of course, significantly reducing the number who walked each day from the suburbs to their work (still totaling 400,000 in London in 1854).[100] Thus the railways not only greatly increased the amount of domestic travel and the number of travellers of low socio-economic standing, but also became for urban labourers the everyday passage between work and home that the footpath was for rural labourers.

This freeing of people from the economic necessity of walking, which had palpable effects by the early 1800s and has continued to grow in force and speed right up to the present day, clearly makes it possible to practise and think about voluntary walking, and about walking as travel, as something done 'at ease, by choice' and as having benefits like those of true travel. However, the whole project of freeing people from walking was undertaken not to enable people to choose walking but to enable them to enjoy the results of destination with even less trouble about the process of travelling than before. This is evident in the case of Shanklin, a small village connected to the rail system in 1864: 'No sooner had the first sounds of a locomotive whistle been heard . . . than the editor of a local newspaper grumbled that many of the visitors brought by the railway had had "great difficulty in finding the beauty spots" and that not only improved signposting, but better roads and gas lighting, were urgently needed.'[101] For this editor, beauty is confined to 'spots' which must be made as painlessly accessible as possible.

[100] Ibid. 134, 135.   [101] Ibid. 124.

In short, the rise of the railroads actually fuelled the growing popularity of walking tours, presumably because one could now arrive relatively painlessly at the places where one did want to walk, without the gruelling task of walking all the way, say, from Calais to the Alps.[102] Peripatetic practice and theory arise out of the growing realization of true travel, peripatetic's challenge to the older tradition remaining dependent upon true travel's continuing material success.

[102] Marples, *Shanks's Pony*, 137.

2

Replacing Cultivation

DURING the same period of time in which the transport revolution allowed travellers to approach the ideal of destination-oriented travel and encouraged new attention to the process of travel, the accelerating enclosure of agricultural land in England contributed to a double displacement of small farmers and rural labourers. Not only did the appropriation of common lands and the reorganization of open fields literally remove these people from the lands they cultivated, either directly or through gradual impoverishment that forced freeholders off their lands and labourers into wandering, but the accompanying changes in the rural landscape displaced even those who retained their economic and physical positions by rendering unrecognizable the shapes and experiences and perspectives which had defined the localities in which they lived and worked. Thus enclosure, like the transport revolution, directed attention toward process and change; and, as the transport revolution altered the socio-economic content of walking in such a way that walking, with its particularly accessible process, could be regarded as a mode of travel, so enclosure revealed walking as an instrument of reappropriation of common lands and perspectives that simultaneously stabilized old local forms and opened those forms to extra-local use and interpretation.

In the literature of this period, an increasing dissatisfaction with a pictorial aesthetic which favours effortlessly attained, optimal perspectives indicates a growing awareness of accelerating material change and the need for a poetic perspective that somehow accounts for such change. At the same time georgic, which imagines the farmer's laborious rural life as mediating between past and future, rural and urban, and civilizing and destructive appropriation, is generally understood to disappear as a separate genre, and cultivators rarely appear without some qualification of their mediative capacity.[1] William Cowper, John Thelwall, James Plumptre, Jane

---

[1] For post-18th-cent. texts, standard interpretative practice conflates georgic and pastoral into a single retrospective rural mode called 'pastoral', a move with which I will take issue in the next chapter.

Austen, and John Clare, with varying degrees of consistency, all
turn to pedestrian perspective as the appropriate alternative to the
disembodied views usually characterized as 'Fancy's flight', implicitly recognizing the possibilities of walking's new material
context. Cowper and Clare also, although again very differently,
associate walking with rural labours and the effects of enclosure.
As we read these partial approaches to peripatetic and consider
their material context, the strength of Wordsworth's choice of
the walker to fill the ideological space from which the farmer
was being expelled becomes clear: the localizing yet travelling
action of walking replaces cultivation, not only in the formal sense
of metaphorical substitution, but in the sense of redefining cultivation in its extended sense as being both placed and moving,
stable and changing.

Virgil's ideal cultivator, whether he is the prosperous farmer of
Book II with many labourers in his employ or the Corycian man
whose own working of a small plot produces happy self-sufficiency,
directs his labour into his land, and it is this placement of his care
which preserves the wellbeing of both his family and his nation:
'The farmer cleaves the earth with his curved plough. | This is his
yearlong work, thus he sustains | His homeland, thus his little
grandchildren' (*Georgics*, II. 513-15). Virgil prefaces this description of the farmer's labour with warnings against the destructive
mobility and manufactured wealth of politicians, soldiers, and city
dwellers:

> One is prepared
> To plunge a city's homes in misery
> All for a jewelled cup and a crimson bedspread;
> Another broods on a buried hoard of gold. . . .
> . . . .
> Men revel steeped in brothers' blood, exchange
> The hearth they love for banishment, and seek
> A home in lands beneath an alien sun.   (II. 504-6, 510-12)

Virgil does not shrink from investigating the similarities of cultivation and conquest, especially as potentially violent appropriations of territory. Clearly, however, he regards the exiled, wandering military livelihood, depending as it does upon mobility and
portable wealth, as dangerously unstable, and looks to the settled,
land-wealthy farmer for a conservative antidote.

Enclosure undermined contemporary English models of Virgil's metaphor, appropriating small freeholds and common lands that sustained the independent farmer and agricultural labourer and so disassociating these cultivators from their lands and their means of livelihood. In assessing John Clare's reactions to this trend, Raymond Williams warns against visualizing some pre-enclosure age of agrarian bliss: 'There was no fall from Eden, but rather a new phase of the long conquest and repression of working country people by wave after wave of landlords and masters. . . . the broad tendency of conquest and appropriation, using every kind of legal and illegal means, had begun long before any time to which Clare could trace his ancestors and was to continue, in new ways, long after him.'[2] This useful correction offers a longer, narrower view that clarifies our perceptions of the material history of land use in England. Yet, given both a much briefer timespan and the inevitable interpenetration of the personal and ideological with the material, Clare's sense of some present crisis is no less accurate. Despite the gradual rise of enclosures from the sixteenth century on, at the middle of the eighteenth century 'roughly half of the area under plough in English agriculture remained to be enclosed'.[3] During the next 125 years—Gray identifies 1755 to 1870 as the period of greatest change—almost all of that land was formally enclosed, so that 'by the end of the nineteenth century an open-field township in England had become a curiosity'.[4] Dahlman, indeed, says that the open-field system was 'virtually non-existent' by the *middle* of the nineteenth century.[5] Whatever parameters one chooses, there can be little question that, from the mid-eighteenth century on, the process of enclosure was 'enormously accelerated' by a complex of factors including 'the need to fashion an agrarian countryside to serve the expanding markets of the towns and colonies', Parliament's consequentially favourable attitude toward enclosing lands to improve production, the increasing sophistication of large-scale farming techniques, and 'the gradual improvement of transport

---

[2] Raymond Williams, in the introduction to John Clare, *John Clare: Selected Poetry and Prose*, ed. Merryn and Raymond Williams (London and New York: Methuen, 1986), 14.

[3] Carl J. Dahlman, *The Open Field System and Beyond* (Cambridge: Cambridge University Press, 1980), 168.

[4] Howard Levi Gray, *English Field Systems* (Cambridge, Mass.: Harvard University Press, 1915), 110, 10.

[5] Dahlman, *Open Field System*, 168.

facilities . . . lowering the costs of taking the agricultural products to the urban markets'.[6]

The specific effects of enclosure in given areas are controversial, but there is general agreement that 'the dispossession of the small landed proprietor—before or after enclosure—was usual. The degradation of the labourer after the loss of his common "rights" was very usual'.[7] A response to historians who discount the importance of this effect of enclosure for the national economy states the case more forcefully: 'enclosures lead to highly complex economic changes—changes that are technically progressive, since they give rise to greater efficiency and specialization, but are simultaneously socially disastrous to labour, since in themselves, they produce, by inexorable economic logic, an initial and appreciable decline in the standard of living of peasants and so of the working population as a whole'.[8] In short, as the appropriation of both smaller freeholds and common or waste lands created larger farms (or private parks) and improved agricultural production, it simultaneously displaced small freeholding farmers and reduced labourers' chances of both living wages and supplementary income based on commons rights. Thus increasing agricultural wealth paradoxically impoverished the countryman.

The growing scarcity of ideal Virgilian cultivators in late eighteenth- and nineteenth-century literature parallels the economic displacement associated with enclosure. Representatives of a stable, successful yeomanry like Jane Austen's gentleman-farmer, Robert Martin, become as rare as actual English freeholders who can maintain an independent subsistence. Wordsworth's freeholders —the Wanderer's parents, Michael and Isabel, the unfortunate sheep-herder in 'The Last of the Flock'—suffer straitened circumstances despite their industry and virtue; R. D. Blackmore

---

[6] Ann Bermingham, *Landscape and Ideology: The English Rustic Tradition, 1740–1860* (Berkeley: University of California Press, 1986), 9; Dahlman, *Open Field System*, 167–8. For a succinct summary of the enclosure movement and some cogent remarks on the 'familiar pattern of actual loss and imaginative recovery' described in artistic as well as literary representations of the agrarian landscape in the 18th cent., see Bermingham, *Landscape and Ideology*, 9–11.

[7] W. E. Tate, *The English Village Community and the Enclosure Movements* (London: Victor Gollancz, 1967), 90.

[8] Jon S. Cohen and Martin L. Weitzman, 'Enclosures and Depopulation: A Marxian Analysis', in William N. Parker and Eric L. Jones (ed.), *European Peasants and their Markets: Essays in Agrarian Economic History* (Princeton, NJ: Princeton University Press, 1975), 176.

places John Ridd's heroic mixture of independence, prosperity, and rough rural virtue in the seventeenth century, where it can command a certain nostalgic credulity; even Hardy's Gabriel Oak appears an anomaly in a world of poor husbandmen, of Sergeant Troys and Farmer Boldwoods. This literary depopulation of the countryside represents an England where cultivation no longer secures either the prosperity of the individual or the stability of the nation. Enclosed farmlands, indeed, are insistently imagined as deserts emptied of value by agriculture itself, from the 'endless wastes of corn' on 'Salisbury Plain' to Clare's lovingly remembered commons, 'All leveled like a desert by the never weary plough' ('Remembrances', 48).

In fact, enclosure unsettled the rural landscape as thoroughly as the rural economy. W. G. Hoskins, discussing the parliamentary enclosures from the time of George II on, notes that 'within a year or two years of the passing of the [enclosure] act', the majority of affected parishes underwent

a complete transformation, from the immemorial landscape of the open fields, with their complex pattern of narrow strips, their winding green balks or cart-roads, their headlands and grassy footpaths, into the modern chequer-board pattern of small, squarish fields, enclosed by hedgerows of hawthorn, with new roads running more or less straight and wide across the parish in all directions. . . . A villager who had played in the open fields as a boy, or watched the sheep in the common pastures, would have lived to see the modern landscape of his parish completed and matured, the roads all made, the hedgerow trees full grown, and new farmhouses built out in the fields where none had ever been before. Everything was different: hardly a landmark of the old parish would have remained.[9]

If not literally desert, this new landscape might as well have been a trackless wilderness to its inhabitants, for whom crucial interpretative signs that guided movement and evoked emotion

[9] W. G. Hoskins, *The Making of the English Landscape* (Harmondsworth: Penguin, 1955), 179. Hoskins figures his own work of recovering *The Making of the English Landscape* as a pedestrian task, closing his chapter on 'Parliamentary Enclosure' with a hypothetical walk 'in the pastoral, remote country on the borders of Leicestershire and Rutland' that passes 'in a walk of nine or ten miles through a landscape modelled in five different centuries', in separate enclosures dating from 1496 to 1842. 'So, behind every generalization', Hoskins writes, 'there lies the infinite variety and beauty of the detail; and it is the detail that matters, that gives pleasure to the eye and to the mind, as we traverse, *on foot* and unhurried, the landscape of any part of England' (pp. 209–10, emphasis mine).

had vanished forever. Thus, at the same time as the rewards of staying in one place, of farming a freehold or working at one trade, diminished, and as the transport revolution increased the speed of travel between places, the rural landscape underwent changes so rapid and significant that everyone lived as if they were travelling, the country changing around them even if they did not move.

Neither true travel, with its emphasis on destinations, nor Virgilian cultivation, with its crucial placement in the land, generates useful aesthetic standards for an age in which even freeholding farmers experience accelerating changes in their physical surroundings that mimic movement from place to place. The problem which must be solved is a complex one. The culture needs continuity as the individual needs memory, and yet there is all this change and movement which seems to break the continuity of tradition, place, time, speed, at both levels. In the mid-nineteenth century, Ruskin sets the resolution of this dissonance as the first task of those who look at 'modern landscapes' in poetry or painting (his examples are Scott and Turner):

we find ourselves on a sudden brought under sombre skies, and into drifting wind; and, with fickle sunbeams flashing in our faces, or utterly drenched with sweep of rain, we are reduced to track the changes of the shadows on the grass, or watch the rents of twilight through angry cloud. And we find that whereas all the pleasure of the mediaeval was in *stability*, *definiteness*, and *luminousness*, we are expected to rejoice in darkness, and triumph in mutability; to lay the foundation of happiness in things which momentarily change or fade; and to expect the utmost satisfaction and instruction from what is impossible to arrest, and difficult to comprehend.[10]

Now the individual or culture framing an idyllic future must, as Schiller suggested, comprehend motion in its vision of continuity and stability.[11] In the experienced world, as in the represented,

[10] John Ruskin, *Modern Painters*, vol. iii (Chicago and New York: Belford Clarke & Co., n.d.), 271–2.

[11] For a discussion of Schiller's requirements for idyll see Lore Metzger's discussion of Schiller's *On the Aesthetic Education of Man* and *On Naive and Sentimental Poetry* in her *One Foot in Eden: Modes of Pastoral in Romantic Poetry* (Chapel Hill and London: University of North Carolina Press, 1976), 7–42. She describes Schiller's 'master problem' for the writer of idyll: 'how to introduce dynamic life into a still center, tension and energy into tranquility and repose, aspiration into fulfillment, theory into praxis, the subjunctive into the indicative mood' (p. 38).

people need to know how to see and interpret an environment which is increasingly mutable, both because the environment itself is rapidly changing and because people are moving through it at greater and more varied speeds. Moreover, they need to see it in ways that permit some kind of memorial continuity so that they can reflect on and act on that environment, rather than passively suffering it. When I speak of 'aesthetic standards', then, I am not only speaking of standards for artistic representation and interpretation, but also of actual physical modes of perception which may be selected for their everyday material usefulness.

Wordsworth demonstrates concern for this everyday aesthetic usage in his arguments against the Kendal and Windermere railway project, commenting that the 'good [of experiencing natural beauty] is not to be obtained by transferring at once uneducated persons in large bodies to particular spots', but instead by encouraging 'little excursions with their wives and children among neighbouring fields, whither the whole of each family might stroll'.[12] His condescension toward the vacationing labourers would be more annoying if he did not go on to criticize the wealthier (and presumably better-educated) tourists he saw driving through the Alps where he once walked as a 'fellow-traveller' with stream and road: 'instead of travellers proceeding, with leisure to observe and feel, [they] were pilgrims of fashion hurried along in their carriages, not a few of them perhaps discussing the merits of "the last new Novel," or poring over their Guide-books, or fast asleep'.[13] Clearly, his full argument represents a direct rejection of the true travel aesthetic as it affects the everyday practice of people of all classes. The crucial thing, Wordsworth plainly says, is not to gain knowledge of any particular place or places, but to be able to see and examine the moving passage between places, the process of change itself. And the perspective from which this may be accomplished, he says with equal clarity, is that of the excursive pedestrian.

For Wordsworth, as we shall see, that perspective is also the ideal poetic perspective, one which permits the representation of idyll by combining movement and stability in a recurring scrutiny

[12] William Wordsworth's letter of 9 Dec. 1844 to the *Morning Post*, appended by Ernest de Selincourt to his 1906 edition of Wordsworth's *Guide to the Lakes* (repr. Oxford: Oxford University Press, 1970), 152.
[13] A second, undated letter to the *Morning Post*, also appended to Wordsworth, *Guide*, 163–4.

of process. Even before Wordsworth accomplishes his extension of georgic into peripatetic, in fact, a number of crucial texts mimic pedestrian perspective, imaginatively identifying that perspective with the aesthetic qualities that peripatetic theorists will explicitly assert as advantageous: an intimate knowledge of travelled space acquired by natural pace; a continuous, traceable path of perceptions and so of memories from destination to destination; a sense of limited perspective requiring continued movement, continued process, continued expansion. These texts mark an approach to peripatetic's mediative solution from the eighteenth-century poems, linked to Wordsworth's *Excursion* by generic affiliation and/or by their use of pedestrian characters or events, that favor a mode of perception called 'excursive' and characterized as effortless flight.

John Gay's *Trivia; or, the Art of Walking the Streets of London* (1715) exploits the incongruity of a pedestrian-poet by means of a georgic 'parody' which humorously proposes the substitution of walker for cultivator that Wordsworth will later propose seriously.[14] Instead of Virgil's 'What makes the corncrops glad, under which star | To turn the soil . . . and wed your vines | To elms', Gay's opening lines are:

> Through Winter Streets to steer your Course aright,
> How to walk clean by Day, and safe by Night,
> How jostling Crouds, with Prudence, to decline,
> When to assert the Wall, and when resign,
> I sing: Thou *Trivia*, Goddess, aid my Song,
> Thro' spacious Streets conduct thy Bard along;
> By thee transported, I securely stray
> Where winding Alleys lead the doubtful Way,
> The silent Court, and op'ning Square explore,
> And long perplexing Lanes untrod before.[15]

Trivia, indeed, proves the proper muse for Gay's song. W. H. Williams's notes identify 'Trivia' as the 'epithet of Diana as worshipped where three ways meet'; the Latin sense of a crossroads leads to the English 'trivial', which first designates the commonplace

---

[14] Dwight L. Durling, *Georgic Tradition in English Poetry* (New York: Columbia University Press, 1935), 41.

[15] John Gay, *Trivia; or, the Art of Walking the Streets of London*, introd. W. H. Williams (London: Daniel O'Connor, 1922), Book I, lines 1–10. Further quotations from Gay will be cited in the text by book and line number.

and everyday, and then the unimportant and little esteemed.[16] Gay's joke depends on just this movement: elegant suggestions of divine inspiration and Roman roads descend toward advice on an activity his audience perceives as commonplace and unimportant. He fills the serious, classical forms of Virgil's *Georgics* with 'insubstantial' matter, and so makes them humorous. Gay's first book, for instance, makes fun of the contrast between the labours of the Virgilian farmer and those of the London walker. Titled 'Of the Implements for Walking the Streets, and Signs of the Weather', it offers the equivalent of the *Georgics*' description of 'the armament | Tough country-dwellers use', advising the walker on the selection of shoes and coats and canes—and just so we don't miss the point, reminds us that 'when too short the modish Shoes are worn, | You'll judge the Seasons by your shooting Corn' (Virgil, I. 160–1; Gay, I. 39–40). Instead of Ceres' gift of the plough, we are told of the origin of pattens in the sufferings of one 'blue-ey'd Patty', a maiden beloved of Vulcan who literally gets cold feet:

> This *Vulcan* saw, and in his heav'nly Thought,
> A new Machine Mechanick Fancy wrought,
> Above the Mire her shelter'd steps to raise,
> And bear her safely through the Wintry Ways.
> Strait the new Engine on his Anvil glows,
> And the pale Virgin on the Patten rose. (I. 271–6)

Trivia's facetious casting of poet as walker has two interesting effects which foreshadow the serious peripatetic, and so contrast sharply with other eighteenth-century forerunners of Wordsworth's *Excursion*. The first of these is an emphasis on the actual physical sensations of walking. Gay's descriptions of the rain and cold and mire that afflict the walker, and of the dangers of getting lost or mugged in the mazy London streets, certainly feed the reader's expected dislike for walking. Together with their suggested remedies, however, they also suggest that walking can be a conscious labour which, when done well, confers certain benefits on the walker. In this sense these descriptions work much like the opening of the *Excursion*, in which the narrator's difficult walk to the ruined cottage seems to produce the benefits of the Wanderer's tale.

The nature of those benefits is the second result of the poet appearing as walker, for Gay gives his pedestrians the superior

---

[16] Williams in Gay, *Trivia*, 60.

physical, economic, and moral health Virgil gave his model farmer at the end of Book II of the *Georgics*. Because 'no Coach to frequent Visit rolls, I Nor for your Shilling Chairman sling their Poles', pedestrians evade a list of physical ills including jaundice, asthma, gout, and gallstones (II. 379–88). Moreover, Gay's walker lives a thrifty but sufficient life. From handbills he 'learns the cheapest Tailor's Name' (II. 420), and from the various markets he may well 'supply the Wants of Life, I Support thy Family, and cloath thy Wife (II. 427–8), while avoiding the waste and heartless excess of the wealthy who ride in coach and chair:

> This Coach, that with the blazon'd 'Scutcheon glows,
> Vain of his unknown Race, the Coxcomb shows.
> Here the brib'd Lawyer, sunk in Velvet, sleeps;
> The starving Orphan, as he passes, weeps;
> There flames a Fool, begirt with tinsilled Slaves,
> Who wastes the Wealth of a whole Race of Knaves.
> That other, with a clustring Train behind,
> Owes his new Honours to a sordid Mind.
> This next in Court Fidelity excells,
> The Publick rifles and his Country sells.
> May the proud Chariot never be my Fate,
> If purchas'd at so mean, so dear a Rate;
> O rather give me sweet Content on Foot,
> Wrapt in my Vertue, and a good *Surtout*!   (II. 455–68)

That last line, in which virtue is as easily assumed as an overcoat, delivers the parodic thrust which prevents *Trivia* from being mistaken for a serious precursor of peripatetic. Still, Gay's formal substitution of walker for farmer in the georgic mode generates some of the same associations crucial to Wordsworthian peripatetic: walking becomes a conscious physical labour which produces physical, economic, and moral health, and the proper perspectives for poetry.

These associations are conspicuously missing from Richard Savage's *The Wanderer* (1729). Judson Lyon describes *The Wanderer* as being 'composed largely of peripatetic dialogue between the Wanderer and the Hermit', and sets forth various points of contact between this poem and Wordsworth's *Excursion*: the Hermit's similarity to the Solitary, the relation of epitaphs in a graveyard, the alternation of dialogue and natural description, and

the presentation of 'commun[ion] with nature as the highest religious act'.[17] To this summary I would add the beggar of Canto V
who reappears as 'The BARD, whose Want so multiplied his Woes,
| He sunk a Mortal, and a Seraph rose'.[18] Now a good angel, this
bard wanders the earth disguised in various shapes of mendicancy,
'Inspiring Patience in the Heart of Woe', much like the Old
Cumberland Beggar or the Wanderer, depending on which aspect
of the character one emphasizes (v. 334).

Eventually, however, 'The Seraph flitts away', his walking as
easily thrown off as the rest of his disguise (v. 393). So, too, is the
peripatetic façade of Savage's poem: flight is its natural mode,
while what walking there is, as the invocation and its echoes
suggest, remains purely contemplative rather than predominantly
laborious, virtually ungrounded in physical sensation. The narrator
anticipates 'my Flight' in these terms:

O'er ample Nature I extend my Views;
Nature to rural Scenes invites the Muse:
She flies all public Care, all Venal Strife,
To try the *Still*, compar'd with *Active* Life.

· · · · · · · · ·

Come, CONTEMPLATION, whose unbounded Gaze,
Swift in a Glance, the Course of Things, surveys;
Who in *Thy-self* the various View can'st find
Of Sea, Land, Air, and Heav'n, and human Kind;
What Tides of Passion in the Bosom roll;
What Thoughts debase, and what exalt the Soul;
Whose Pencil paints, obsequious to thy Will,
All thou survey'st, with a creative Skill!   (I. 11–14, 19–26)

This poetic perspective is at once unbounded and immobile. The
Muse's flight arrives at a high perspective from which all things

---

[17] Judson Stanley Lyon, *The Excursion: A Study* (New Haven, Conn.: Yale
University Press, 1950), 34–5. Lyon claims the distinction of having written the
only book-length study of the *Excursion*. Kenneth Johnston's *Wordsworth and The
Recluse* (New Haven, Conn. and London: Yale University Press, 1984) offers an
extensive reading of the *Excursion*, resituating it as part of *The Recluse*, that is
generally more interesting and useful to a contemporary reader. Lyon's older work
nonetheless proves more useful to me here because of his interest in textual sources.
[18] Richard Savage, *The Wanderer*, in *The Poetical Works of Richard Savage*,
ed. Clarence Tracy (Cambridge: Cambridge University Press, 1962), Canto V, lines
281–2. Further quotations from Savage's *Wanderer* will be noted by canto and line
number in the text.

can be observed without further movement. Both flight and subsequent observation are effortless. No attention is given to the
physical realities or possible sensations of flight, or to the scenes
'between' the unseen point of departure and the instantly attained
destination. Once at the viewpoint of the poem, interior and exterior—'Thy-self' and 'Sea, Land, Air', etc.—are equally and easily
accessible to the poet. All that is seen is held still for perception
as in a painting, a single still frame that may be surveyed at
leisure.

Canto IV of Savage's poem exemplifies the bodiless flitting of
fancy as a mode of 'travel' and of poetic perception. Having parted
from the Hermit—'The Mountain he, I the City gain'd'—at the
end of Canto III, the Wanderer reports,

> Still o'er my Mind wild *Fancy* holds her Sway,
> Still on strange, visionary Land I stray.
> Now Scenes crowd thick! Now indistinct appear!
> Swift glide the *Months*, and turn the varying Year!   (IV. 1–4)

Certainly there is a sense of moving perception here, but it is
dreamlike and distorted, with views piled upon each other or
fading from sight as they do in imaginative rather than physical
vision. The Wanderer's 'journey' from the city to the scene of the
canto's main action is equally dreamlike: his Fancy 'wafts [him]
on', to Winter's violent withdrawal, the sun's movement through
the zodiac, the song of the lark, the sunrise, and so forth, for
nearly 200 lines before he suddenly descends into a scene. Proclaiming 'Be this my Seat', he materializes at a grotto filled with
strange lights and vapours; the Hermit, supernaturally apprised of
the Wanderer's location, also appears, and the two wander off
together. How either the Wanderer or the Hermit 'actually' arrives
at the cave is never clear, nor do we particularly care. There is no
georgic insistence here upon the necessity of some physical act to
ground the imaginative; the walk of the body is subordinated to
the flight of the mind, which quite literally moves out of the body
and then returns with effortless ease, representing views linked by
mental rather than physical process.

For Savage, in short, it is not walking but flight which is excursive
and, therefore, the poetic mode of perception and expression. This
is, indeed, the case in much of what precedes Wordsworth. In
discussing the origin of the title of *The Excursion*, Lyon notes

that ' "Excursive," a word of rather infrequent usage, enjoyed considerable currency in the eighteenth century'.[19] Lyon cites as an example the final line of this passage from Thomson's *The Seasons* (1726–8):

> To me be Nature's volume broad displayed;
> And to peruse its all-instructing page,
> Or, haply catching inspiration thence,
> Some easy passage, raptured, to translate,
> My sole delight, as through the falling glooms
> Pensive I stray, or with the rising dawn
> On fancy's eagle-wing excursive soar.[20]

Walking is an implicit mode for the translation of Nature's book, but 'falling', 'glooms', and 'stray' suggest that the pedestrian's translation will literally fall away from the original into obscurity and error. His fancy, on the other hand, 'soars'—effortlessly flies, glides with unbeating wings—to a broad and illuminated perspective above the text, suggesting a clear and complete reading.

The opening of 'Winter' confirms the terms of this comparison. Although the narrator presents the new season through sixteen lines of peripatetic description—'When with frequent foot . . . Pleased have I wandered through your rough domain; | Trod the virgin snows' and so forth—he then invokes the Muse who

> Skimmed the gay Spring; on eagle-pinions borne,
> Attempted through the Summer-blaze to rise;
> Then swept o'er Autumn with the shadowy gale.
> And now among the Wintry clouds again,
> Rolled in the doubling storm, she tries to soar,
> To swell her note with all the rushing winds,
> To suit her sounding cadence to the floods;
> As is her theme, her numbers wildly great.   (20–7)

These lines suggest the physical sensations of flight far more vividly than most evocations of poetic flitting, but the panoramic visions which follow still obliterate the poet's original walk: we soar above rather than trudge through 'Winter'.

---

[19] Lyon, *Excursion*, 32.
[20] James Thomson, *The Seasons*, in *The Seasons and The Castle of Indolence*, ed. James Sambrook (Oxford: Clarendon Press, 1972), 'Summer', lines 192–8. Further quotations from *The Seasons* will be indicated in the text by book title and line number.

David Mallet's *The Excursion* (1728), the work which prompts
Lyon's enquiry into Wordsworth's title, follows this same familiar
pattern. Mallet's *Excursion* parallels Wordsworth's in a number
of ways, which Lyon enumerates as fused natural and intellectual
sojourns, 'a panegyric on Newton, a discussion of the deity
"infus'd" through nature . . . an expression of the popular idea of
a graduated scale or chain of beings . . . [and] the use of nature
as the vehicle and even as the object of didacticism'.[21] Moreover,
Mallet groups labourers, shepherds, and travellers as exemplifica-
tions of industry, and describes a forest 'whose solitary walks |
Fair *Truth* and *Wisdom* love', hinting at some of the associations
among cultivation, walking, and poetry that are developed by
Wordsworth.[22]

Typically, however, the arguments of Mallet's poem are preceded by an address to Fancy in which flight is clearly designated
as the poetic/excursive mode; the plan of the poem covers vast
extents of terrestrial space and time and then devotes its final
canto to 'a survey of the solar system, and of the fixed stars' (66).
These early suggestions are eventually confirmed by a clear picture
of the poem's dominant mode of travel and perception:

> O'er [nature's] ample breast,
> O'er sea and shore, light Fancy speeds along,
> Quick as the darted beam, from pole to pole,
> *Excursive traveller.*   (80–1)

Note again the swift, effortless passage of Fancy, and its multi-
layered characterization as 'light'—'light' in the sense of that lack
of weight which permits it to move at the speed of light, 'quick as
the darted beam', and 'light' in the sense of illuminated or illuminating as the 'darted beam' itself. In the terms of Mallet's *Excursion*, to be an 'excursive traveller' is precisely to be light, weightless,
airborne, instantaneously swift, illuminating—not at all pedestrian.
The last lines of the poem make the contrast between the flight
of fancy and the walk of the body deliberate: as we contemplate
angels and the mind of God in the void of deep space, we find 'no
paths to guide imagination's flight', a final line which marks quite

[21] Lyon, *Excursion*, 32.
[22] David Mallet, *The Excursion*, in *The Works of David Mallet Esq. In Three
Volumes. A New Edition Corrected* (London: A. Millar & P. Vaillant, 1759), 70.
Further quotations from Mallet's *Excursion* will be noted in the text by page number.

plainly the limits of the foot and the excursive power of the wing (110).

It is important to remember that, until the first brief voyage of the Montgolfiers' balloon in 1783, human flight is wholly imaginative, and that, until commercial air-travel in the twentieth century, very few people actually experienced flight.[23] Thus, when an eighteenth-century fancy 'flies', it is indeed fancy which does so: no human physical counterpart is implied and the resulting perspective is indeed imagined—rather well, really. Only rarely, however, does this perspective represent continuous movement. The opening of Thomson's 'Winter' is an exception, but even Thomson imitates the sensations of a bird, not those of a human aviator. Typically, the eighteenth-century flight of fancy resembles not a continuous fly-by but rather a series of glances from a single landing-point or from a number of landings unconnected by reports of physical flight. In fact, what these accounts most resemble are the actual eighteenth-century travel accounts that we examined earlier. Despite his grumbling about bad roads and so forth, Johnson's preoccupation with destination makes the process of travel nearly invisible, which, besides implying that the physical processes of travel *should* be transparent, ensures that each 'sight' remains as neatly framed as a landscape in a Claude glass or a view from Rievaulx Terrace. Fancy's flight is equally effortless: the reader at once attains a perspective which, if panoramic, none the less gives the sense of singularity and stasis, as if all that is visible

---

[23] As the previous discussion suggests, the literary tradition of imaginative flight is extensive. See W. B. Carnochan's *Confinement and Flight: An Essay on English Literature of the Eighteenth Century* (Berkeley: University of California Press, 1977) for a discussion of imaginative flight as an (ultimately excursive) escape from (sometimes salutary) imprisonment or seclusion: 'As the eighteenth-century prison is to pastoral—that is, a displaced image—so are these flights, vertical or linear, to quest. . . . that flight characteristically turns back on itself like the line drawn out at length to a circle' (pp. 103–4). The Continental tradition includes Velez de Guevara's *El diabolo conjula* (1641), in which the devil's flight opens the social interiors of Madrid to criticism, and Le Sage's derivation of Velez, immensely popular in its time, *Le Diable boiteux* (1707). Flight as a vehicle of social satire evolved toward flight as an entrance to Utopia, as in Restif de la Bretonne's *La Decouverte australe par un Homme-valant, ou Le Dedale français* (1781), in which this 'new French Dedalus' founds a rational Utopian community. Meanwhile, in an anticipation of Baudelaire's *flâneur*, the role of social discovery and satire falls to the walker: in Restif's *Les Nuits de Paris* (1788), a pedestrian snoop called 'the owl'—a trace of the original flights retained in this characterization—wanders through the city, observing and commenting on human activities.

will be held for us to view in whatever order and time we may wish. The panorama of fanciful flight becomes 'the view', framed in a hemispherical glass, with little sense of arrival or departure or passage through. Indeed, the particular bounds broken by the excursions of fancy are the bounds of usual physical travel: if fancy must eventually return to the body, completing the excursive movement, any interval of physical travel is literally passed over, as Savage's Wanderer seems teleported from the city to the grotto.

In discussing the effect of landscape painting on the contemplation of both actual and represented landscapes, John Barrell notes that the Claudian landscapes which influenced Thomson and other eighteenth-century poets are characterized by 'a fairly high viewpoint' and a sense of 'tremendous depth'.[24] However, he criticizes characterizations of this sense of depth by the late eighteenth-century landscape painter Richard Wilson and twentieth-century art critic Michael Kitson, who respectively comment that 'you may walk in Claude's pictures and count the miles', and speak of 'the imaginary traveller in Claude's landscapes'.[25] Although Barrell is concerned with how the eye travels through the picture, and lapses into language like 'how far and how rapidly we are travelling through [Claude's] landscapes', he quite properly observes that the metaphor of the traveller 'is not a helpful one, at least insofar as Kitson seems to suggest that the traveller is conscious only of what he sees along his path, and never looks up into the distance'.[26] That distant horizon, Barrell argues, is arrived at immediately—read 'effortlessly'—by the eye, and only then does the exploration of the passage between foreground and distance commence. In this process of exploration, too, Barrell detects perceptions quite different from those of a walker bound by our ordinary physical laws. The horizontal bands of light and dark which direct the viewer's eye are also bands of scale which establish perspective, not through the Renaissance method of 'a gradual diminution in the size of things', but through 'a series of abrupt leaps': 'to cross one of Claude's bridges is to step into something like Lilliput'.[27]

As Barrell's comment indicates, the whole idea of stepping through a Claude is wrong-headed. Wilson's metaphor is sufficiently

---

[24] Barrell, *Idea of Landscape*, 8.   [25] Ibid.
[26] Ibid. 9, 8.   [27] Ibid. 11, 10.

early (he died in 1782) to suggest some need, much like that which develops in the poetry of the period, for an aesthetic which foregrounds the physical processes and successive, limited view-points of the walker. More simply, it may suggest that Wilson's whole idea of walking was more like Savage's than Wordsworth's, and that he used 'walking' merely as a formal indication of travel. In either case, Claude's pictures themselves effortlessly instal their viewers at a selected viewpoint which provides immediate access to any perspective within that framed/enclosed view—a kind of perspective clearly preferred by actual eighteenth-century travellers and walkers looking at landscapes, as well as by admirers of Claude. Choosing such a viewpoint might well involve 'a considerable amount of jockeying for position, of screwing up the eyes, of moving back and forth, of rearranging objects in the imagination', but it is plainly of little or no importance for painter, poet, or travel-writer to communicate any sense of physical process or succession once the optimum perspective is established.[28]

By the time we get to Wordsworth's 'Peter Bell' (1798), the effortlessness of flight and the accessibility of panorama have become aesthetic barriers rather than stimulants. The narrator imagines and at first enjoys the flying boat, a wonderful fusion of bodiless fancy and mechanized transport, which carries him out to the stars. But he enjoys the return to earthly sights even more than the journey out, and the boat (suddenly possessed of a life of its own) scolds him for his timidity:

> Go creep along the dirt and pick
> Your way with your good walking stick,
> Just three good miles an hour.
> Sure in the breast of full grown poet
> So faint a heart was n'er before;
> Come to the poet's wild delights,
> I have ten thousand lovely sights,
> Ten thousand sights in store.   (73–80)

But the narrator responds that the fairy visions the boat promises him are those of a bygone time, 'when poets lived in clover', and that he must get back to the world as it is (116). Sure enough, he walks back to his garden, where he has promised to 'relate the tale | Of Peter Bell the Potter' to some friends, arriving 'somewhat out

---

[28] Ibid. 5.

of breath, | With lips, no doubt, and visage pale, | And sore too
from a slight contusion' (134–5, 151–3). The real damage, however,
seems to have been done by his fancy's flight: the poet starts in
mid-narrative and has to be reminded by his audience of the need
to tell the tale from the beginning. 'Who is Peter?' asks one auditor,
while others complain that ''tis a downright riddle' and that they
are 'wandering in a wood' (164, 165, 158). The narrator's aerial
dalliance has unfitted him for poetry, making him skip effortlessly
over what must be taken step-by-step, through the narrative and
its limited but successive views, to achieve a continuous and intimate knowledge of the narrative path. Despite his grumbling
about his 'two poor legs', it is plainly the use of those legs and the
gradual recollection of the pedestrian perspective that make him a
fit poetic guide.

William Cowper's *The Task* (1784) moves toward this preference for pedestrian poetic perspectives, setting up the conventional
equation between fancy's flight and excursive poetic capacity but
then undermining it. A line cited by Lyon as an example of
eighteenth-century uses of 'excursive', for instance, caps a passage
which denigrates fanciful soaring by linking it with idleness and
sightseeing:

> As he that travels far, oft turns aside
> To view some rugged rock or mouldering tower,
> Which seen, delights him not; then coming home,
> Describes and prints it, that the world may know
> How far he went for what was nothing worth;
> So I with brush in hand and pallet spread,
> With colours mixed for a far different use,
> Paint cards and dolls, and every idle thing
> That fancy finds in her excursive flights.[29]

Cowper's imaginary traveller seeks 'a view' in proper eighteenth-
century fashion (notice that the 'rugged rock' and 'mouldering
tower' which are viewed also suggest high vantage-points), but
the traveller's description of that view turns out to be 'worthless'.
Moreover, the narrator's own views and descriptions appear equally

---

[29] William Cowper, *The Task*, in *The Poetical Works of William Cowper*, ed.
William Benham, Globe Edition (London: Macmillan, 1908), Book IV, lines 234–
42. Further quotations from Cowper's *Task* will be cited in the text by book and
line numbers.

worthless, characterized as 'painted' and 'idle', and so linked to
the worldly, citified pursuits he attacked in the twenty lines prior
to this passage. Yet 'idle things' are precisely what 'fancy finds in
her excursive flights', suggesting that the effortless panoramas of
fanciful flight are not fit poetic perspectives.

This passage is part of the larger argument of Book IV, 'The
Winter Evening', in which the arrival of the newspaper by post
provides an opportunity for a reverie contrasting the virtuous
recreations of rural domesticity with the card-playing and theatre-
going of idle city society. The reading of the paper seems to instal
the narrator at an effortlessly achieved, panoramic perspective on
world affairs:

> Thus sitting, and surveying thus at ease
> The globe and its concerns, I seem advanced
> To some secure and more than mortal height,
> That liberates and exempts me from them all.   (IV. 94–7)

Again, however, for the reader who recognizes the narrator's literal seat as a sofa, the prime emblem of idleness in *The Task*, the
ease of this perspective threatens the worth of the narrator's observations. Cowper rescues his narrator, in fact, by making it clear
that his ability to take in this view depends upon the labours—
specifically, the travels—of other men:

> [Man] travels and expatiates, as the bee
> From flower to flower, so he from land to land;
> The manners, customs, policy of all
> Pay contribution to the store he gleans;
> He sucks intelligence in every clime,
> And spreads the honey of his deep research
> At his return, a rich repast for me.
> He travels, and I too. I tread his deck,
> Ascend his topmast, through his peering eyes
> Discover countries, with a kindred heart
> Suffer his woes, and share in his escapes;
> While fancy, like the finger of a clock,
> Runs the great circuit, and is still at home.   (IV. 107–19)

As 'travels' and 'expatiates' become 'gleans' and the various verbs
of honey-making, so travel and expatiation (or 'walking about',
from *ex(s)patiat-*) become metaphorically the labour of those
traditionally georgic bees which signify successful cultivation

and culture-building. Cowper's full poetic argument is, in fact, georgic in its advocacy of cultivating labour, although he disembodies that labour: the ideal farmer, although he does not 'govern only or direct, | But much performs himself', confines himself to work 'demanding skill rather than force' (III. 403, 407). When, later in Book IV, an embroiderer cultivates 'the well-depicted flower | Wrought patiently into the snowy lawn', her needlework producing 'buds, and leaves, and sprigs, | And curling tendrils', and mixing with others' cultivation of history, poetry, and music by the rural fireside, all of the georgic images and plays upon cultivation are there *except* the representation of actual farming. Like the embroiderer's 'farming', the narrator's 'walking' is well distanced from the original physical labours which support the metaphor, and yet the original terms are insisted upon. Just as the embroidery's retracing of the work of cultivation seems to save it from being a painted vanity, so the narrator redeems his easy perspective by his imaginative retracing of the traveller/walker/honey-maker's route. Fancy does not fly here but runs, and in a most curious fashion, like the hand of a clock that circles round but 'is still at home'. This is not departure and return in true excursive (or expatiatory) fashion, but the mock excursion of a fancy circumscribed by time and domesticity, its flights grounded in the perspectives of actual human travellers.

Cowper's addition of 'expatiates' to 'travels' reminds us that Book I of *The Task* specifies walking as the particular kind of travel that opposes the idleness of 'The Sofa'. Immediately following his mock-heroic account of the sofa's origin, the narrator tells us that although 'The Sofa suits the gouty limb', he will escape the jaded appetite and disease that produce and result from idleness:

> For I have loved the rural walk through lanes
> Of grassy swarth, close cropped by nibbling sheep
> And skirted thick with intertexture firm
> Of thorny boughs; have loved the rural walk
> O'er hills, through valleys, and by rivers' brink
> E'er since a truant boy I passed my bounds
> To enjoy a ramble on the banks of Thames;
> And still remember, nor without regret,
> Of hours that sorrow since has much endeared,
> How oft, my slice of pocket store consumed,

Still hungering, penniless and far from home,
I fed on scarlet hips and stony haws,
Or blushing crabs, or berries that emboss
The bramble, black as jet, or sloes austere.
Hard fare! but such as boyish appetite
Disdains not, nor the palate undepraved
By culinary arts, unsavoury deems.
No Sofa then awaited my return,
Nor Sofa then I needed.   (I. 103–27)

This passage invites comparison with Gay's *Trivia*, especially where
Gay commends the healthy effects of walking as opposed to coach-
riding. (In fact, in the lines preceding the above passage, Cowper
describes a chaise as a kind of travelling sofa.) The echo of Gay is
enhanced by the georgic modality and intermittently facetious tone
of *The Task*. In some respects, however, the passage prefigures
Wordsworth's *Excursion* and *Prelude*. The walks this pedestrian
loves, unlike Gay's, are rural and lined with Virgilian sheep; the
thought of current walks recalls earlier excursions—literally breaking bounds—as a 'truant boy' who harvests physical and moral
sustenance from nature. This more serious comparison accurately
foreshadows Cowper's increasingly serious attacks on idleness and
his championing of the georgic solution to cultural degradation.

As Book I continues, its parodic or facetious qualities fade, so
that they remain associated with the idleness of the sofa, and
Cowper's anticipation of Wordsworthian peripatetic becomes more
pronounced. After representing walking as a sign of physical and
moral health, the narrator addresses the 'dear companion of my
walks, | Whose arm this twentieth winter I perceive | Fast locked
in mine', and recalls a representative stroll:

How oft upon yon eminence our pace
Has slackened to a pause
   .   .   .   .
Then with what pleasure have we just discerned
The distant plough slow moving, and beside
His labouring team, that swerved not from the track,
The sturdy swain diminished to a boy.

                              (I. 154–5, 159–62)

What follows is a Thomsonian/Claudian sweep from this first
pictorial element toward 'Groves, heaths, and smoking villages
remote', but the community of pedestrians recovering a georgic

prospect which eventually includes cattle and a herdsman's hut
has a familiarly peripatetic shape (I. 176).

This same shape reappears just a hundred lines later, this time
preceded by a pedestrian passage through—rather than a view
of—a landscape:

Descending now (but cautious, lest too fast)
A sudden steep, upon a rustic bridge,
We pass a gulf, in which the willows dip
Their pendent boughs, stooping as if to drink.
Hence, ankle deep in moss and flowery thyme,
We mount again, and feel at every step
Our foot half sunk in hillocks green and soft

  .   .   .   .

The summit gained...

  .   .   .   .

                  Now roves the eye,
And posted on this speculative height
Exults in its command. The sheepfold here
Pours out its fleecy tenants o'er the glebe.
At first, progressive as a stream, they seek
The middle field; but scattered by degree,
Each to his choice, soon whiten all the land.
There from the sunburnt hayfield, homeward creeps
The loaded wain...

                         (I. 266–72, 278, 288–97)

One of the first things we notice about the way to the summit is
that it is emphatically not a painted landscape experienced primarily through the eye: the body must balance cautiously on a steep
incline, the willows' 'thirst' suggests human exertion, and the feet
sink into a soft ground dampened by moss and scented by thyme.
Moreover, the viewpoint of the passage is specifically, sensually
pedestrian, emphasizing the action of the feet—notice the reiteration
of 'ankle', 'step', 'foot'—which must step successively through each
experience—first the descent, then the bridge, then the ascent. As
if the eye were cast down to watch the footing, there is no preview
of the ground ahead or effortless attainment of perspective. At
every point the body's physical labours and limitations (as well as
abilities) define perception.

Even upon the 'speculative height' the eye is not quite so
'commanding' as it might seem. Although once again it passes

from the foregrounded georgic prospects of sheepfield and haywain toward the distant woods and river, some part of the view remains hidden: 'There lost behind a rising ground, the wood | Seems sunk, and shortened to its topmost boughs' (I. 305–6). Despite its elevation, this is a grounded view from which some things, although contained within the circle of the horizon, are not visible.

It may well be that the much-discussed localization of nineteenth-century landscapes, poetic and otherwise, does not derive so much from the inclusion or exclusion of localizing objects, but from the representation of successive, limited viewpoints. M. H. Abrams, who repeatedly describes the establishing landscape of his greater Romantic lyric as 'not only particularized . . . [but] precisely localized, in place, and sometimes in time as well', none the less spends the bulk of his argument on how the speaker's feelings 'displace the landscape as the center of poetic interest', thus differentiating his lyric from 'local poetry' in which 'the order of the thoughts is the sequence in which the natural objects are observed'.[30] Clearly, then, Abrams's sense of precise localization does not arise from an accurate rendering of 'things as they are'. Wordsworth himself says that he has completely rearranged the landscape of the Lakes to produce the landscape of the *Excursion*— for instance, having the Wanderer and narrator travel up Langdale vale and on into Little Langdale, but then, 'as by the waving of a magic wand', transforming this small valley into the larger arena of Grasmere vale (*PW* v. 375–6). This fits Barrell's description of the *eighteenth*-century landscape: 'a theatre where the poet's own moral reflections are acted out; where the objects do not so much give rise to the reflections, as the ready-made and waiting reflections justify the inclusion of this or that object in the poem'.[31]

Yet even at its most didactic the *Excursion*, not to mention the much earlier 'Tintern Abbey', gives the *impression* that reflections arise from objects, because those objects, however selected, are presented successively, as contiguous parts of a limited but moving view that mimics the pedestrian perspective. Here, as the narrator and the Wanderer approach the Solitary's retreat, they discover a child's play-house:

[30] M. H. Abrams, 'Structure and Style in the Greater Romantic Lyric', in Harold Bloom *et al.* (ed.), *From Sensibility to Romanticism* (New York: Oxford University Press, 1965), 534, 540, 552.

[31] Barrell, *Idea of Landscape*, 35.

So, to a steep and difficult descent
Trusting ourselves, we wound from crag to crag,
Where passage could be won; and, as the last
Of the mute [funeral] train, behind the heathy top
Of that off-sloping outlet, disappeared,
I, more impatient in my downward course,
Had landed upon easy ground; and there
Stood waiting for my Comrade. When behold
An object that enticed my steps aside!
A narrow, winding entry opened out
Into a platform—that lay, sheepfold-wise,
Enclosed between an upright mass of rock
And one old moss-grown wall;—a cool recess,
And fanciful! For where the rock and wall
Met in an angle, hung a penthouse, framed
By thrusting two rude staves into the wall
And overlaying them with mountain sods;
To weather-fend a little turf-built seat

   .   .   .   .

      the whole plainly wrought by children's hands!
Whose skill had thronged the floor with a proud show
Of baby houses, curiously arranged;
Nor wanting ornament of walks between,
With mimic trees inserted in the turf,
And gardens interposed.   (II. 403–20, 423–8)

These pedestrians' negotiation of a tricky descent, unlike that described in *The Task*, does not resolve into any 'speculative height'.
Wordsworth immediately foregrounds the limitation of the narrator's view by the slopes that 'rise' around him as he descends,
shutting out his view of the funeral procession. The narrator stops
for a moment but then walks on into that 'narrow, winding entry',
seeing first the platform, and then (drawing closer) how it is made,
and then (near enough for comparisons now) how large it is (big
enough for him to sit on), and finally the details of the children's
play village, right down to minature walks which rather charmingly
suggest that he might continue his exploration into this tiny village,
were he only small enough. These successive revelations imitate the
unfolding of a locality to the pedestrian traveller who follows its
paths towards an intimate knowledge of its topography. The
walker's perceptions are limited, to be sure, by his passage inside—

as he descends the sloping path he loses sight of the other side of the hill—but that limitation invites further movement and observation by its very incompleteness, and by the satisfying progress of the explorations of the interior of his narrow passage. And we as readers trace the narrator's increasingly sure apprehension of the play-house, so that when, a few lines later, he finds a damaged copy of Voltaire and the Wanderer reflects upon the likelihood of the Solitary's death, we have a sensation of naturalness, as if the reflections do indeed arise from objects observed in the course of a walk through a landscape and into a locality. Yet this play-house is without any reported source in Wordsworth's actual experience: it is, so far as I know, a pure fiction.

Thus, although a nineteenth-century landscape may be no more 'real' or 'local' than an eighteenth-century one in terms of selection and arrangement of features, its artificiality is masked by the reader's sensation of natural movement and perspective—the very movement and perspective, in fact, which would be the lot of a local resident using footpaths to get where he is going. The reader feels that the landscape is particularized, localized, because he feels that he could walk through it and replicate the perspectives of the poem. Hence the popularity of those books and tours that help the tourist retrace Wordsworth's walks in the Lakes, or Jane Austen's in Bath. In fact, these 'retracings' are themselves often rearrangements or reconstructions of presumed walks. The historical actuality is not the crucial issue: what is important is the sensation, the mimicry, of the original form—in short, the peripatetic aesthetic.

In *The Task*, the movement toward this peripatetic aesthetic and its supporting mode remains entangled in the desire for effortless panorama. Barrell remarks that in I. 288–97 above, '[Cowper] is anxious to describe the view more particularly than his remote station will allow, and after a few lines has quite descended, so to speak, into the landscape . . . [but later] demands that we imagine ourselves on the high viewpoint we previously seem to have abandoned'.[32] Barrell does not notice the peripatetic approach to the summit—a good example of the customary invisibility of the pedestrian in literature, even in cases where observing him is helpful—but his sense of the confusion of the wide

---

[32] Ibid. 56–7.

view from the summit and the intimate, particularized views common to the foot-traveller is quite accurate. In fact, although the
last two books of *The Task* are titled 'The Winter Morning Walk'
and 'The Winter Walk at Noon', they include just two brief allusions to the physical process of walking and make no sustained
attempt at mimicking a pedestrian perspective.[33] At the beginning
of 'Winter Morning', for instance, the narrator flits past cattle,
herdsman, woodsman, dog, chickens, wild birds, streams, and trees,
finally arriving at the ice palace of the Russian empress and so at
meditations on government. Subject rather than physical contigu-
ity (or its imitation) links these observations: the movement from
well-fed chickens in the yard to winter-killed birds in the forest is
generated by their identity as birds and their contrasting fates in
winter, not by their succession along the pedestrian's line of travel.
Neither this penultimate book nor the poem as a whole returns to
any imitation of the physical quality of walking or of pedestrian
perception.

   As in the case of Gay's *Trivia*, however, the introduction of the
walker into the georgic permits walking advantages traditionally
accorded to farming: health, productive labour, and the virtues
of rural life. Moreover, Cowper's occasional mimicry of pedestrian
perspective suggests an additional benefit: a new standard for
aesthetic judgement and artistic perspective that can claim to anchor
these processes of abstraction in material needs and processes, just
as georgic metaphorically grounds poetry in the earth. A similar
transitional case is John Thelwall's *The Peripatetic* (1793), 'which
blended the serial essays of the eighteenth century with a narrative thread and lyric interludes . . . [and] may have influenced
[Thelwall's] friend Coleridge's conception of the shape that
Wordsworth's great philosophical poem *The Recluse* was to take,
as well as the actual shape of *The Excursion*'.[34] Lyon suggests more
direct influence, enumerating specific similiarities in episode, character, and attitude between Thelwall's work and Wordsworth's
Excursion, and, although Wordsworth himself made light of his

---

[33] One of these allusions occurs at the beginning of 'Winter Morning' and the
other about 300 lines into 'Noon'. For a related confusion see the beginning of
Book III, where the narrator appears at first to be walking but within a few lines
spurs his horse.
[34] Donald Reiman in his introduction to John Thelwall, *Ode to Science; John
Gilpin's Ghost; Poems; The Trident of Albion* (repr. New York and London:
Garland, 1978), p. v.

relationship with Thelwall, he did indeed own a copy of *The Peripatetic*.[35]

Reading Thelwall could scarcely have given Wordsworth any model for the mimicry of pedestrian perspectives. The narrative thread of *The Peripatetic* is a walking tour, to be sure, but the book's organization into innumerable little titled prose 'chapters', occasionally inlaid with poetry, creates a whimsical jarring far more reminiscent of Sterne (whom the narrator, in fact, names as his pattern) than evocative of Wordsworth. About a hundred pages into the first volume, for instance, we read: 'The Street', an account of the travellers' setting out despite hazy weather; 'The Vernal Shower', a recollection of an earlier walk on which the narrator felt 'one of the earliest inspirations of the Muse' (lark-song, of course—flying inspiration); 'Legal Consistencies', which comments on the political implications of that previous walk, undertaken to deliver papers to a debtor; 'The Sonnet', which discusses sonnets and poetic form; and 'Bermondsey', an abrupt return to the orginal walk which has now reached an unpicturesque country churchyard. Typically, nothing perceived between the street and the churchyard is reported—no feature of the landscape, no sensation of the walkers. It is as if the narrator had been lifted up outside his inn and dropped down into the Bermondsey churchyard, the interval filled with contemplation of various nearly random subjects—larks,

---

[35] Lyon's claims that 'Wordsworth had known Thelwall personally for many years' and that he 'develop[ed] a great respect for Thelwall's ability to write blank verse' seem a rather enthusiastic reading of Wordsworth's letter of 16 Nov. 1838 to Thelwall's wife (Lyon, *Excursion*, 37). In fact, Wordsworth says that 'Circumstances were not favourable to much intercourse' between the two poets, recalling only three meetings, while his 'great respect' for Thelwall's blank verse is couched in these coolly qualified terms: 'Mr. Coleridge and I were of opinion that the modulations of [Thelwall's] blank verse were superior to those of most writers in that metre' (*Letters of William and Dorothy Wordsworth: The Later Years*, ed. Ernest de Selincourt, 2nd edn., rev. Alan G. Hill, vol. vi (Oxford: Clarendon Press, 1982), 639, 641). See also Johnston's discussion of the relationships among Coleridge, Wordsworth, and Thelwall, detailing the organizational and thematic influences of Thelwall on Wordsworth (Johnston, *The Recluse*, 11–14). Johnston gives Thelwall more credit than I am willing to, but then Johnston regards the walking in both works as a 'mere' metaphor or structural device, calling it 'the peripatetic metaphor' and commenting on some of Wordsworth's shorter poems that 'they all follow the rudimentary plot which Wordsworth, left to his own devices at this time, could hardly vary: walking along a road, he meets somebody who tells him his or her life-story' (pp. 14, 6). To Johnston, clearly, the proliferation of peripatetic narrators, characters, and plots in Wordsworth signals a passive failure of imaginative vigour.

debts, poetry—as unaffected by the process of travel as if he had
been snoozing on a magic carpet.[36]

Significantly, however, the narrator's explanation for these digressions is not the soaring of a winged muse, but the excursive
impulses of a foot-traveller:

> If, in the foregoing digressions, I should appear, according to thy better
> judgment, to have wandered too far from the point, thou wilt be kind
> enough to remember, that, as I am only a foot traveller, the bye path to
> the right and to the left is always as open to me as the turnpike road: and
> that if, on the present occasion, I have been rambling somewhat too long
> among the fields and green allies of poetical digression, thou art, never-
> theless, bound in gratitude to excuse me, since I have been induced to go
> purely for thy sake.[37]

Here the excursive senses of trangressing boundaries by leaving
the expected line of narrative, and of the transgressions themselves
being the 'main line', are attached directly to the pedestrian mode
of travel and perception. The opening sections of The Peripatetic,
moreover, are sprinkled with references to the physical and intellectual advantages of walking. 'From the peripatetic habits of the
ancient philosophers,' the narrator argues, 'and the attachment
to rural life displayed by them all, in opposition to the practice
of modern students, who are in some degree compelled, by the
institutions of society, to bury themselves in large cities', comes
the ancients' longevity and the moderns' 'proverbially debilitated'
health.[38] Here is that association of walking, philosophy or study,
and 'rural life' we saw in Gay and Cowper, which, if unaccom-
panied in Thelwall's text by georgic affiliations, suggests that
same walking/poetry/cultivation nexus Wordsworth sustains in his

---

[36] The Observant Pedestrian; or, Traits of the Heart: In a Solitary Tour from
Cærnarvon to London, by 'The Author of The Mystic Cottager' (London: William
Lane, 1795) achieves much the same effect as Thelwall's Peripatetic, and by the
same means: representing itself as a record of a foot-journey, it offers episodic
meditations generated by destination rather than by process. See also its two se-
quels, Farther Excursions of the Observant Pedestrian (London: R. Dutton, 1801)
and the significantly titled Observant Pedestrian Mounted; or a Donkey Tour to
Brighton. A Comic Sentimental Novel in Three Volumes (London: W. Simpkin &
R. Marshal, 1815).

[37] John Thelwall, The Peripatetic; or, Sketches of the Heart, of Nature and
Society; in a series of Politico-sentimental Journals, in verse and prose, of the
Eccentric Excursions of Sylvanus Theophrastus; supposed to be written by himself
(1793; repr. New York and London: Garland, 1978), 105.

[38] Ibid. 14.

poetry. Despite the absence of sustained mimicry of peripatetic labour or of the limited, successive, contiguous views it produces, *The Peripatetic* associates walking with philosophy and poetry, uses it as narrative structure, emphasizes its excursive shape and recollective capacities. These changes imply, almost inevitably, the change in aesthetic which is their logical extension.

James Plumptre's *The Lakers: A Comic Opera in Three Acts* (1798) also lacks any mimicry of pedestrian perspectives, but represents walking as educative travel undertaken by gentlemen whose health, morality, aesthetic judgement, and class standing equal or surpass those of true and picturesque travellers. In the process of satirizing burgeoning tourism in the Lake District, this published but unperformed play also registers the growing accept-ability of the pedestrian touring which had begun with Joseph Budworth's trek in 1792. Plumptre enthusiastically participated in this trend, making three tours of the Lakes between 1796 and 1799 in which he covered more than 1,774 of a total 2,236 miles on foot. We know, too, that by July 1799 Plumptre had read Wordsworth's 'An Evening Walk' (1793).[39] Although 'An Evening Walk', composed in 1788-9 (and thus before Wordsworth's sojourn on the Continent during the Long Vacation of 1790), relies on a traditionally pictorial aesthetic, its placement of the poet as walker is suggestive, and there is the possibility that Plumptre had already read it when he wrote his play.[40]

Certainly *The Lakers* is much like 'An Evening Walk' in raising the value of pedestrian practice by associating or equating it with the still-admired picturesque. Our hero in this romantic comedy of errors is Sir Charles Portinscale, an accomplished picturesque traveller who regularly visits Keswick to gain 'health and amusement'

[39] Bicknell and Woof, *Discovery of the Lake District*, 38-9. See also their de-scriptions of Plumptre's published and unpublished notes on his walking tours in the Lakes and elsewhere, which include 'A list of travelling requisites' (pp. 36-9).

[40] See e.g. Geoffrey Hartman's description of 'An Evening Walk' as 'a gallery of discrete pictures' (*Wordsworth's Poetry, 1787-1814* (Cambridge, Mass. and London: Harvard University Press, 1987), 93). Hartman goes on to argue that something more than 18th-cent. loco-descriptive poetry is going on here, but con-tinues to emphasize its essentially pictorial aesthetics: 'Like the Dutch painters, except that his gaze is kinetic, Wordsworth gives every trait of nature its due, building larger prospects out of minutiae, and never sacrificing the part to the picturesque' (p. 94). In linking 'An Evening Walk' with loco-descriptive poetry, Hartman also notes that 'The poem's plan [is] ultimately based on Virgil's *Georgics*, which proved country matters could be the substance of a sustained poetry' (p. 93).

from 'surveying' its 'wonders'.[41] In his disguise as a local guide, Sir
Charles discourses upon the scenery, composing it as Gray or
Gilpin might:

This spacious amphitheatre of picturesque mountains, with the pellucid
waters lying at their base, variegated with islands, adorned with wood,
or clothed with the sweetest verdure, presents a picture as fine as the
imagination can form. You look directly across the lake, for three miles,
into the gorges of Borrowdale, where Castle Crag guards the tremendous
pass. . . . (17)

Sir Charles's travel practices, perspectives, and aesthetic discourse
appear in favourable contrast to those of destination-oriented true
travellers, whose oblivious ignorance to their natural surroundings
is a prime target of Plumptre's satire. In the play's first scene, Sir
Charles joins the landlord of the local inn in deriding Sir Incurious
Hurry, who 'drives post through the country every year, with his
carriage windows up, and never gets out but to eat, drink, and
sleep' (2). Sir Hurry foreshadows Bob Kiddy, the comic villain of
the piece, who travels 'To tell the merits of each inn' and seeks
only culinary views: 'Gone to see the water fall! that's rum enough.
I'll see a good stream of wine before the day's out' (36, 35). Sir
Charles and the landlord admire, on the other hand, the purposeful
attentiveness to nature and locality of a sporting traveller, Tom
Angle, who 'knows the time of every fly, from the green-drake to
the palmer-fly' and spends every day in fishing or shooting (2). Sir
Charles, sprinkling his picturesque commentary with proper names,
directions, descriptions of weather, and local history, demonstrates
the importance of such a thorough knowledge of one's ground
to proper aesthetic practice, specifically to the selection and composition of edifying picturesque views.

But Plumptre also derides the picturesque traveller in the character of Miss Beccabunga Veronica, the primary obstacle to Sir
Charles's courtship of her niece, Lydia. Miss Veronica's relentless
application of 'picturesque' to every object and situation, and her
indiscriminate use of picturesque methods, strip both her discourse
and her practice of meaning. Using a Claude glass's differently
coloured lenses to view the scene described by Sir Charles above, ·

[41] James Plumptre, *The Lakers: A Comic Opera in Three Acts* (London: n.p.,
1798), 1. Further quotations from Plumptre's *Lakers* will be noted in the text by
page number.

Miss Veronica successively calls the scene 'gorgeously glowing', 'gloomily glaring', and 'frigidly frozen' (19). Then, sketching the view, she substitutes Alps for hills, an abbey for a church, a castle for a house, and proposes recolouring it for what she thinks is good Gilpinesque effect: 'an orange sky, yellow water, a blue bank, a green castle, and brown trees' (21). Her companions complain that they cannot recognize either her verbal or her pictorial representations as the view before them. In Miss Veronica's fanatically uncritical hands, picturesque methods have become the means of disguising rather than of revealing the artistic essence of a landscape.

Miss Veronica proves incompetent at everything she does, but especially at two pursuits directly linked with her aesthetic failures: botanizing/husband-hunting and walking. Although Plumptre develops no genuine georgic in *The Lakers*, he does sustain a running pun on 'husbandry' that substitutes botanizing for the more usual farming or gardening, by having his characters equate botanical knowledge with sexual skill. Miss Veronica is manifestly a dreadful botanist, misusing Latin terms and botanical concepts with the same *élan* with which she misuses her Claude glass, but her husband-to-be considers her claim to competence as one of the primary reasons to marry her—she is, he admiringly says, 'deeply versed in the mysteries of the loves of plants' (52). She, in turn, rationalizes her marriage to a servant by reminding herself that 'he is a botanist, he is picturesque'—she actually looks at him through her Claude glass at this point—and then declares that their marriage would be 'perfectly botanic' (58).

Miss Veronica botanizes, husband-hunts, and seeks the picturesque by means of local pedestrian excursions, and, sure enough, is also an incompetent walker who ignores the physical demands of walking, its process, and turns her excursions into opportunities for picturesque posing. She shows up for an ascent of Skiddaw on a rainy day in a thin, fragile costume incongruously mixing classical and rustic elements which Sir Charles criticizes on both practical and aesthetic grounds: 'You would have found that dress rather too light and airy for that cold atmosphere', he comments, and then goes on in an aside to the audience, 'A Grecian nymph in a Scotch plaid, upon the mountains of Cumberland!' (27). Sir Charles, on the other hand, succeeds in 'husbandry', walking, and picturesque practice: he gains Lydia's hand, is able to guide their party on pedestrian tours of the locality and, although we do not observe his walking, by implication takes his authoritative views from places reached on foot.

The appearance of two Pedestrians in the latter part of the play solidifies the role of pedestrian practice in the maintenance of good 'husbandry' and proper artistic perspectives, partly by redefining walkers as potentially respectable, moral men and walking as educative travel. When the Pedestrians enter at the end of Act II, Kiddy questions them about their mode of travel, utterly bemused at their assertion that their reason for walking is not simply poverty but preference as well: 'Why, they're crack'd. What then, if you had money, you wouldn't walk?' The First Pedestrian replies that not only expense but loss of independence and convenience are spared, while 'Exercise secures appetite and sleep; the contemplation of the works of nature and of man affords amusement and exercise to the mind, and health results from both' (37, 38). Moreover, the Second Pedestrian claims, they have learned from their travels, gaining moral insight from their observation 'that human nature is pretty much the same in every place and in every condition' (38). The Pedestrians quickly display their moral superiority, at first opposing and then actually preventing Kiddy's senseless duel with Sample (and thus permitting Sample's marriage to Anna).

Significantly, the aesthetic superiority of the picturesque traveller and the moral superiority of the pedestrian are represented as mutually dependent: the Pedestrians share Sir Charles's enthusiasm for viewing the wonders of Keswick, while Sir Charles joins them in chastising Kiddy for his murderous deceptions; and Miss Veronica's example implies that aesthetic and pedestrian competency go hand in hand. Significantly, too, the end of the play once again emphasizes the Pedestrians' respectable social and economic standing. Asked for their names by Sir Charles, who comments on the discrepancy between their words and their appearance, the First Pedestrian responds, 'We trust, Sir, that we are gentlemen, though thus habited, and taking our tour on foot to gain a knowledge of our country and of mankind' (59). The Pedestrians then join in the closing song (gaining almost the last word in the play), figuring their pleasurable, healthful pedestrian experience as 'solid wealth' preferable to 'power [or] riches':

We will still, our aim pursuing,
For improvement travel on,
Men and manners still be viewing,
Making all we see our own.   (61)

Plumptre contains his redefinition of walking as deliberate, respectable, cultivating travel in a comic opera form which echoes,
despite the essentially serious function of the Pedestrians themselves, the laughter of incongruity that drove Gay's satire. For all
the ridicule directed at the unthinking picturesque traveller, *The
Lakers* provides no alternative aesthetic: the Pedestrians speak of
viewing 'the wonders of Keswick' in the same terms as Sir Charles,
and the dramatic form offers no opportunity for extended narrative
mimicry of pedestrian perspectives. But Plumptre's tactics of redefinition, his association of walking with accepted artistic practices and perspectives, and the terms of that redefinition closely
approach Wordsworth's, most notably, perhaps, in the explicit
assertion that walkers can be gentlemen.

With Plumptre, we pass into the period during which the great
change in attitudes toward walking occurred. Although Cowper,
Thelwall, and Plumptre stand out because of their generic and
influential associations with Wordsworth, their work is no more
than representative of the increasing literary visibility of the pedestrian in the late eighteenth and early nineteenth centuries. In Jane
Austen's novels, which frame the window of attitudinal and
practical change, a taste for walking and respect for other pedestrians become signs of the virtues Austen ascribes to the best of
the English landed gentry and freeholders. Gentlemen and gentle-
women are distinguished as readily by their willingness, even their
desire, to walk as by their common sense, independence of opinion,
unostentatious economy, country living, and what Mr Knightley
calls 'English delicacy towards the feelings of others'.[42] In *Pride and
Prejudice* (1813), Elizabeth Bennet's three-mile walk to Netherfield
to attend her sister's illness demonstrates good sense and sisterly
devotion, and contrasts sharply with the fastidious distaste of Miss
Bingley, who accuses her of 'conceited independence, a most
country-town indifference to decorum' and enviously wonders
if 'this adventure has rather affected [Mr Darcy's] admiration of
[Elizabeth's] fine eyes'. Elizabeth's leniency toward Darcy no doubt

[42] Austen, *Emma*, 166.

derives in part from his resistance to this slur: although he has agreed that he 'would not wish to see [his] sister make such an exhibition', his direct response to Miss Bingley's gibe is that Elizabeth's eyes 'were brightened by the exercise'.[43]

A parallel situation develops in *Emma* (1815), where Mr Knightley's substantial rationality finds partial expression in his preference for walking: 'Mr. Knightley keeping no horses, having little spare money and a great deal of health, activity, and independence, was too apt, in Emma's opinion, to get about as he could, and not use his carriage so often as became the owner of Donwell Abbey.'[44] 'Emma's opinion' here is shockingly like that of Mrs Elton, whose repeated references to her brother-in-law's two carriages, especially the elegant barouche-landau, indicate her excessive attention to appearances and her self-satisfaction—faults which Emma shares and must curb before she can be a fit mate for Mr Knightley. In both novels, indeed, the union of hero and heroine with which Austen accomplishes her consolidation of English values is a union of walkers who reach mutual understanding and plight their troths on the paths of forests and gardens.

These are brief examples from novels in which the full impact of such contrasts depends upon the articulation of a number of scattered incidents, but they accurately indicate the direction in which Austen takes her play with society's traditional readings of carriage and foot-travel.[45] Her treatment of characters who are preoccupied with what we might call the manners of travel, who read foot-travellers as 'country-town' people of low status and flash barouche-landaus as proof of their own importance, empties the carriage of nobility, leaving it a mere pound-sign. The differences between carriage-riders and walkers thus signal not only differences between the values of individuals but between what Austen perceives

[43] Austen, *Pride and Prejudice*, in *The Novels of Jane Austen*, ed. R. W. Chapman, vol. ii (Oxford and New York: Oxford University Press, 1965), 36.

[44] Austen, *Emma*, 223.

[45] Ronald Blythe disagrees, noting that although carriage-riding is bad in *Emma*, 'walking is worse'. His examples of unhappy walkers, however, are Emma in her most snobbish days, Frank Churchill, Mr Elton and Harriet Smith, certainly not the characters the novel advances as role models for its readers. While Jane Fairfax's insistence on walking to the post office does indeed 'cause consternation', it plainly represents her independence and unwillingness to play the fool to Frank Churchill; as Blythe himself notes, it is the action of an 'emancipated woman' (Blythe in *Emma*, 471).

as the values of the literally mobilized *nouveau riche* and those of the traditional landed culture.

There are no peripatetic poets in Austen, nor does her dialogue-rich style offer much in the way of descriptive passages that might represent the peripatetic aesthetic. In *Northanger Abbey* (written 1798–9), however, Austen closes a sustained comparison of carriage and foot travellers with a tongue-in-cheek episode of Claudian landscape viewing. Catherine Morland's plans for a country walk with the Tilneys are twice disrupted by the falsehoods of John Thorpe, who in each case wants her to join a driving party. His first intervention is successful, but when Catherine learns that Thorpe has taken it upon himself to excuse her from her second engagement to walk with the Tilneys, she hurries off—on foot, as Austen carefully emphasizes—to undo the misunderstanding. As the walking party itself proceeds, its principal features are discussions of what the walkers read and of how to look at what they see. In each case the Tilneys work to develop Catherine's aesthetic vocabulary and range: her sole descriptive term for books, 'nice', provokes Henry Tilney's gentle ridicule, and both brother and sister apply more serious arguments on behalf of reading history as well as novels. When the Tilneys turn to a discussion of the landscape's 'capability of being formed into pictures', Catherine discovers that she knows 'nothing of drawing—nothing of taste'.[46] The 'taste' which Catherine lacks is that pictorial eighteenth-century taste for elevated, framed views, and the Tilneys readily take up her education on this point, talking to her 'of foregrounds, distances, and second distances—sidescreens and perspectives—lights and shades; and Catherine was so hopeful a scholar that when they gained the top of Beechen Cliff, she voluntarily rejected the whole city of Bath as unworthy to make part of a landscape'.[47]

Like Plumptre, Austen invites us both to laugh at and to applaud her characters' earnest practice of popular aesthetics. The narrator seems to be poking fun at the artificial conventions of the party's Gilpinesque landscape viewing, just as she is at Gothic conventions —closely associated with theories of the picturesque, as *The Mysteries of Udolpho* and *The Romance of the Forest* demonstrate—throughout *Northanger Abbey*. Still, as the Tilneys allow

---

[46] Austen, *Northanger Abbey*, in *The Novels of Jane Austen*, ed. R. W. Chapman, vol. v (Oxford and New York: Oxford University Press, 1969), 110.
[47] Ibid. 111.

Catherine to admire Mrs Radcliffe's novels as one kind of good reading, Austen allows us to admire the pictorial aesthetic as one kind of landscape viewing and to applaud, albeit with a knowing smile, Catherine's start at forming thoughtful, informed, aesthetic standards. That Catherine makes this start on a rural stroll suggests Austen's consciousness of the aesthetic implications of deliberate pedestrianism, even though that consciousness does not develop into any imaginative alternative to Claudian conventions.

John Clare, on the other hand, does offer an alternative. Clare's poetry differs from Austen's fiction in more than genre, tending to be descriptive rather than dialogic, particularized rather than generalized, earnestly lyrical rather than coolly distanced. In his countryman's England, as in that of Austen's country squires, walking is associated with traditional land-based values, economic and otherwise, which the author perceives as disappearing and which he wants to preserve. Clare's predominantly lyrical voice, however, together with his many pedestrian narrators and characters—nearly as common in Clare as in Wordsworth—creates the deliberate link between poet and pedestrian that one misses in Austen and facilitates Clare's own particular imitation of pedestrian perspectives.

In *The Idea of Landscape and the Sense of Place*, John Barrell gives much thought to how Clare sees landscapes, or rather to how Clare represents such perceptions. Barrell describes Clare's representations as being designed 'to reveal [a poem's images] all as parts not so much of a continuum of successive impressions as of one complex manifold of simultaneous impressions', primarily by means of making deliberate connections between clauses in ways that deny the subordinations such connections would usually enforce. Drawing from his primary example, 'Emmonsails Heath in winter', Barrell argues that 'The only way we can reconcile, in the first four lines for example, the notion that the images there are all of equal importance, and the notion that the two clauses introduced by "while" are nevertheless in some sense subordinate, is to understand that for Clare the experience of seeing the leaves of the brake is somehow inseparable from the experience of seeing the heron: they are both parts of the same complex impression, not just this *and* that, but this *while* that.'[48] Finally, Barrell suggests,

---

[48] Barrell, *Idea of Landscape*, 157.

this method re-creates a 'circular' sense of place like that which 'might be characteristic of an unimproved, open-field imagination': 'the images in the poem become like beads on a necklace: they cannot change places with each other, but can be told in a circle in such a way that we lose the sense of a beginning and end, and so of one sort of order.'[49]

Barrell emphasizes Clare's evocation of simultaneity and his awareness of the disorder inherent in particularity and multiplicity, primarily because Barrell himself aims to draw these qualities into our definitions of form. None the less, he describes a duplex effect much like that characteristic of representations in which the peripatetic aesthetic is at work. Clare represents simultaneous perceptions, but must use separate words and clauses to do so; the images he forms with these words and clauses are particular, multiple, discrete, and yet Clare's syntax renders them continuous; the sense of place he re-creates by these means is circular, and yet can be told 'like beads', like discrete and ordered items, and yet comes round into itself again. Limited, successive, yet continuous views—linear, traceable, yet cyclical movement—Barrell appears to be describing, in part, the peripatetic aesthetic applied.

Clare himself says plainly that he is making a deliberate move away from extensive, elevated views toward things as they are seen by the foot-traveller. These three stanzas from 'The Flitting', the first of the poems associated with Clare's removal from Helpston to Northborough, propose this shift almost as directly as does the opening of Wordsworth's 'Peter Bell':

> Give me no high flown fangled things
> No haughty pomp in marching chime
> Where muses play on golden strings
> And splendour passes for sublime
> Where citys stretch as far as fame
> And fancys straining eye can go
> And piled untill the sky for shame
> Is stooping far away below
>
> I love the verse that mild and bland
> Breaths of green fields and open sky
> I love the muse that in her hand
> Bears wreaths of native poesy

[49] Ibid. 162–3.

Who walks nor skips the pasture brook
In scorn—but by the drinking horse
Leans oer its little brig to look
How far the sallows lean accross

And feels a rapture in her breast
Upon their root-fringed grains to mark
A hermit morehens sedgy nest
Just like a naiads summer bark
She counts the eggs she cannot reach
Admires the spot and loves it well
And yearns so natures lessons teach
Amid such neighbourhoods to dwell   (153–77)

The 'native poesy' Clare prefers obviously possesses several distinctive qualities. Its subjects and images are natural, rural, and common rather than 'fangled', urban, and rare, and the ideal methods and forms of poetry, now represented by wreaths made of flowers and grasses rather than by music drawn from golden-stringed lyres, reflect these choices. The fundamental change which produces these distinctions, however, is a change in the poet's chosen mode of perception, and the new aesthetic appears to be peripatetic. Clare rejects not just 'fangled things', but 'high flown' art whose favourite views are of immense height and breadth. 'Fancys straining eye' suggests, of course, fancy's flight—the high viewpoint required to see this mythical city of art, which itself leaves the sky 'stooping far away below', and the sheer insistence on the visual which transforms perception into picture—but it also suggests a breakdown in the system. No longer is such flight effortless, for writer or reader; the eye strains to see into the furthest distance, but cannot quite find the limiting frame, and the resulting poetry is itself strained, forced, and straining to the reader.

Clare's muse, meanwhile, 'walks nor skips the pasture brook | In scorn', but pauses on its bridge to look at how the willows hang across the stream, and then sees a moorhen's nest among the willow roots, and then counts the eggs in the nest. She does not fly to some high vantage point to gain a broader view, or strain her eyes toward the horizon, but instead chooses greater and greater 'limitation', seeing first a whole scene with horse and brook and bridge and trees, then willows only, then the nest at their roots, and finally the tiny eggs within the nest. The succession of limited, even progressively limited, scenes paradoxically removes other barriers and limitations, producing emotional intimacy which connects the person with the place and vivid memory which makes the past present. Clare, indeed, does not separate these 'two' effects: 'a love and joy | For every weed and everything', for the details that only close and deliberately limited views of a place can reveal, *is* 'A feeling kindred from a boy | A feeling brought with every spring' ('Flitting', 189–92).

These last lines sound particularly Wordsworthian, but Clare's pedestrian/poet differs from Wordsworth's in at least two important respects. For one thing, he thinks of his walking and poetic re-collection not as labour but as leisure. 'The Flitting' gives some hint of this in the criticism of the old aesthetic as 'straining', and in the relaxed and prolonged halting of its pedestrian muse upon the bridge. 'Stray Walks' and 'Careless Rambles' both revel in wandering 'sweet leisures aimless road', always coupling walk-ing with Clare's insistent 'musing': 'roam and think', 'think and roam', 'then wander home | And oer the beautys we have met . . . muse', 'Stray Walks' puts it, and 'Careless Rambles' concludes, 'mid the velvet moss I musing tread | Feel[ing] life as lovely as her picture seems' ('Stray Walks', 26, 1, 11, 13–14; 'Careless Rambles', 13–14).

'Sunday Walks' develops these associations at some length, directly contrasting the walker's everyday work with his leisurely, musing strolls. The title immediately suggests that walking is part of the traditional sabbath rest. Clare, in fact, makes walking prime among the sabbath's blessings, first by showing us a rural labourer whose 'ear at leisure dwells | On the soft soundings of his village bells', as 'He takes his rambles just as fancys please' ('Sunday Walks', 1–2, 4). Walking, unlike flight, does not strain fancy but relaxes into the pleasure of following one's own inclination. This licence matches nicely with the auditory image of the bells, which in England often follow no melody or rule, but peal up and down and across the scale with pleasant abandon, so that we can think of the non-musical rambling as a parallel case of sanctified chaos.

As Clare's pedestrian wanders down the grassy strips that separate fields and into sunken lanes bowered with hedges, he hears the 'hum of bees were labours doomed to stray | In ceasless bustle on his weary way' and the calls of various animals 'From rustics whips and plough and waggon free | Biting in carless freedom oer the leas' (29–30, 34). The contrast between the labouring bees and

the unyoked animals rather emphatically disrupts any connection
to the georgic mode that the agricultural vistas of the poem may
have tempted us to make, clearly preferring an Edenic freedom
and leisure that more readily suggest the pastoral. Although Clare's
pedestrian 'muses with a smile | On thriving produce of his earlier
toil' (41–2), enjoying the sight of 'browning wheat ears and oat
bunches grown | and pea pods swelld by blossoms long forsook |
And nearly ready for the scythe and hook' (44–6), the experience
that helps 'His musing marvel[s] home to natures cause' (50) is
not his prior labour but his present leisure:

> A six days prisoner lifes support to earn
> From dusty cobwebs and the murky barn
> The weary thresher meets the rest thats given
> And thankfull sooths him in the boon of heaven
> And sabbath walks enjoys along the fields   (59–63)

The images are agricultural, and the pedestrian/poet is a labourer,
and yet Clare distinguishes sharply between labour and both walking and poetry-making. Labour dooms and imprisons, providing
merely 'lifes support'. But leisure, embodied in walking and 'musing', gathers a rich imaginative harvest which includes the recognition of a creative power 'Who rules the year and shoots the
spindling grain' (54). As the poem shifts into first-person meditation, and then into hymn or prayer, this distinction does not fade:
the poetic narrator asks, 'free from labour let my musings stray |
Were foot paths ramble from the public way', and closes with
thanks to 'the lord of sabbaths' who has granted this day for
walking 'As leisure dropt in labours rugged way | To claim a
passport wi the rest to heaven' (99–100, 141–2).

   This particular difference between Clare's and Wordsworth's
walkers strikes me as moving evidence of the gap between the
class standing and literary acceptance of the two poets, and of
the extraordinary success of the latter's ideology. Wordsworthian
peripatetic asserts the extension not just of a traditional literary
mode, but of a working concept of 'the good life', by placing the
walker where the farmer stood as cultivator, preserver, reformer,
and (of course) poet. All of this depends upon initially accepting
farming, walking, and poetry-making as interchangable labours, in
practice as in representation. This from Wordsworth, whose labours
were walking and poetry. But Clare, who laboured at ploughing,

reaping, threshing, herding cattle, and gardening tells us plainly that next to his work amid dusty cobwebs and murky barns, walking and poetry-making appear as the sweet pursuits of paradise (briefly) regained, a true sabbath rest. From Clare's point of view, a decision to use georgic as the parent stock of peripatetic would surely involve an unconscionable equivocation on 'labour'.

The other difference between Clare's pedestrian/poet and Wordsworth's resonates with Clare's removal of walking from the workday world in that it too points towards the pedestrian's desire to rest in some unchanging, paradisaical place. As our discussion of 'The Flitting' suggests, Clare mimics pedestrian perspectives partly in order to re-establish the limiting frame he feels should be there but cannot find from the vantage-point set by the eighteenth-century aesthetic. His emphasis, in fact, falls on limitation rather than succession, so that his pedestrians tend to tighten their perceptual focus, looking more and more narrowly into a single scene, as in 'The Flitting', or, as in 'The Morehens Nest', 'catching little pictures passing bye':

then I walk and swing my stick for joy
And catch at little pictures passing bye
A gate whose posts are two old dotterel trees
A close with molehills sprinkled oer its leas
A little footbrig with its crossing rail
A wood gap stopt with ivy wreathing pale
A crooked stile each path crossed spinny owns
A brooklet forded by its stepping stones
A wood bank mined with rabbit holes—and then
An old oak leaning oer a badgers den
Whose cave mouth enters neath the twisted charms
Of its old roots and keeps it safe from harms
Pick axes spades and all its strength confounds
When hunted foxes hide from chasing hounds
                                        ('Morehens Nest', 65–78)

These tightly focused perceptions no doubt contribute to what Barrell terms the simultaneity of Clare's representations, not only because each momentary place seems coeval in time with the others, but because each seems itself to be held or 'caught' in time, excluding changes. The muse of 'The Flitting' 'cannot reach' the eggs in the moorhen's nest , nor can these hunters dig out the fox; each vision of the walk—the gate, the close, the bridge—although connected by our knowledge that the speaker is walking and so sees successively, remains perceptually intact, a pure and undisturbed memory.

Clearly, Clare's pedestrian poets, who 'love with [their] old hants to be' ('Flitting', 91), retrace familiar ground with very different motives and effects from Wordsworth's excursive walkers. When the narrator of 'Michael' revisits the sheepfold, or the Wanderer in the *Excursion* returns to Margaret's cottage, they both perceive and accept change. In fact, their primary business is to account for and interpret the changes they perceive in people and places in such a way that those changes somehow resolve into a moral lesson, specifically a lesson that helps others (including the reader) understand and accept change in their own lives. Indeed, although Wordsworth's pedestrians do stop and reflect in the way Hartman labels as the 'halted traveler' motif, we understand walking as the crucial instrument of their perception and useful interpretation of change because excursive walking itself moves and changes and passes on, always returning to an always different place. Clare's pedestrians, on the other hand, seek continually to refind a familiar place that remains familiar and unchanged, so that despite Clare's declared turn toward a pedestrian aesthetic, his perceptual stress often falls upon pause rather than upon motion. Thus, where the narrator of the *Excursion* walks into his increasingly fine perception of detail, seeing at last a miniature town that suggests, atomlike, a world within a world, space still to be explored, the muse of 'The Flitting' stops to look into a nest of eggs where she sees, finally, *eggs*—still, secure, and for all their implicit capacity, a period to her vision.

In fact, Clare's poems about birds' nests, which he planned to collect in a separate volume, develop the implications of his perceptual emphasis most clearly. Eleven of these thirty-eight poems have explicitly pedestrian speakers and/or characters, and so much is made of the difficulty of finding birds' nests unless one is on foot that the observations of the other twenty-seven implicitly depend on the pedestrian perspective. Indeed, aesthetic concerns much like those addressed in 'The Flitting', are clearly part of the complex of ideas and feelings Clare explores in these important poems. Birds naturally suggest the winged muse, and birds nesting, especially when they include the nightingale and the skylark, suggest the muse grounded and at home, a vivid image of Clare's 'native poesy'. The birds themselves are often characterized as recluses—'Thou hermit hunter of the local glen'—and their nests as being 'For secresy and shelter rightly made' ('Sand Martin', 1; 'Birds Nests', 12). Often a walker does not know 'he tramples near its nest': 'Had not the old bird heard us trampling bye I And fluttered out—we had not seen it lie I Brown as the road way side' ('Fern Owls Nest', 8; 'Pettichaps Nest', 11–13).

The small beauties of the birds' eggs, meticulously described in nest after nest, should be secure enough in such seclusion, as should the productions of the native poet, and yet fear of invasion and destruction pervades these poems. The walker-poet sees, represents, and so preserves the nest, the eggs, the home of poesy and its fruits. 'We'll let them be', says the finder of 'The Pettichaps Nest', and the speaker of 'The Nightingales Nest' concludes, 'We will not plunder the music of its dower I . . . We'll leave [its eggs] still unknown to wrong I As the old woodlands legacy of song' ('Pettichaps', 27; 'Nightingales', 69, 91–2). Yet dangers remain, and Clare's language and imagery rather surprisingly cast these dangers in the forms of walking.[50] In 'The Fern Owls Nest', the woodsman may indeed trample the nest with his careless and 'heavy tread'; 'Where fear encamps' around the snipe's nest, 'The trembling grass I Quakes from the human foot', and the birds 'dread I The very breath of man I Hiding in spots that never knew his tread' ('Fern Owls', 7; 'To the Snipe', 3–6, 37–9). That same pettichap's nest which the poet finds by chance and carefully preserves astonishes him by its proximity to a road: 'For fears rude paths around are thickly spread I And they are left to many dangers ways' ('Pettichaps', 28–9). Still another nest is guarded from a road by a brook:

Right pleasant brook Im glad ye lie
Between them and the road
They're not all friends that wander bye
And faith is ill bestowed
Hid from the world their green retreat
The worlds ways never knew
But much I fear they'd quickly meet
Its cares if in its view

('In the hedge I pass a little nest', 25–32)

---

[50] Virgil twice pictures the destruction of birds' nests by ploughmen, at II. 207–12 and at IV. 510–16, and Wordsworth twice translated this last passage, which compares Orpheus to a grieving nightingale (*PW* i. 284 and n.).

In this stanza Clare's difficulties show crystal-clear. The speaker's 'wandering bye' shapes both his initial experience, permitting him to see and appreciate the nest, and his representation of that experience, and so acts to preserve both nest and memory of nest. But because Clare 'stops' walking metaphorically, by naming it 'leisure' ('rest' or 'pause') and by representing his perceptions while walking as simultaneous and/or as 'caught' in time, the very movement of walking itself—stepping down the road, changing perspectives, passing through time/space—threatens the nest and his representation of it. His wording makes it very clear that this is a problem of pedestrian perception: if the nest were 'in view' of the road it would be more easily threatened by faithless strangers—by inconstancy, in fact, and change. The speaker concludes that he himself will walk only on well-known paths, and offers this as advice to the reader: 'chuse not haunts that many know | . . . For ye are sure to find a foe | Where many pass for friends' (41, 47–8). But to stop walking, or even to 'stop' walking, is surely to lose the very perspectives which, in Clare's scheme of things, properly shape poetry and preserve the walker's perceptions.

Moreover, Clare overtly chooses pedestrian perspective as a remedy for the change and motion he fears. His conscious recognition of that choice in 'The Flitting' occurs immediately after his removal to Northborough in 1832, an event Raymond Williams calls, 'in terms that now recover their literal meaning—unsettling, dislocating'.[51] The small physical distance from Helpston to the Northborough cottage—just three or four miles—plainly embodied great psychological distances for Clare, from first love to present indifference, from youth to middle age, from countryman to poet, from native to stranger, all of which had to be encompassed by his already troubled mind. In 1841, after his mental breakdown and three years of treatment at Matthew Allen's asylum, Clare tries to bridge these distances by precisely the method he proposes in 'The Flitting': he escapes on foot from the asylum, walking back toward Northborough in the confused belief that there he will be reunited with his 'first wife', the girl he loved in his youth in Helpston. His prose account of the journey, which focuses on the difficulties of finding his way and his determination to go on, suggests that

---

[51] Williams in Clare, *Selected Poetry and Prose*, 11.

Clare longingly imagines his youth as an unchanging locale recoverable by his pedestrian quest. It also poignantly demonstrates the materiality of his fears: because Clare is walking through country he does not know, he is forced to keep mostly to main roads, afraid to take footpaths lest he get lost. Even so he often loses his way; his journey is lengthened by miles, he runs out of money and is slowed still further by hunger and tiredness, and he is taken into custody not long after he finally comes to familiar ground. Back in the asylum, he writes, 'Returned home out of Essex and found no Mary—her and her family are as nothing to me now though she herself was once the dearest of all—and how can I forget' ('[Journey out of Essex]', 437). Displaced from his native ground, envisioning an unchanging Edenic home that lies just down some familiar path, Clare finds himself lost in the distances of his own recollections.

Clare's titular rejection of the eighteenth-century aesthetic, then, of 'flitting' as a mode of poetic perception, is also a rejection of his own flitting to Northborough, and of the flitting of time and love and hope. Even before this crucial trauma and the conscious pedestrian aesthetic of 'The Flitting', walking appears as a way to the localized and the settled, as in the birds' nest poems, all of which were written between 1824 and 1832. Like Austen, Clare senses the potential of the peripatetic aesthetic in dealing with the accelerating changes that have rendered the eighteenth-century aesthetic so unsatisfying, and he actually goes on to develop his own representations of pedestrian perspectives. Yet, like his pedestrian escape from the asylum and for essentially the same reasons, the experiment fails: Clare's pedestrian-poet strives mostly to exclude motion and change, and so his poetry threatens its own mode.

The key to this conundrum may be that, for Clare, walking—and particularly his kind of walking, countryman's walking—is an integral part of the way of life being destroyed by enclosure. Much has been written about Clare's reactions to enclosure, and I will not add to the basic debate except to agree with Williams (and essentially with Robinson and Powell) that 'Enclosure . . . in Clare's verse, is a complex and shifting term. . . . The closure of commons, the stopping of paths; loss of labour and of wages; the ploughing of meadows and the felling of trees: all these, on different occasions, and often effectively and rhetorically combined, are the felt consequences of what is at once the "mildew" and the "tyranny" of enclosure.'[52] What I do wish to pursue a bit further is the relatively unremarked effect of enclosure on walking—'the stopping of paths', among other things—and the implications of that effect for the empirical and metaphorical relations between walking and farming.

Williams describes Clare's poem 'The Mores', which 'some editors call . . . "Enclosure"' as 'an impassioned attack on those who have caused the moors to suffer the fate of the commons, turning men and animals off the land in the pursuit of gain'.[53] This description emphasizes Clare's cognizance of enclosure's paradoxical destruction of the countryman's agrarian wealth by agricultural development, and Clare does indeed speak directly to this point in 'The Mores': 'Inclosure came and trampled on the grave | Of labours rights and left the poor a slave' (19–20). But the poem's primary concern is enclosure's restraint of walking, both as an aesthetic and as an empirical act. It opens with an evocation of the moors before enclosure, 'one eternal green | That never felt the rage of blundering plough':

> Unbounded freedom ruled the wandering scene
> Nor fence of ownership crept in between
> To hide the prospect of the following eye
> Its only bondage was the circling sky   (7–10)

Here is Barrell's 'circular sense of place', and something of the unbounded prospect of an eighteenth-century vantage-point. Eventually, however, the characterization of this scene as 'wandering' resonates with a later passage in which Clare shows walking as the proper mode in which to view the countryside:

> Each little path that led its pleasant way
> As sweet as morning leading night astray
> Where little flowers bloomed round a varied host
> That travel felt delighted to be lost
> Nor grudged the steps that he had taen as vain
> When right roads traced his journeys end again
> Nay on a broken tree hed sit awhile
> To see the mores and fields and meadows smile
> Sometimes with cowslaps smothered—then all white
> With daiseys—then the summers splendid sight

---

[52] Williams in Clare, *Selected Poetry and Prose*, 15.   [53] Ibid. 232.

Of corn fields crimson oer the 'headach' bloomd
Like splendid armys for the battle plumed
He gazed upon them with wild fancys eye
As fallen landscapes from an evening sky
These paths are stopt—the rude philistines thrall
Is laid upon them and destroyed them all
Each little tyrant with his little sign
Shows where man claims earth glows no more divine
On paths to freedom and to childhood dear
A board sticks up to notice 'no road here'   (50–70)

In this passage 'wandering' plainly means walking the country paths, both becoming 'lost' and finding one's way again by means of those paths in that familiar excursive movement which breaks bounds but always returns. Moreover, having an unbounded perspective does not mean being able to see everything at once, or seeing from on high—even the landscapes in 'wild fancys eye' are 'fallen . . . from an evening sky'—but being able to walk where one has always walked, seeing the fields successively in flower and in grain, returning to places beloved in childhood and enjoyed at leisure.

Clare sees the loss of this pedestrian freedom as no small part of enclosure's slavery. Indeed, the full shape of 'The Mores' suggests that these twenty lines on walking—precisely one-quarter of its length—form the core of the poem. The opening picture of the unenclosed moor, and the following descriptions of prosperous country life before enclosure, of free-ranging herds and herdsmen and of roaming gatherers of uncultivated fruits and flowers, all underscore the necessity of freedom to wander in old paths. Each reminiscence closes with a direct accusation against enclosure's economic tyrannies and aesthetic depredations, setting up a rhetorical equation between the countryman's freedom to wander, his economic prosperity, and his aesthetic enjoyment of natural scenes, especially those remembered and loved from his earliest days. Thus 'The Mores' represents path-closing not only as an effect of enclosure and an emblem of its depredations but as one of its most powerful agents of change which, by changing people's physical paths, changes what they see and how they see it, cutting them off from crucial areas of their cultural and personal histories.

Clare's poetic account of enclosure's effects on old ways of walking and seeing matches well with other brief literary and historical accounts which imply a similar relationship between the forms of agriculture and those of walking. The open-field land- scape described by Hoskins, with its small, scattered, oddly shaped fields and broad commons, shaped the old forms of walking Clare loves so well. Definite paths traced the movements of labourers and farmers between fields, commons, villages, and homes. At the same time, the principle of common access to certain lands, plus the relatively small extent of cultivation, allowed free wandering and open vistas. Kim Taplin's description of the pre-enclosure walker's relatively unrestricted choices, in fact, suggests the route followed by the labourer at the beginning of 'Sunday Walks': 'although there were well-beaten tracks linking regular destinations, one might still wander at will through common or uncultivated land and by a variety of ways along the balks dividing the narrow strips where crops were grown'.[54]

Enclosure changed these choices in a variety of ways. Some of the footpaths which followed the old field boundaries simply vanished under the new cultivation, obliterated by the plough. Other paths, curiously enough, achieved their first legal status as public ways across private lands because they appeared on the maps which accompanied awards of enclosure. For the most part, however, the award maps were 'intent on becoming authorities for the future rather than sources of information about the past'.[55] Barrell describes these maps as annihilations of existing topography which simply omitted old boundaries, roads, and paths and wrote in the clean, broad outlines of private holdings and projected highways, making the rural landscape more immediately access- ible to outsiders uninitiated in the mysteries of local roads and fields but destroying the intimacies common access once allowed.[56]

As enclosure proceeded, then, many paths and rights of way fell into the twilight zone between physical landscape and legal map, and walking became an uncertain guerrilla tactic which, as the experience of the walker in 'The Mores' demonstrates, might or might not become trespass. Even legally established footpaths could be closed for a variety of reasons and under a variety of authorities. Until 1815, in fact, private landowners simply put up barriers or 'no trespassing' signs—sometimes with spurious

[54] Taplin, *English Path*, 5.   [55] Gray, *English Field Systems*, 14.
[56] Barrell, *Idea of Landscape*, 94–6.

attributions to official decisions—to discourage the use of paths across their lands, and the 1815 Act of Parliament requiring two Justices of the Peace to close a public right of way quickly became a joke: 'It was currently reported that one magistrate would jovially ask another to dinner, giving as a reason that he wanted his concurrence in stopping up a footpath.'[57] Thus, when Mr Knightley says that he will not '[move] the path to Langham . . . turning it more to the right that it may not cut through the home meadows . . . if it were to be the means of inconvenience to the Highbury people', he is exhibiting an admirable and unusual sensitivity to the old common rights of the villagers.[58] Complaints about this state of affairs, including a diatribe in an 1829 legal textbook on the tendency of justices to close footpaths as favours to 'proprietor[s]' without regard for public needs, eventually led to an 1835 Act transferring the power of such closings to juries, and reforms proceeded from there.[59]

Thus, although enclosure legitimated some footpaths by officially mapping them, it more often provided legal means for closing, moving, or destroying parts of the paths and ended common access to unpathed moors and heaths. The cumulative impact on the everyday economy of the countryman must have been large: fields and villages once easily accessible by a cross-county path or route might now be reached only by some more roundabout path or public road, perhaps reached easily only by cart or horse, and so might fall out of a labourer's practical range of daily access. Great pieces of one's personal life, too, might be appropriated. Taplin stresses the crucial part footpaths played in courtship for country-dwellers of all classes, and Clare and Wordsworth write incessantly of memories and emotions recovered by the retracing of old paths, the retravelling of old routes.[60]

For the poet, indeed, the stopped footpath presents a serious aesthetic problem, compounded by its implication of the dominance of legal, monetary forms over his personal and artistic forms. Cowper alludes to this difficulty as his narrator descends from that 'speculative height' in *The Task*:

> The folded gates would bar my progress now,
> But that the lord of this enclosed demesne,

[57] Webb, *King's Highway*, 203.   [58] Austen, *Emma*, 128.
[59] Webb, *King's Highway*, 231.   [60] Taplin, *English Path*, 65–84.

> Communicative of the good he owns,
> Admits to me a share: the guiltless eye
> Commits no wrong, nor wastes what it enjoys.   (I. 330–4)

Notice that the narrator's eye, as well as his foot, may be guilty of trespass. What can be seen by the walker is now owned, and might be stolen or wasted, but is instead transferred in shares to the narrator, who only then may enjoy it. Enclosure transforms pedestrian perception, the fundamental form and content of this part of *The Task*, into a commodity, its value ('the good') appropriated and distributed by means that potentially separate the poet from his material, the poem from the experience in which it is grounded, and that can deny the poet his work. For Clare this threat has, in a sense, already been fulfilled: although he disassociates walking from labour and from economic function, poetic walking vanishes, 'stopped' either by Clare or by a path-closer, even as the farming of a small freehold and the independent labour of a countryman vanishes.

But enclosure's disruption of old forms of walking also foregrounds the elements of British law which permit those same old forms to disrupt, both physically and aesthetically, the process of enclosure: 'not only was there general access to commons, prior to enclosure, but there were actual paths which were regarded by ancient custom as rights of way even where no written by-laws existed in relation to them; and the law even today [1979] says that a path which it can be proved has been used "as of right" for a period of twenty years or more shall be deemed to be public'.[61] Usage, in other words, determines access—which means that walking is actually a means of preserving the unenclosed character of the countryside, of appropriating or reappropriating land for common use.

Wordsworth himself makes deliberate use of this principle on at least one occasion. David McCracken, noting that Wordsworth 'championed public footpaths', draws our attention to John Taylor Coleridge's reminiscence of an 1836 walk with Wordsworth 'through the Glenridding Walks':

I remember well, asking him if we were not trespassing on private pleasure-grounds here. He said, no; the walks had, indeed, been inclosed, ˙

[61] Ibid. 28.

but he remembered them open to the public, and he always went through them when he chose. At Lowther, we found among the visitors, the late Lord W——; and describing our walk, *he* made the same observation, that we had been trespassing; but Wordsworth maintained his point with somewhat more warmth than I either liked, or could well account for. But afterwards, when we were alone, he told me he had purposely answered Lord W——stoutly and warmly, because he had done a similar thing with regard to some grounds in the neighbourhood of Penrith, and excluded the people of Penrith from walking where they had always enjoyed the right before. He had evidently a pleasure in vindicating these rights, and seemed to think it a duty.[62]

Justice Coleridge's confusion over this incident—his inability to 'well account' for Wordsworth's vigorous defence of public access, and his equivocal response to Wordsworth's sense of duty—reflects the simultaneously conservative and subversive quality walking acquires during this period of enclosure. On one hand, what Wordsworth does in the Glenridding Walks is not only perfectly legal, but actively supportive of the new forms of enclosed England, legitimating public rights of way and so opening the once insular countryside to travellers. On the other hand (as his companion plainly senses), because such a walk appeals to older legal and topographical forms, maintaining local idiosyncrasies that enclosure tends to destroy, it subverts private claims to enclosed lands, insisting on some degree of common access. The walker appropriates his path, and yet his appropriation undoes the appropriations of enclosure in both method and result: his possession is the direct result of his labour, and, although he is privately enriched, whether in poetic association or in easy access to village and field, his gain impoverishes no one and actually opens similar opportunities for anyone who wishes to follow in his footsteps.

When the walker is a poet, even private lands along his path are metaphorically unenclosed; we become tenants in common, enriched by the poetic fruits the walker gathers, enjoying individual access to a mutual estate. Thus Wordsworth can claim in *Home at Grasmere* that he and Dorothy possess 'unappropriated bliss' by '[finding] means I To walk abreast, though in a narrow path, I

---

[62] David McCracken, *Wordsworth and The Lake District* (Oxford and New York: Oxford University Press, 1985), 3; Alexander B. Grosart, *The Prose Works of William Wordsworth*, vol. iii (London: Edward Moxon, Son, & Co., 1876), 425 and n.

With undivided steps': the walkers' possession of their path is real, physical, enriching, and yet leaves the path, the bliss of life at Grasmere, still unappropriated, available to all, even offered to all by means of poetry (85, 177–9). It is a miracle of loaves and fishes, a bottomless pitcher, continually renewing the resources it consumes.

When Wordsworth imagines walking as a cultivating labour, then, using georgic as the literary stock upon which to graft his walking poems, he produces an ideological hybrid of enormous potential. Walking itself provides continuously moving perception at a human pace, so that the walker experiences change as a process which he is able to retrace, both physically and memorially. Wordsworth's excursive walking, in particular, balances the elements of change and continuity, and emphasizes the walker's ability to retrace his steps and comprehend the changes he sees. All this speaks to the growing dissatisfaction with the eighteenth-century pictorial aesthetic visible in Cowper and Austen and Clare, who sense the advantages of adopting an aesthetic based on pedestrian perspectives, and speaks also to similar problems and needs liable to be felt in everyday aesthetic practice. Moreover, walking's material capacity to appropriate paths for common use means that when it is also imagined as georgic labour, it replaces cultivation, regrounding civilizing labour in efficacious material action and relocating the rural countryside both in its own local character and in its significance to the life of England as a nation. How Wordsworth accomplishes this imagining will be our next concern.

3

Walking Where the Sower Dwelt

WHEN Wordsworth entitled *The Excursion*, he selected a word which describes a very particular sort of journey—in this case, a very particular kind of walking. 'Excursion' derives from the Latin *excurrere*, 'to run out', and the *Oxford English Dictionary* lists its primary English meaning as 'The act of running out; escape from confinement; "progression beyond fixed limits" (J[ohnson])', and so forth. By 1700, however, 'excursion' had also come to mean 'A journey, expedition, or ramble from one's home, or from any place with the intention of returning to it', so that both the idea of breaking bounds and the idea of returning to them are contained within the same term. The literary version of 'excursion', 'excursus', involves this same double movement, being defined as 'A detailed discussion (usually in the form of an appendix at the end of a book, or some division of it) of some point which it is desired to treat more fully than can be done in a note' or 'A digression in which some incidental point is discussed at length'— discourse which departs significantly from the main text, in other words, but which none the less bears upon it, and from which the reader returns to the main line of enquiry.[1] The *Excursion* can be considered as a series of such digressions, or as a single excursus in itself, a dramatic interlude between the first and third books of *The Recluse* which, as Wordsworth projected them, were to 'consist chiefly of meditations in the Author's own person' (*PW* iv. 368). But the excursion to which the title most literally refers is the walking tour undertaken by the narrator and the Wanderer, which itself involves various smaller excursions, departures from a main line and returns along it, both remembered and performed by the walkers. The Wanderer does not wander in the bad old sense of aimless, socially disruptive walking, but instead returns continually along paths already walked, effecting connection and stabilization as he goes.

---

[1] The definitions in this paragraph are drawn from the *OED* entries for 'excur', 'excursion', and 'excursus'.

Wordsworth never used the term 'excursive walking', but I introduce it to distinguish what Wordsworth called 'walking' and 'wandering' from the previous uses of those words. Just as proponents of true travel implicitly redefine 'travel' by using that word to refer to process-less, destination-oriented travel, so Wordsworth shows us walkers who choose to retrace old paths and return repeatedly to certain locations, and, by calling this 'walking' and 'wandering', redefines these terms to include the deliberate intention of return. This implicit redefinition of 'walking' as excursive walking, walking which accomplishes both wilful movement beyond previous bounds and relocation at the walk's origins, counters the threat of wandering with a promise of return. Moreover, it formally reshapes 'walking' to resemble educative travel (the traveller going out and returning with his new knowledge) and appropriative local walking (the walker opening the countryside to travellers and maintaining its local identity), thus tapping into the positive potential uses and interpretations of pedestrian action. Finally, excursive walking's capacity for relocation and replacement permits serious comparisons with Virgilian cultivation along lines that John Taylor and John Gay found ludicrous.

In *The Prelude, Home at Grasmere*, and 'When first I journeyed hither' ('When to the attractions of the busy world'), Wordsworth represents excursive walking as an agent of home-making and nation-building, and shows the coincidence of its deliberate returns with the recollective action of poetry. These varieties of cultivation—civilizing, stabilizing, poetry-making—are of course those derived from the concrete term of agriculture in Virgil's *Georgics*. Here, however, such cultivation derives from excursive walking rather than farming. 'Salisbury Plain', 'The Old Cumberland Beggar', and *The Excursion* set up the comparison even more plainly, juxtaposing walking and agriculture in such a way as to associate the two acts and yet repeatedly demonstrating the superior capacities of walking as cultivating labour. In these poems I read the development of a previously unrecognized literary mode that I name 'peripatetic', an extension of georgic with excursive walking as the concrete term of its metaphors of cultivation.

The first fifty lines of *The Prelude* represent a crucial instance of Wordsworth's ongoing redefinition of 'walking' and 'wandering'. As the narrator walks out of the city, he speaks of that departure as a release from imprisonment into free wandering and yet as an instrument of locating himself in a chosen home:

> Now I am free, enfranchised and at large,
> May fix my habitation where I will.
> What dwelling shall receive me? in what vale
> Shall be my harbour?
> .   .   .   .
> The earth is all before me. With a heart
> Joyous, nor scared at its own liberty,
> I look about; and should the guide I choose
> Be nothing better than a wandering cloud,
> I cannot miss my way.   (I. 9–12, 15–19)

The cadence of these lines so smooths the narrator's transitions between placement and wandering that we are scarcely aware of them. From 'a house | Of bondage' he walks out to freedom not only to wander, to go where he chooses, but also freedom to 'fix [his] habitation', to place himself where he chooses. He recognizes the possible dangers of liberty but asserts that he cannot stray from the right path, which clearly also means that he cannot fail to place his new abode correctly. Indeed, his assertion appears to be that *because* his wandering is free he will not stray: 'The earth is all before me' leads directly, without guidance, to 'I cannot miss my way'.

Again, although he asks, 'whither shall I turn | By road or pathway, or through open field', and imagines as a guide 'any floating thing | Upon the river' (I. 29–30), the narrator resolves this brief worry about undirectedness into the pleasure of determining his own living place:

> Enough that I am free; for months to come
> May dedicate myself to chosen tasks;
> May quit the tiresome sea and dwell on shore.
> If not a settler on the soil, at least
> To drink wild water, and to pluck green herbs,
> And gather fruits fresh from their native tree.   (I. 33–8)

With lack of direction, then, comes self-direction and with wandering—now clearly deliberate wandering—comes placement: he will not travel (the verb suggests itself) but dwell on shore. Yet he will create that dwelling in movement, living not as a settled cultivator but as a gatherer of wild nourishment. As such a gatherer he must move to live, and yet claims in that movement to make himself a home.[2]

The sense of such lines, that the stable placement of a human life is enabled by movement, appeals so strongly to those who live in the constant movement of technological cultures that we must exert a certain effort to remain aware that Wordsworth *constructs* this sense by means of smooth rhetorical transitions between the terms of wandering and settlement. In the process of these transitions he invests 'wandering' with positive value once foreign to that term: wandering becomes not a relaxation of body and mind, a withdrawal from community—although he continues to play upon those older ideas—but a deliberate, directed labour undertaken to make self and home. He repeats the construction so frequently, both in the *Prelude* and elsewhere, that the idea becomes 'natural', its working nearly invisible. The famous passage beginning 'Fair seed-time had my soul', for instance, opens its crucial remembrances with the 'transplanted' boy walking rather than rooted, 'wander[ing] half the night among the Cliffs | And the smooth Hollows' (I. 305, 309, 314–15). The image of the seed alone contains both placement and growth; and when the seed-time is revealed as a time of wandering, the wandering takes on the character of deliberation despite its rambling quality and

---

[2] David Simpson's rich and informative reading of 'Gypsies' in *Wordsworth's Historical Imagination: The Poetry of Displacement* (New York and London: Methuen, 1987) responds to this strain in Wordsworth as juxtaposition, rather than conflation: 'Wordsworth's displacement . . . takes two antithetical but entirely cognate forms: a strenuous over-identification with places and communities (as in *Home at Grasmere*), and a near-complete remoteness from all human contingencies. Wordsworth is a poet who always wants both to retire to a chosen vale and to sally forth along the roads and over the hills—and wants both at once' (p. 48). Simpson, whose primary concern is the displacement of Wordsworth's imaging of writing 'in the language of work and property' by his 'propensity for the vocabulary of idleness and vagrancy', rhetorically recognizes connections among poetry, labour, and walking throughout his book (p. 2). His chapters on ' "Gypsies" ', 'Poets, Paupers and Peripatetics: The Politics of Sympathy', and 'Structuring a Subject: *The Excursion*' should be read alongside my work: they offer an intensely focused discussion of Wordsworth's restive efforts to identify his work with traditionally productive labours, and provide detailed domestic histories for individual Wordsworth poems. For Simpson, however, walking and wandering (he does not distinguish between them, accepting Wordsworth's redefinition) remain varieties of movement that contrast with the placement of propertied people, and, despite their connection in Wordsworth with poetic composition, function as leisurely departures from the constraints of labour. In identifying shepherding, rather than the Wanderer's peripatetic peddling, as Wordsworth's ideal occupation, Simpson misses Wordsworth's assertion that walking itself is labour (p. 47).

becomes a cultivation of the seed, a placing of the child in land and love, a venturing out and a returning to home.

The seed-time passage also gives us a glimpse of the way Wordsworth shifts through the metaphorical terms of georgic into those of his own representation of walking as cultivation. In that move from seeding through transplanting into wandering, Wordsworth not only suggests that walking is cultivation but leaves the impression that walking supersedes Virgilian cultivation, taking on its functions and altering its original terms. As this passage continues, in fact, the agricultural metaphor gives way to descriptions of the narrator's night walks. The closing images embody the moral pressure of the natural world, felt by the narrator as he hurries along after stealing birds from others' traps, as 'Low breathings coming after me, and sounds | Of undistinguishable motion, steps | Almost as silent as the turf they trod' (I. 330–2). Even where the narrator's walking wanders in the bad sense, straying toward criminality, Wordsworth reasserts the function of walking as cultivation, rendering the narrator's moral correction in pedestrian terms as well. Agricultural images, meanwhile, have disappeared.

The *Prelude's* narrator intends his excursive walks, his returns in memory to observe the self being made, as construction and confirmation of a fit perspective from which to conduct poetic labour, and the figuring of that perspective as a travelling one has never been in much doubt (although its specifically pedestrian quality has excited little comment). But *Home at Grasmere*, which seems to insist so powerfully on placement, retreat, and containment, also develops a poetic perspective which moves not just within the vale of Grasmere but out of it and back, and which does so specifically by walking.[3]

The narrator first remembers looking down into Grasmere vale and imagining himself moving about it like birds, and like the eye in a Claudian landscape:

> flit[ting] from field to rock, from rock to field,
> From shore to island, and from isle to shore,
> From open place to covert, from a bed
> Of meadow-flowers into a tuft of wood,

---

[3] Stephen Gill's text is 'the earliest complete one, MS B', which still includes the lines later attached as a 'Prospectus' to the *Excursion*. See Gill (ed.), *Poems*, 695–6 for a brief discussion of the rather complex composition history of the poem.

From high to low, from low to high, yet still
Within the bounds of this huge Concave; here
Should be my home.   (37–43)

Later, when he has taken up residence there, we get a lovely
passage of birds' circling flights within the vale, 'Hundreds of
curves and circlets high and low, I Backwards and forwards,
progress intricate' (298–9). But the narrator prefaces these images
with his realization that 'like them I I cannot take possession of
the sky' (287–8). Indeed, the 'lonely pair I Of milk-white Swans'
he identifies with himself and Emma are missing; and his other
comparison of the two of them with birds reflects the siblings'
condition before they come together as a household again, when
they were 'like Birds I Which by the intruding Fowler had been
scared, I Two of a scattered brood' (322–3, 173–5). However
beautiful and seductive the contained, circling perspective of Grasmere's birds may seem, the narrator cannot use it to make Grasmere
his home.

How he does come into possession of Grasmere's 'unappropriated
bliss' is by walking (85).[4] His sad separation from Emma ends when,
'Remembering much and hoping more', they 'found means I To
walk abreast, though in a narrow path, I With undivided steps'
(177–9). As he and Emma arrive in Grasmere 'on foot I Through
bursts of sunshine and through flying snows', their entrance somehow animating trees and streams, they see things from a perspective like and yet unlike that of birds in circling flight: 'All things
were moved; they round us as we went, I We in the midst of them'
(219–20, 235–6). 'All things' round back toward the walkers, as
if they were a still centre, and yet they move along a path that
leads through the vale, out of it as well as in. There is return—
the narrator returning to the place he first saw as a boy—but not
containment, circling but not flitting. Thus the passage places the
pedestrians at the moving centre of circles, holding the circling as
Grasmere does, but also moves them through and into the vale.[5]

---

[4] Kurt Heinzelman offers a complementary discussion of the Wordsworths' home-
making activities, focusing on the difference between William's and Dorothy's
ideas of and procedures for domestic settlement, in 'The Cult of Domesticity:
Dorothy and William Wordsworth at Grasmere', in Anne Mellor (ed.), Romanticism and Feminism (Bloomington: Indiana University Press, 1987).

[5] See Karl Kroeber's Romantic Landscape Vision: Constable and Wordsworth
(Madison: University of Wisconsin Press, 1975) for a contrary (and now tradi-

So they come into Grasmere, 'A pair seceding from the common world' (249). The narrator tells us it is a place where 'old | Substantial virtues' are preserved by solitude and 'local circumstance', where 'Labour . . . preserves | His rosy face', and 'where he who tills the field | . . . is Master of the field | And treads the mountain which his Father trod' (466–7, 467, 440–1, 462–4). Yet, as the last image suggests that this preservation of settled rural virtues is not accomplished solely by placed labour, so the narrator does not make his home simply by 'seceding' and stopping. Nor is his home-making movement, as he imagined it would be, a flitting from spot to spot within Grasmere's magic bounds. Instead he realizes participation in this community of 'untutored Shepherds' and homely virtue as a continuation of his foot-journey into the vale:

> the inward frame,
> Though slowly opening, opens every day.
> Nor am I less delighted with the show
> As it unfolds itself, now here, now there,
> Than is the passing Traveller, when his way
> Lies through some region then first trod by him
> (Say this fair Valley's self), when long hung mists
> Break up and are beginning to recede.
> How pleased is to hear the murmuring streams,
> The many Voices, from he knows not where,
> To have about him, which way e'er he goes,
> Something on every side concealed from view,
> In every quarter some thing visible,
> Half-seen or wholly, lost and found again,
> Alternate progress and impediment,
> And yet a growing prospect in the main.   (694–709)

The 'inward frame', it seems to me, is many things: the frame of self, the frame of poetic vision, Grasmere itself, home, the local place of labour and life. The narrator observes this opening as if he were a pedestrian passing through the frame (he moving in the midst of things), from and to what lies beyond, through limited, successive visions of what lies within (all things moving round

tional) assessment of the birds' circling flight as the ideal movement of the poem, the one which marks the self-sufficient containment of Grasmere Vale (pp. 120 ff.). Also, for perceptive comments on the interplay between circles and paths in Wordsworth, see John Elder, *Imagining the Earth: Poetry and the Vision of Nature* (Urbana and Chicago: University of Illinois Press, 1985), 97, 103.

him). Indeed, the passage through accomplishes the opening, the 'growing prospect'. The narrator's visions cannot literally be those of first passage. He is a resident here, and yet he understands the essence of his residency, of what it means to have a home in Grasmere, to be wandering. He sees the vale as a pedestrian passing through a place not known, and yet because the narrator lives there, the passage must be a return and all that he sees 'lost and found again'. Grasmere becomes indeed 'A Centre, come from wheresoe'er you will', but, in order to experience it as centre, come, and go, he must (167).

One of the particular difficulties in assessing this redefinition of walking and wandering is our knowledge that Wordsworth himself was a constant, vigorous pedestrian who repeated the out-and-in movement of excursive walking on every scale from international travel to garden strolling. His 1790 pedestrian tour through France, Italy, Switzerland, and Germany, so unusual in its day that Wordsworth and his companion kept their plans for the Long Vacation from their families and the Cambridge authorities, began a long series of vagabond adventures:

From the time of his first tramp across France until he settled at Grasmere (1790–99) [Wordsworth] was seldom long in one place; and although poverty, poetry, and family cares precluded many long trips thereafter it is amazing how many short excursions he made . . . Indeed he and his friend Mathews had for a time some idea of becoming vagrants, and, according to his sister, he went to Orleans to qualify himself to become 'the travelling companion to some young gentleman.'[6]

While he lived in Grasmere and later at Rydal, Wordsworth satisfied his vagrant urges in adult versions of the youthful rambles he reports in the *Prelude*, local walks that began and ended at home, usually within a single day. Dorothy Wordsworth's journals record one or more walks of this sort almost every day, to Ambleside, Penrith, Keswick, Easedale Tarn—the list even of common destinations is extensive. My own random sample of the Grasmere journals yields six successive entries, dated 19–24 October 1800, noting William and/or Dorothy walking, most of them actually beginning with variations of the 19th's 'We rose late and walked' (up Loughrigg Fell in this case), and flanked by two entries

[6] Raymond Dexter Havens, *The Mind of a Poet*, 2 vols. (Baltimore: The Johns Hopkins Press, 1941), ii. 416.

that specifically note no walking.[7] Little wonder Thomas De Quincey estimates Wordsworth's lifetime pedestrian distance at '175 to 180,000 English miles'.[8]

Dorothy's accomplishments in this vein must have fallen little short of William's mark. She was his constant companion through many years of walks, including the 1797 tour with Coleridge along the Somerset coast during which many of the *Lyrical Ballads* were composed and, of course, the daily excursions from Grasmere and Rydal. Morris Marples points out one remarkable day in 1794 when she walked thirty-three miles with her brother.[9] Such vigorous pedestrianism in a woman excited vigorous reproaches: Dorothy's great-aunt wrote a letter chastising her for 'rambling about the country on foot', obviously an unladylike undertaking. Dorothy responded with some warmth (considering the careful politeness of her reply) that her walks showed her both healthy and frugal, and that they 'procured me infinitely more pleasure than I should have received from sitting in a post-chaise'. Certainly the great-aunt's reproaches did little to restrain Dorothy, although perhaps the older lady would be comforted to know that Dorothy walking, like Dorothy writing, is still most often regarded as William's companion: she does not wander 'in an unprotected situation'.[10]

But then traditional accounts of William's walking treat it as a kind of subsidiary companion to his poetry too. David McCracken's *Wordsworth and The Lake District*—a fine instance of the traditional 'walking in Wordsworth' book, filled with wonderful juxtapositions

[7] Dorothy Wordsworth, *Journals of Dorothy Wordsworth*, ed. Mary Moorman, 2nd edn. (Oxford: Oxford University Press, 1971), 46–8.

[8] Thomas De Quincey, *Recollections of the Lakes and the Lake Poets*, ed. David Wright (Harmondsworth: Penguin, 1970), 135.

[9] Marples, *Shanks's Pony*, 90.

[10] *The Letters of William and Dorothy Wordsworth: The Early Years*, ed. Ernest de Selincourt, 2nd edn., rev. Chester L. Shaver, vol. i (Oxford: Clarendon Press, 1967), 117. See Meena Alexander for a brief but evocative reading of Dorothy Wordsworth's walking/writing as an act of escape and a celebration of displacement (*Women in Romanticism: Mary Wollstonecraft, Dorothy Wordsworth and Mary Shelley* (Savage, M.: Barnes & Noble, 1989), 78–99). Alexander understands 'the activity of walking [as] just one facet, if the most palpable one, of a fascination with mobility that drew her into the very process of the natural world, both her seeing eye and the world that entered into visibility haunted by movement and change' (p. 95). This account still makes walking merely analogous to ways of thought, but recognizes the need to cope with the flux of experience, the affinity for pedestrian perspectives, and the relation between walking and writing.

of geographical, biographical, and literary material—offers a standard treatment of perhaps the most famous example of a poem 'inspired' by a walk, 'I Wandered Lonely as a Cloud'. McCracken identifies the probable location of the field of daffodils, quotes the poem in full, notes the changes William has made from the 'facts of 15 April 1802', gives Dorothy's journal entry, and marks the particular qualities and words William's poem drew from the entry.[11] McCracken's conclusion about all this, buttressed by the fact that the poem was written two years after the event, is that 'The experience of that time and that place provided crucial raw material, but before it could become a poem it had to be transformed by memory and imagination.'[12]

In this formulation Dorothy's journal entry clearly falls, like 'experience', into the less important category of 'raw material'. McCracken establishes the 'facts' of the experience by appealing to that entry as if it were unmediated experience, unshaped by any artistic intent. Even given the obvious intentional differences between journals and poetry, this seems a rash subordination. So, too, McCracken leaves their walking, an action deliberately emphasized by the poem's first line, in the exterior realm of experience—'crucial', but superseded by the functions of memory and imagination. Yet his initial approach to 'I Wandered Lonely' carefully locates the 'actual' site of Wordsworth's walk, and at the end of the book he offers maps and directions for the reader who wants to walk there, and elsewhere, 'In the Footsteps of Wordsworth'. The insistence on retracing the walk to its 'real' location suggests that by, following the 'same' paths, we can come to the 'same' place, the place of poetic perception, and recover what Wordsworth saw and thought. The unexamined assumption that the recovery of the real walk precedes the reading, as it did the writing, of the text, reiterates the claims of the poetry itself, but obscures the sources of its own origins through the rhetorical subordination of the material to the imaginative.

This double bind, the result of later ideological recastings of peripatetic values, makes it difficult to see what Wordsworth's practice and his poetry assert: that walking does not merely provide the raw materials of writing, but is physically linked with the process of composition. Wordsworth composed 'Tintern Abbey'

---

[11] McCracken, *Wordsworth and The Lake District*, 143.   [12] Ibid. 145.

on a four-day walk to Bristol with Dorothy (it was finally written down when they arrived), and writes in the *Prelude* of walking and composing with Coleridge in 1797:

> Murmuring of him who, joyous hap, was found
> After the perils of his moonlight ride,
> Near the loud waterfall; or her who sate
> In misery near the miserable Thorn.   (XIII. 400–3)

Wordsworth habitually walked while composing, whether he had sweeping scenery or stimulating companionship or not, repeating the returning motions of excursive walking in whatever space was available. Emerson reports in *English Traits* that his 1833 interview with Wordsworth included a turn about the garden, where Wordsworth 'showed [Emerson] the gravel walk in which thousands of his lines were composed'.[13] And this bit of verse, 'intended', de Selincourt tells us, 'as the motto for a group of poems', gives us the feel of this less grandiose stepping:

> Orchard Pathway, to and fro,
> Ever with thee, did I go,
> Weaving Verses, a huge store!   (*PW* ii. 488)

Lightly written as these lines are, they plainly claim not just the gathering of information or material by pedestrian means but the physical coincidence between walking and talking, between the out-and-back movement of excursive walking stripped to its basics and the making of lines of verse.

Wordsworth's poetry extends what might otherwise be read as idiosyncratic practice into an instrument of public renovation by insisting on this coincidence between pedestrian and poetic process, on the laborious character of these coincident actions, and on common human access to both. When the earliest version of *Home at Grasmere* moves into what becomes the prospectus for the *Excursion*, the home perspective created by the narrator's excursive walking becomes the one from which he will make poetry that will 'live, and be | Even as a light hung up in heaven to chear | Mankind in times to come' (1032–4). At the end of the *Prelude*, the arduous pedestrian ascent of Snowdon and memories of the *Lyrical Ballads* walking tour resolve into a proclamation that

---

[13] Ralph Waldo Emerson, *Selected Writings of Emerson*, ed. Donald McQuade (New York: Modern Library, 1981), 511.

the narrator and his friend, as 'joint-labourers in the work' of humanity's 'redemption', will 'speak | A lasting inspiration, sanctified | By reason and by truth' that will teach others (XIII. 439, 441, 442–4). Now the practice moves out into the world: walking becomes not just home- or self-making, but a making of poetry, a cultivation, a teaching of renovated humanity. Nor does it remain a solitary pursuit but, even when practised individually, functions as communal labour.

'When first I journeyed hither' demonstrates Wordsworth's insistence on the coincidence of the physical process of walking and poetry making, his figuring of both as labour, and his opening of this potentially private practice into broad public renovations.[14] Here the poet recalls a time early in his residence at Grasmere when bad weather prevented his customary long walks. He seeks, in the shelter of a nearby fir-grove, 'A length of open space where I might walk | Backwards and forwards long as I had liking | In easy and mechanic thoughtlessness' (37–9). Despite what we know of Wordsworth's habits of composition, 'easy' and 'thoughtlessness' suggest that at this point in the poem the speaker regards walking as leisurely, as a rest from both physical and intellectual work. The grove attracts him, in fact, by its character of still seclusion. He describes it as a 'Commodious harbour, a sequestered nook', a 'safe covert', and reads a bird's nest built near the ground as 'Sure sign . . . that they who in that house | Of nature and of love had made their home | Among the fir trees' had found security and quiet there (9, 11, 21–3). But the firs are so thick that Wordsworth cannot establish his walkway, 'And, for this cause . . . loved the shady grove | Less than [he] wished to love a place so sweet' (39–40).

The passionate terms of these lines, together with the characterization of the fir-grove as a potential home, suggest that Wordsworth's inability to walk in the grove also frustrates his settlement in Grasmere, a project whose importance is signalled by

[14] Gill's early text was composed 1800–4. Simpson tracks the revisions leading to and following the version of this poem published in 1815, 'When to the attractions of the busy world', commenting especially on the increased conditionality attached to the speaker's perception that John has made the path (*Wordsworth's Historical Imagination*, 36–7). Later versions also slightly recess the home-making/ journeying nexus into the body of the poem, naming a preference for 'studious leisure' as the motivation for this home-making—a claim undercut, I think, by the later clear need for laborious walking to achieve placement.

the first lines of the poem: 'When first I journeyed hither, to a home | And dwelling of my own' (1–2). When he cannot walk in the grove, he feels that he cannot love it, cannot enter and possess it. During a visit from his brother John, however, William discovers that John has found a way to walk in the grove:

A hoary pathway traced around the trees
And winding on with such an easy line
Along a natural opening that I stood
Much wondering at my own simplicity
That I myself had ever failed in search
Of what was now so obvious.
. . . .
                              at once I knew
That by my Brother's steps it had been traced.
. . . .
                         that more loth to part
From place so lovely he had worn the track,
One of his own deep paths! by pacing here
With that habitual restlessness of foot
Wherewith the Sailor measures o'er and o'er
His short domain upon the Vessel's deck
While she is travelling through the dreary seas.   (57–62, 64–5, 68–73)

Several things about the speaker's account of John's path are worthy of note. First, the path was plainly 'there' before John walked it: its 'easy line | Along a natural opening' (note the suggestions of narrative in the terms 'line' and 'opening') should have been 'obvious' to William. Second, this path bears legible traces of John's 'habitual' pacing of the deck when he is at sea, which in turn resembles that very 'easy and mechanic' pacing William sought to perform in the grove. The poem rhetorically associates this kind of 'ease', however, with 'naturalness' rather than with mechanism, and with public action rather than with private contemplation.[15] Thus, the poem asserts, John's walking reads the path out of the grove, tracing its contours in such a way that not only the natural line of the path but the idiosyncratic lines of John's own style of

[15] My thinking here, although bent toward a different end, owes something to Barrell's account of transference of crucial adjectives ('deep' or 'lofty') from concrete to abstract nouns (from 'lofty cliffs' to 'lofty thoughts') and how Wordsworth manages this transference so as to produce 'fiduciary symbols' which we 'trust' as carriers of meaning (*Poetry, Language and Politics* (New York: Manchester University Press, 1988), 137–67).

walking, a style integral with his labours for the East India Company, are legible to William. Further, these lines are legible specifically as poetry, for William attributes John's pedestrian success to 'Undying recollections' of nature which have made John 'A silent poet' (85).

The crucial turn here is John's performance of walking as labour, as habitual, repetitive, restless—literally 'without rest'—movement and as thoughtful, recollective, poetic work. This performance, the sequencing of the narrative insists, brings about William's rhetorical, emotional, and physical possession of the grove: he names the path for his brother and, 'lov[ing] the fir-grove with a perfect love', walks there often (94). In this narrative, in fact, leisurely walking simply does not exist. William can walk in the grove only by walking as his brother walks, literally retracing John's footsteps, doing this regularly and with sustained attention, thinking as he goes:

> when Thou,
> Muttering the verses which I muttered first
> Among the mountains, through the midnight watch
> Art pacing to and fro the Vessel's deck
> In some far region, here, while o'er my head
> At every impulse of the moving breeze
> The fir-grove murmurs with a sea-like sound,
> Alone I tread this path, for aught I know
> Timing my steps to thine, and with a store
> Of indistinguishable sympathies
> Mingling most earnest wishes for the day
> When We, and others whom we love shall meet
> A second time in Grasmere's happy Vale.   (105–17)

Walking performed laboriously, and performed while labouring, opens a path closed to the leisurely walker; it places John in the landscape, in name, in material trace, and in his own memory, and enables William's physical and metaphorical home-making. Moreover, the conclusion of the poem both demands and promises the maintainance of these acts of relocation and settlement by the continued movement of the two men's mutual pedestrian practice. As they walk, retracing each others' (and their own) physical and poetic paths, they synchronize mountain and ocean, poetic and economic labours, private home-making and public nation building. The imagery—muttering, walking, 'impulse[s]' of a 'moving breeze', the ocean itself—emphasizes flux and change, yet

the rhetorical juxtapositions make continuous movement the
foundation of hopes for the brothers' reunion in Grasmere, now
a 'happy Vale' functioning as the stable receptacle of their future
and as an ideal community encompassing, at the least, those
'others whom we love'.[16]

If John ploughed instead of walked, if William were a farmer
instead of a poet, we would have no trouble in recognizing this
poem as georgic and their mutual labours as Virgilian cultivation
sustained by Roman fraternity. Such a reading is complicated,
however, by more than a shift in metaphor. Traditional literary
historical accounts of pastoral and georgic at the end of the
eighteenth century argue that 'georgic' ceases to be a functional
critical term on two grounds: the disappearance of the recently
popular classical georgic; and the results of a debate between
neoclassical and rationalistic conceptions of pastoral. John Chalker
studies *The English Georgic* almost exclusively through eighteenth-
century texts; Dwight Durling follows *The Georgic Tradition
in English Poetry* into the nineteenth century, primarily by means
of works 'strongly influenced by the georgic tradition', and praises
the form as 'tenacious', but notes that 'after 1810 the [georgic]
impulse begins definitely to wane'; Richard Feingold says bluntly
that 'after 1800 . . . the georgic simply disappeared'.[17] Perceptions
of a post-eighteenth-century failure of the georgic mode may be
hardened by the remarkable surge of interest in and composition
of georgics during the eighteenth century, the reasons for which
Chalker summarizes in his introduction, and by the fact that, .
as Anthony Low notes, 'few georgics were apparently written in
England between 1500 and 1700'.[18] All this inclines us toward the

---

[16] Simpson's reading of 'When to the attractions' in *Wordsworth and the Figurings
of the Real* (Atlantic Highlands: Humanities Press, 1982) also identifies John's
walking with labour—'Work is done upon the grove'—but understands this work
as obsessive and intrusive, deriving from John's essential alienation ('to the extent
that he cannot make a distinction between work and leisure') and constructing
mediated communication (rather than 'direct discourse') between the brothers via
the alienation of nature (pp. 37, 38). I am drawn to this account, which suggests
that walking may function here as 'improving' rather than unenclosing the grove,
but my primary emphasis lies on the overt constructions of the poem, what it
wishes to *claim* walking accomplishes.

[17] Durling, *Georgic Tradition*, pp. x, 192, 101; Richard Feingold, *Nature and
Society: Later Eighteenth-Century Uses of the Pastoral and Georgic* (New
Brunswick, NJ: Rutgers University Press, 1978), 1.

[18] Anthony Low, *The Georgic Revolution* (Princeton, NJ: Princeton University
Press, 1985), 4.

designation of an 'English Georgic Age', neatly bounded by century figures.

Moreover, the late eighteenth century saw an escalation of 'the centuries-old debate over whether pastoral should imitate golden-age shepherds, as the neoclassic critics maintained, or whether it should imitate real English shepherds, as the rationalistic school insisted'.[19] As Max Keith Sutton notes, industrialization, together with changes in literary taste, drove these positions still further apart: 'For the pastoral to survive the post-Augustan demand for realism, it needed either to escape the demand by becoming more mystical, as it does in Blake and Palmer, or to blend more fully with the georgic tradition in representing the real pain and labor of rural life.'[20] Wordsworth's 'Michael', subtitled 'A Pastoral', typifies the latter solution: the poem attempts a rationalistic pastoral in that it purports to show actual rural conditions, including Michael's and Isabel's and Luke's laborious maintainence of their freehold.

Now, obviously a 'pastoral' which valorizes labour—the logical outcome of the rationalist desire—is also, or is instead, a georgic. Feingold, in fact, regards the blending of genres suggested by this latter alternative as an ongoing process in the eighteenth century:

The georgic with its emphasis on work, and the pastoral, taking pleasure and tranquillity for its ambience, do not in [the eighteenth century] split apart each into its own generic reserve, the first for the treatment of public, the second of private, experience. Instead we find each coloring the other, quite freely combined within single poems as if to announce an idea of optimal civilization, a blend of *otium* and *ponos* itself figuring forth an ideal pattern of life in a good social order.[21]

But Wordsworth's rhetorical move in the subtitle of 'Michael' maps the imposition of a very different appearance on to this practical blending of genres: as the practice of rationalistic pastoral gains ground, 'georgic' vanishes into 'pastoral'.

This shift carried forward into twentieth-century literary critical language and, as we shall see, has only recently been challanged.

---

[19] Metzger, *One Foot in Eden*, 3. See J. E. Congleton's *Theories of Pastoral Poetry in England, 1684–1798* (Gainesville: University of Florida Press, 1952), 75–114.

[20] Max Keith Sutton, 'Truth and the Pastor's Vision in George Crabbe, William Barnes and R. S. Thomas', in Richard F. Hardin (ed.), *Survivals of Pastoral* (Lawrence: University of Kansas Publications, 1979), 36.

[21] Feingold, *Nature and Society*, 17.

Some readers, dissatisfied with either classical term, reach for other terms to describe georgic and pastoral impulse or form in a literary work. 'Rural' is a favourite, as in Glen Cavaliero's *The Rural Tradition in the English Novel* and W. J. Keith's *The Poetry of Nature: Rural Perspectives in Poetry from Wordsworth to the Present.*[22] Feingold nominates ' "bucolic" to designate works which express a judgement of the moral quality of civil society by explicit or implicit reference to rural experience'.[23] More commonly, critics confirm the late eighteenth-century rhetorical move, subordinating the discussion of georgic to that of pastoral, as Sutton does, or describe georgic elements as 'pastoral'. A prominent example of the latter is Leo Marx's treatment of 'The Bean-Field' in Thoreau's *Walden* as pastoral, despite Marx's display of traditionally georgic valuations of the balance between the civil and the wild or natural and of agrarian labour in that chapter.[24]

To a certain extent, this latter response may have permitted 'pastoral' to survive as a useful interpretative term, since it can be expanded to include all sorts of rural images and values. It may also have contributed to the relatively broad range of dates given for the 'death' of pastoral by broadening the category itself: Frank Kermode says pastoral ends 'with Marvell', whereas Feingold places its decline to 'something to be either contemned or rescued' at 1800 with the disappearance of georgic, and the editors of *A Book of English Pastoral Verse*, John Barrell and John Bull, are content to defer 'The impossibility of writing a credible version of Pastoral' to the Victorian era.[25] Barrell and Bull, in fact, discuss Wordsworth's development of a 'more satisfactor[ily] bourgeois' pastoral in which 'hard work is an essential element'.[26]

As this latter example suggests, however, the submergence of

---

[22] Cavaliero's study covers 1900–39. Obviously neither his 'rural tradition' nor Keith's is identical with either pastoral or georgic. They do, however, include recognizable elements of both, most notably the inevitable discussion of country life as opposed to city life—the shared concern which permits the conflation of pastoral and georgic in the first place.

[23] Feingold, *Nature and Society*, 16.

[24] See this chapter in Leo Marx, *The Machine in the Garden: Technology and the Pastoral Ideal in America* (New York: Oxford University Press, 1964).

[25] Frank Kermode, *English Pastoral Poetry: From the Beginnings to Marvell* (London: George G. Harrap & Co., 1952), 42; Feingold, *Nature and Society*, 1; John Barrell and John Bull, ed., *A Book of English Pastoral Verse* (New York: Oxford University Press, 1975), 431.

[26] Barrell and Bull, ed., *English Pastoral Verse*, 428.

'georgic' in 'pastoral' limits or confuses critical judgements in unfortunate ways. To say that both georgic and pastoral elements appear in a single work or 'colour' each other is not, after all, to say that georgic and pastoral are 'the same', nor does the conflation of the two traditions necessarily imply the disappearance of either. Indeed, only by referring to the original distinctions between the two can we adequately determine the degree of their conflation and/or survival in individual literary works. This seems especially important given the various influential readings of pastoral, notably those by Raymond Williams, Renato Poggioli, and Thomas G. Rosenmeyer, which regard pastoral as an upper-class idealization disguising lower-class misery, and thus a mode of which we are well rid.[27] Barrell and Bull follow this line, arguing that pastoral's 'function is to mystify and to obscure the harshness of actual social and economic organization'.[28] When they comment that 'Wordsworth is perfectly willing to acknowledge that the work his rustics perform is arduous, and may cause suffering', and that he links this labour with both material gain and natural harmony, however, they identify this value system as 'his version of Pastoral', failing to acknowledge its clearly georgic antecedents.[29] Whatever one thinks of Barrell and Bull's attitude toward pastoral, their permissive shifts between 'pastoral' as the classical genre and 'pastoral' as that expanded mode elsewhere called 'rural' or 'bucolic' disable interpretation by obscuring the possible significance of georgic forms and values.

Ironically, in fact, Barrell and Bull's use of 'pastoral' in the late eighteenth-century sense unintentionally perpetuates its darker ideological function: the 'disappearing' of rural labour into a softened, idealized, naturalized landscape now named, despite its complicating interior representations, as the site of leisurely contemplation. In 'The Landscape of Labor: Transformations of the Georgic', John Murdoch comments on the ideological dimensions of the orginal shift in terms, and demonstrates the usefulness of

[27] Raymond Williams, *The Country and the City* (London: Chatto & Windus, 1973); Renato Poggioli, *The Oaten Flute: Essays on Pastoral Poetry and the Pastoral Ideal* (Cambridge, Mass.: Harvard University Press, 1975); and Thomas G. Rosenmeyer, *The Green Cabinet: Theocritus and the European Pastoral Lyric* (Berkeley: University of California Press, 1969).
[28] Barrell and Bull, ed., *English Pastoral Verse*, 4.
[29] Ibid. 428.

recovering (by uncovering) 'georgic'. By the mid-eighteenth century, Murdoch argues,

the absorption of the Georgic into the collective cultural consciousness, into a region almost *beyond* consciousness and therefore beyond question, requires that it should become practically invisible . . . . Its origins in political revolt require concealment; its dependence on hard, unremitting labor requires it as well. So various things happen: the Georgic is assimilated to the Pastoral, so that in literature and painting they are often almost indistinguishable.[30]

In painting this means that 'the labor of ploughing, harrowing, seeding, and mowing was entirely transposed into its material effects', the elements of a cultivated landscape such as fields and herds and woods which 'themselves have been subsumed into what we would call abstractions'.[31] Murdoch, reading an 1817 Julius Ibbetson print depicting (among other things) a peasant on the road with a load of firewood gathered from common lands, goes on to discuss the apparent intervention and simultaneous collusion of the picturesque aesthetic in this process. In picturesque scenes like Ibbetson's, 'Labor returns to the landscape' in representations of labourers and the implements of their labour, and in the roughness of sketching itself. But, Murdoch argues, picturesque labour is subsistence labour, a 'Mindless', naturalized labour assimilated to an aestheticized landscape and thus lacking any consciousness which might effect change or initiate rebellion.[32] Apparently re-inscribing rural labour in the English landscape, the picturesque excludes the disturbing potential of classical georgic.

As Murdoch's earlier consideration of the print's inscription, 'To the Manes of Gilbert Wakefield', shows, Ibbetson's representations also enforce the most conservative message of eighteenth-century English georgic. Wakefield, whose first major work was an edition of the *Georgics* in 1788, was imprisoned in 1799 for writing a 'Reply' to the Bishop of Llandaff's 'Address to the People of Great Britain' in which Wakefield argued, among other things, that the British labourer had little to fear from a French

[30] John Murdoch, 'The Landscape of Labor: Transformations of the Georgic', in Kenneth R. Johnston *et al.* (ed.), *Romantic Revolutions: Criticism and Theory* (Bloomington: Indiana University Press, 1990), 190.
[31] Ibid. 190–1.   [32] Ibid. 191, 192.

invasion. Murdoch points out that, despite his apparently radical stance, Wakefield's use of Aesop's Ass, which sees no difference between the labour required by its master and that which might be required by its master's enemy, as an illustration of the British labourer's position in the Napoleonic wars leaves the necessity of labour itself unquestioned. Marvelling that 'a political statement of such instantly subversive import [as Wakefield's reply] could at the same time disclose such a profound acceptance of the political status quo'—'In terms of class politics, the real message of the fable is that Labor is inevitable'—Murdoch traces Wakefield's formulation to his understanding of the *Georgics*, which 'provide the defining myth of the prosperity that can be achieved through hard work in the aftermath of rebellion and civil war'.[33] Thus Ibbetson's print, despite its overt gestures toward contemporary liberal political ideals and its potentially sympathetic images of labour, also points, through Wakefield and his reiteration of Aesop and Virgil, to a hidden georgic moral: 'the lot of the laborer is nonnegotiable'.[34]

Whatever we may identify as the real message or moral, Murdoch could not have fully assessed either the subversive impact of labourers returned to the landscape or the hidden conservative compulsion toward acceptance of labour's lot if he had not recognized, in this early nineteenth-century image, the still-functioning political and aesthetic strategies of georgic. 'Assimilation to the pastoral' notwithstanding, it is by digging out the georgic covered by 'pastoral' that Murdoch reads Ibbetson's print and reassesses the political functions of the picturesque.

In adopting this approach, Murdoch enters into a decade-long scholarly discussion of whether the term 'georgic' ought to be revived, especially in application to Romantic literature. Anthony Low's *The Georgic Revolution* presents an extended argument for such a revival. Noting that 'scholars have long recognized certain important qualities of georgic spirit', Low decides that he himself will 'use "georgic" in the same general sense that literary critics have agreed to use "pastoral"':

Like pastoral, georgic is primarily a mode rather than a genre. It is an informing spirit, an attitude toward life, and a set of themes and images rather than anything so definite, say, as a four-book, didactic poem of

---

[33] Ibid. 180, 181.   [34] Ibid. 191.

two thousand lines on the subject of agriculture. . . . As an initial working definition . . . we may say that georgic is a mode that stresses the value of intensive and persistent labor against hardships and difficulties; that it differs from pastoral because it emphasizes work instead of ease; that it differs from epic because it emphasizes planting and building instead of killing and destruction; and that it is preeminently the mode suited to the establishment of civilization and the founding of nations.[35]

Despite Low's comparison, the reintroduction of 'georgic' as a viable critical term would clearly alter the 'general sense' of 'pastoral', permitting recognition of the distinctions that the latter term has so long obscured.

Although Low's extensive discussion of this issue did not appear until 1985, from 1980 on Kurt Heinzelman consistently distinguishes georgic from pastoral, suggesting that the post-eighteenth-century term 'pastoral', with its broad inclusion of all sorts of rural images and values, deceptively cloaks the Romantics' ongoing use of georgic. In ' "Crossing the Wye"—Or, Why Value Landscape?' he seems to advocate, in passing, the reverse of this modal subordination, arguing that 'Tintern Abbey' 'is not a pastoral but a georgic: that is, it mixes the two modes'.[36]

Marjorie Levinson and Annabel Patterson reject Heinzelman's position, especially as applied to 'Michael', on the grounds that his proposed 'economics of the imagination', in which the poetic labours of reading and writing operate as mechanisms of production and exchange, ignores fundamental differences in the kinds of labour involved in poetic and agricultural production. Levinson objects that 'the labor that the poet expends is *not* of the same kind as that which characterizes Michael', specifically in that it lacks purposefulness, the deliberate looking forward to and acting toward a given aim: 'The poetic *locus classicus* for Wordsworth's advocacy of "wise passiveness" in reading and writing is "The Solitary Reaper"; here, the poet effortlessly reaps his mind of a harvest grown from the seeds of random, unlooked-for associations.'[37] Patterson invokes Fredric Jameson's *The Political*

---

[35] Low, *Georgic Revolution*, 8, 7, 12.

[36] Kurt Heinzelman, ' "Crossing the Wye"—Or, Why Value Landscape?', *The Maine Scholar*, 1 (1988), 176. See also Heinzelman's *Economics of the Imagination*, and 'Self-Interest and the Politics of Composition in Keats's *Isabella*' (*ELH* 55 (1988), 159–93).

[37] Marjorie Levinson, *Wordsworth's Great Period Poems: Four Essays* (Cambridge: Cambridge University Press, 1986), 149.

Unconscious to make much the same point, quoting his commentary on the 'intellectual dishonesty' of intellectuals who 'seek to
glamorize their tasks ... by assimilating them to real work on the
assembly line and to the experience of the resistance of matter in
genuine manual labor', a move which, Jameson believes, ignores
the fact that 'writing and thinking are not alienated labor in that
sense'.[38]

These objections seem at first to turn on this question: what
separates 'real' or 'genuine' labour from spurious labour? Levinson
states that real labour, or, rather, that labour which Michael does
and with which the Wordsworthian poet wishes to associate his
work, is distinguished by purposefulness; she also implies that
labour is distinguished by effort, presumably deliberate rather than
accidental. Patterson, by way of Jameson, defines it as 'genuine
manual labor', which Jameson has already described (in words
which Patterson omits in her quotation) as 'real work on the
assembly line' and 'the experience of the resistance of matter'.[39]

In considering certain dimensions of this latter definition (naturally enough, given its source), we become aware that we live
in a time in which it is scarcely possible to utter 'labour' without
its Marxist inflection. I do not wish, even were it possible, to
erase that inflection. But I think we must distinguish between our
usage in describing the theory and practice of our own writing,
Wordsworth's usage in a similar situation, and our usage in
evaluations of Wordsworth's representations of labour. Wordsworth
may have thought of labour as purposeful and as involving effort
and even, although not in Jameson's eloquent words, as 'the
experience of the resistance of matter'. But it would have been
impossible for him to think of 'real' or 'genuine' labour as being
'alienated labor in that sense'—to quote Patterson, who voices
Jameson's implication, 'in Marx's sense'.[40] Murdoch points out,
for instance, that eighteenth-century conceptions of georgic labour

---

[38] Fredric Jameson, *The Political Unconscious: Narrative as a Socially Symbolic
Act* (Ithaca, NY: Cornell University Press, 1981), 45.

[39] See Patterson's quotation of Jameson on p. 278 of her *Pastoral and Ideology:
Virgil to Valéry* (Berkeley and Los Angeles: University of California Press, 1987).
Her omissions, while perhaps sensible in her context, are somewhat reductive,
making 'genuine manual labor', rather than asssembly-line work and 'experience
of the resistance of matter *in* genuine manual labor', the thing to which these
intellectuals are assimilating their labours (emphasis mine).

[40] Ibid. 278.

(with which Wordsworth would have been thoroughly familiar) included genteel ' "head-work," the labor of thought and invention, directing the toil of others', so that when one looks at eighteenth-century landscape paintings and sees 'the figures of the gentry in the landscape, apparently watching the reapers at work, you may take it that the gentry too are working. And the meaning of the landscape thus constructed is that prosperity, the wealth of nations, and happiness are the result, dearly bought, of gentry and laborers working together on the land for the common good.'[41] Murdoch comments on the obvious advantages that such a conception offered 'the ruling classes' but none the less distinguishes the resulting representations from pastoral, the mode which would 'necessitate the maintenance . . . of an Arcadian space, the possibility of Pastoral, as a special privilege for the gentry': 'within the terms of [the gentry's] Georgic ideology, within the terms of their self-identification as members of an Augustan ruling elite, work was part of the common lot of mankind'.[42]

In this analysis Murdoch clearly identifies both his own concept of 'labour', one obviously although quietly inflected with Marxist knowledge, and an eighteenth-century writer or reader of georgic's concept of 'labour'. The former may, and I believe should, be used to criticize the latter, to uncover the conscious and unconscious mechanisms of oppression to which we must responsibly attend. But to refuse to identify Arthur Young's writings as georgic because they valorize head-work, or to say that George Lambert's paintings cannot function as examples of eighteenth-century georgic (as Murdoch contends they do) because they imply that supervision is labour, is absurd. Virgil's prosperous farmer in Book II of *The Georgics*, although shown in the act of ploughing, hires and supervises labourers too; the retelling in Book IV of the story of Aristaeus, whose success in bee-keeping can be restored only by supplications to Orpheus, interlaces agriculture and poetry-making and civilization-building (the bees' hive functioning as the model of a civil state) as metaphorically inseparable varieties of one work, cultivation. Should we then disqualify Virgil's *Georgics*

---

[41] Murdoch, 'Landscape of Labor', 189. Although Murdoch does not cite a specific source, the context of his remarks suggests that the phrase 'head-work' is originally that of Adam Smith, whom Murdoch describes as a 'georgic economist' (p. 189).

[42] Ibid. 190.

from the genre named for it, because supervision and poetic composition (and much of everyday civil life) are not 'genuine manual labour'?

Whether we should use 'georgic' to describe, say, 'Michael', depends not on our definition of 'real' labour but on our definition of georgic labour. Levinson and Patterson's instincts, if not their formulations, are correct: georgic insistently links moral and political labour with common physical labour. Classically, and through the eighteenth century, the primary material term of the georgic metaphor was farming, but there have always been variants—the haluetic, for instance, in which fishing accomplishes the cultivation. If we want to read a text as georgic, we must identify the natural, common act of physical economy which the text defines as a cultivating labour and allies with poetry or nation-building or whatever. Patterson, for instance, attempts such an identification in her own early discussion of *The Excursion* when she proposes 'a new sub-genre, the georgic of the grave', founded upon the physical labour of grave-digging and extended into epitaph-making.[43] Neither Heinzelman's earliest formulation nor Alan Liu's elegantly worked out discussion of Wordsworth's 'economy of lyric', on the other hand, names a specific physical avatar of poetic labour. The crucial character of this omission may be seen in Liu's third 'law' of Wordsworth's lyric economy, in which Liu finally drops his otherwise consistently economic/material language: 'Less is more' and 'To share is to own' resolve toward 'To imagine is to labor'.[44]

My own formulation of Wordsworth's premiss is: 'To walk is to labour'. Reconsider, for instance, the opening lines of that perennial test case, 'Michael':

> If from the public way you turn your steps
> Up the tumultuous brook of Green-head Gill,
> You will suppose that with an upright path
> Your feet must struggle; in such bold ascent
> The pastoral Mountains front you, face to face.
> But, courage! for beside that boisterous Brook
> The mountains have all opened out themselves,
> And made a hidden valley of their own.   (1–8)

---

[43] Annabel Patterson, 'Wordsworth's Georgic: Genre and Structure in *The Excursion*', *Wordsworth Circle*, 9 (1978), 150.

[44] Alan Liu, *Wordsworth: The Sense of History* (Stanford, Calif.: Stanford University Press, 1989), 347–53.

The steps of reader and narrator, the former invited to retrace a path familiar to the latter, carry them from first perceptions of a closed pastoral world into an opening view of a valley once hidden from their view. At first the narrator tells us that this place is 'an utter solitude', uninhabited except for a few sheep (13). But this first view opens again to reveal 'one object which you might pass by': the narrator rhetorically points to 'a straggling heap of unhewn stones' which he reveals as the sign of the first story told to him and the first guide of his poetic impulse (15, 17). He will tell the story again, he says, 'for the sake I Of youthful Poets, who among these Hills I Will be my second self when I am gone' (37–9).

The frame of 'Michael', then, associates excursive walking, not sheep-farming, with poetic composition. These associated labours relocate the sheepfold and open the pastoral landscape to travellers from outside; and while they cannot complete Michael's work, they claim to reappropriate his land to his uses by cultivating the story of his labour, planting its seed in growing poets. Michael's story itself is not only about the failure of Virgilian cultivation but about its potential replacement by excursive walking. The loss of his freehold, the disappearance of the cottage and the light it offered to wanderers, the incompleteness of the sheepfold, and the vanishing way of life represented by the industrious, virtuous Michael and Isabel are attributable directly to Luke's failure to return: Luke walks away to the city and doesn't come back. The moral of the story is not that 'pastoral' values (including the georgic value of self-sustaining labour) have vanished beyond recall, but that the faithful performance of excursive walking might preserve them, if not in Luke's repossession of the land, then in our reappropriation of its value for our use.

If we recognize the coincidence of walking and poetry, and their collective figuration as cultivating labour, then 'Michael' does not merely assert, as Lore Metzger concludes, that 'only the poet's words can restore the pastoral covenant in an iron age'.[45] Instead it offers the far more comforting promise, a georgic promise, that by a common practice, by walking, we may join the poet in the restoration of rural values and the replacement (in both senses) of cultivation. The seductive mechanisms of that simply gorgeous

---

[45] Metzger, *One Foot in Eden*, 158.

poetic surface (which pleasures us even as we wonder just what it is we love—the poet's cool dismissal of his old friends? Michael's willingness to let go of his son in order to hold his land?) become much clearer when we refuse Wordsworth's rhetorical sleight of hand and read his poem not only as pastoral, but as georgic, extended into peripatetic.

'Michael' actually comes fairly late among the various poems in which the cultivation/walking/poetry nexus develops, and presents a relatively optimistic view of the fate of Virgilian cultivation, allowing it to remain a possibility if coupled with excursive walking. Not so 'Salisbury Plain', in which cultivation seems to have become fruitless as warfare and to have lost its stabilizing influence upon the lives of individuals and nations alike.[46] In its first four stanzas, 'Salisbury Plain' favourably compares the life of warlike savages of ancient times with that of the homeless wanderers of Wordsworth's England. 'The hungry savage', fearful of storms and of beasts as fierce and hungry as himself—'famished trains I Of boars', 'bears contending', 'gaunt wolves in armies'—is nonetheless 'strong to suffer, and his mind I Encounters all his evils unsubdued', both because he knows no other way of life and because his ignorance is shared with 'men who all of his hard lot partake, I Repose in the same fear, to the same toil awake (13–18).

Not so the protagonist of the poem, travelling alone across a cultivated desert which, despite its life-giving capacities, is described in terms of death, waste, and battle:

> By thirst and hunger pressed he gazed around
> And scarce could any trace of man descry,
> Save wastes of corn that stretched without a bound,
> But where the sower dwelt was nowhere to be found.   (42–5)

Among these wastes of corn the traveller finds none of the traditional accoutrements of a fruitful rural landscape, no trees (literally 'no shade', phrasing which suggests ghosts and death as well as soothing shadow), no meadows, no brooks, no cottages or, indeed, any signs of habitation. A shepherd who appears in the distance cannot hear the traveller's shout, which is answered only

---

[46] The final incarnation of 'Salisbury Plain' is 'Guilt and Sorrow'. Gill describes its evolution briefly in *Poems*, 685, and extensively in his edition of *The Salisbury Plain Poems of William Wordsworth* (Ithaca, NY: Cornell University Press, 1975). The prefatory material of the first four stanzas of 'Salisbury Plain' disappears in most later versions.

by 'winds that whistling near | Sweep the thin grass and passing, wildly plain; | Or desert lark that pours on high a wasted strain' (52–4). As night falls on this desolate landscape, attended by 'blackening eddies' of carrion-eating crows, the traveller imaginatively resurrects the ancient savagery of the land: 'warrior spectres of gigantic bones, | Forth issuing from a thousand rifted tombs, | Wheel on their fiery steeds amid the infernal glooms' (58, 97–9).

Taking dubious shelter in a roofless hovel, the traveller meets a female vagrant who tells him a tale of ruin unstemmed by successful cultivation. In three stanzas reminiscent of Virgil's luxuriant characterizations of the prosperous farmer (*Georgics*, II. 512–42) and the Corycian man, the woman describes the plenty and peace created by her father's labour and her own, as she first assists him at his fishing and herding and then takes on the tasks of young womanhood:

'Can I forget my seat beneath the thorn,
My garden stored with peas and mint and thyme,
And rose and lilly for the sabbath morn.
.   .   .   .
The merriment and song at shearing time,
My hen's rich nest with long grass overgrown.
.   .   .   .
'Can I forget the casement where I fed
The red-breast when the fields were whitened o'er,
My snowy kerchiefs on the hawthorn spread
My humming wheel and glittering table store . . .'

(235–7, 239–40, 243–6)

But the peace and plenty generated by cultivation cannot mitigate, much less cancel, the exigencies of law and war which gradually appropriate the woman's substance. Her father's 'little range of water was denied', and with his fishing rights curtailed the family's prosperity fails: 'His all was seized; and weeping side by side | Turned out on the cold winds, alone we wandered wide' (260–1).[47] They flee to the daughter's artisan lover, who marries

---

[47] Gill relates this incident to 'a story of local oppression, known to Wordsworth, in which an old couple are tyrannized because they will not sell a field to a large landowner' (Gill (ed.), *Poems*, 685, n. to line 261 of 'Salisbury Plain'). Gill's source is Z. S. Fink, *The Early Wordsworthian Milieu* (Oxford: Oxford University Press, 1958), 88–9, 134–5. The version of 'Salisbury Plain' called 'The Female Vagrant' expands the woman's tale to make this harassment by a landowner explicit.

the girl and founds a new family; but when war breaks out the cities are impoverished, substituting 'for Labour's cheerful hum | Silence and Fear, and Misery's weeping train' (297–8). Eventually the woman, her father already dead, loses husband and children to the 'pains and plagues' of war, and becomes a penniless wanderer.

The closing stanzas of 'Salisbury Plain' present a world in which the reverberations of poverty and war amplify without restraint. 'Oh what can war but endless war still breed?' asks the narrator, and the metaphorical dimension of his query, with its georgic implications of propagation, reminds us that in this poem the laborious cultivation and cultivating labour of the private citizen provides no antidote to military excess (509). What mitigation of the wanderers' lot there is, indeed, springs from their persistent wanderings. As day dawns the man bids the woman 'come after weary night | So ruinous far other scene to view', a scene dominated by 'a lengthening road and wain | Descending a bare slope not far remote' (334–5, 343–4). The pairing of a moving farm wagon, the first sign of viable human culture since the heedless shepherd of the sixth stanza, with a road is not idle: it is the travellers' walk down that hopeful road which brings them at last to the rural paradise they have longed for and mourned:

>   through a narrow valley's pleasant scene
> A wreath of vapour tracked a winding brook
> Babbling through groves and lawns and meads of green.
> A smoking cottage peeped the trees between,
> The woods resound the linnet's amorous lays,
> And melancholy lowings intervene
> Of scattered herds that in the meadows graze,
> While through the furrowed grass the merry milkmaid strays.
>
>   (407–14)

This seductively domestic vision offers no enduring hope in itself, either for the wanderers or for the rest of humanity. The narrator immediately bids them 'Adieu', reminding them that they must soon depart 'friendless' on their 'several road[s]', and draws a cheerless moral from their tale: 'life itself is like this desert broad, | Where all the happiest find is but a shed, | And a green spot 'mid wastes interminably spread' (415–16, 421–3). Yet without their determined seeking there would be no finding of a shed and a green spot. The wanderers' reward, however briefly granted, is 'Comforts by prouder mansions unbestowed. | For you yon milkmaid bears her brimming load, | For you the board is piled with homely bread' (418–20). The traditional fruits of cultivation are gained not by ploughing but by walking, while the slim hopes of the future are extended not to those who sow the seed but to those who walk the road in search of the place where the sower dwells.

While the penniless vagrants of 'Salisbury Plain' are clearly determined pedestrians, the poem does not place any particular stress upon the physical process of walking, nor does it characterize their travels as excursive. This may well be one source of the poem's bleak tone, for in 'The Old Cumberland Beggar' explicitly physical, returning walking produces individual and communal well-being. The protagonist of 'The Old Cumberland Beggar' might be characterized as a hyperpedestrian, so intent upon his steady shuffle that even his eyes walk the road:

> as he moves along,
> *They* move along the ground; and evermore,
> Instead of common and habitual sight
> Of fields with rural works, of hill and dale,
> And the blue sky, one little span of earth
> Is all his prospect.   (46–51)

The beggar's intense focus on the 'prospect' of the road, an extreme version of the pedestrian's limited perspectives, excludes the traditional source of economic self-sufficiency, the 'fields with rural works'. But the placement of his labour in 'one little span of earth', like the Corycian man's tilling of a small freehold, enables the beggar to gather the 'scraps and fragments' which have sustained him in his way of life since the narrator's childhood (10).

The beggar's economic condition, indeed, seems no more precarious than that of the more affluent villagers:

> the easy man
> Who sits at his own door, and like the pear
> Which overhangs his head from the green wall,
> Feeds in the sunshine; the robust and young,
> The prosperous and unthinking, they who live
> Sheltered, and flourish in a little grove
> Of their own kindred, all behold in [the beggar]

A silent monitor

   .   .   .   .

                       and perchance,
Though [the beggar] to no one give the fortitude
And circumspection needful to preserve
His present blessings, and to husband up
The respite of the season, he, at least,
And 'tis no vulgar service, makes them felt.   (108–15, 119–24)

These lines characterize the passive prosperity of the 'easy man'—phrasing which turns my own mind to Virgil's 'happy man', the Corycian man—and his fellows as being as transient as the season of ripeness before harvest; the work of preservation and husbanding is still undone and, it is implied, may remain so.[48] But the returning pedestrian motions of the beggar, the narrator asserts, cultivate feelings which morally enrich individuals and bind them in communal memory.

Moreover, these motions can be read as poetry. Despite his unconsciousness of anything but his daily rounds, the beggar is repeatedly described as a moral text which 'prompt[s] the unlettered Villagers | To tender offices and pensive thoughts' (162–3):

              the Villagers in him
Behold a record which together binds
Past deeds and offices of charity
Else unremembered, and so keeps alive
The kindly mood

    .   .   .   .

And thus the soul,
By that sweet taste of pleasure unpursued
Doth find itself insensibly disposed
To virtue and true goodness.   (79–84, 93–6)

The beggar differs from the *Excursion*'s Wanderer in his utterly inarticulate condition but, like the Wanderer, requires a versifying narrator to retrace his text, making it legible to those who cannot read it directly. Like the Wanderer's narrator, the beggar's narrator accomplishes this poetic tracing by walking—'I saw an aged Beggar in my walk'—and, like the narrator of 'Michael', places

---

[48] For a discussion of the 'happy man' as a recurring motif, see Maren-Sofie Røstvig, *The Happy Man: Studies in the Metamorphoses of a Classical Ideal*, Oslo Studies in English, 27 (Oslo: Akademisk Forlag, 1954–8).

the reader on the road too, meeting the beggar and hearing the narrator as would a fellow-wayfarer. This poem does not explicitly synchronize these walks as 'When first I journeyed hither' does, but the effect of the joint pedestrian labours is very similar: the creation of a community of feeling, the location of value, the opening of the local and private into the extra-local and public.

The walking/cultivation/poetry nexus Wordsworth builds in these poems works both to show excursive walking as a species of Virgilian cultivation and to demonstrate its superiority in that capacity to agriculture. Against the background of a disappearing or subordinated georgic and the simultaneous economic decline of freeholders and rural labourers, his replacement of farmer with walker extends georgic's literary function into an era in which the culturally stabilizing capacity of agriculture seemed to have faded or failed. Although this extension can obviously be traced through a series of smaller poems, a reading of *The Excursion* as peripatetic shows the development of the new mode to better advantage.

Both Geoffrey Hartman and Annabel Patterson identify the *Excursion* with georgic. Hartman comments briefly on the *Excursion*'s 'roots in the topographical and contemplative poetry of the eighteenth century', most notably that of Thomson, Akenside, Cowper, and Dyer, which 'in turn, is best seen as a development of the *Georgics*, a poem containing the same attention to country lore, a similarly loose yet didactic structure, and a respect for the mind that remains close to "the great and permanent objects that act upon it"'.[49] Interestingly enough, Hartman goes on in the same paragraph to discuss the antecedents of the poem's 'ambulatory scheme', although he makes no particular interpretative point in this context.

Patterson's 1978 article, 'Wordsworth's Georgic: Genre and Structure in *The Excursion*', on the other hand, considers the poem as georgic at length.[50] Arguing that the *Excursion* addresses 'the

---

[49] Hartman, *Wordsworth's Poetry, 1787–1814*, 296.

[50] Patterson's *Pastoral and Ideology* reviews her earlier assessment of the *Excursion*, an assessment which she now seems to regard with discomfort. Her section on Wordsworth speaks of him as developing 'the hard pastoral of the mind at serious work', as opposed to the 'soft pastoral' which valorizes leisure (p. 278). Despite the availability of a traditional labour modality—georgic—and her citation of specific passages from the *Georgics* as Wordsworth's 'pastoral sources' (a peculiar displacement), she follows Jameson in maintaining a strict distinction between mental and physical labour (see above). The result of Patterson's subordination

central issues of georgic, as those had been defined by commentaries, translations and parodies of Virgil's poem, and those of Horace, Martial and Lucretius with which it is associated', Patterson notes that Wordsworth's poem is concerned with 'the real nature of country life, the effects of labor on character, [and] the validity, if any, of seclusion'. Moreover, she suggests, the poem is 'meta-didactic . . . [continuing] a metaphor developed by Francis Bacon for his *Advancement of Learning*, where the "Georgics of the mind, concerning the husbandry and tillage thereof" are outlined in the language of planting, manuring, and harvesting, culture perceived as agriculture'.[51] Noting the claims the Wanderer makes for his proposed programme of national education as a mediative force between 'high and low intelligence, culture and agriculture, city and country, rich and poor', she points out that his full claims extend 'beyond the arena of personal justice' into the stabilization of industrializing culture as a whole: 'The "industrious bees" which traditionally epitomize the georgic work ethic are now seen as justifying the Industrial Revolution; and, given proper education, the Wanderer can envisage only good things from a growing population, the basis of a worldwide cultural imperium.'[52]

Patterson then works through the implications of the 'authentic epitaphs' of Books VI and VII to suggest that here 'Wordsworth establishes a new sub-genre, the georgic of the grave'.[53] Specifically, she juxtaposes the Solitary's characterization of the sexton's labour as agricultural labour in Book V, lines 235–7 with the educative force of the epitaphs delivered by the Pastor, noting that the Wanderer requests these epitaphs of the Pastor as if they were bodies to be disinterred: 'The mine of real life | Dig for us.' She goes on to point out that Wordsworth's *Essay upon Epitaphs*, which Wordsworth 'annexed' as a note to Book V, suggests 'a formal relationship between epitaphs in a country churchyard and the central themes of georgic, since the former supply testimony as to

---

of georgic to pastoral is the reduction of the *Excursion* to a sign that Wordsworth 'became temporarily dissatisfied with the pastoral ideology of the *Prelude*' (p. 284). My problems with this assessment are no doubt evident from the full argument of this chapter, but here I will simply point to the fact that Patterson closes her extended discussion of Wordsworthian 'pastoral' with an account of what she herself recognizes as Wordsworthian georgic.

[51] Patterson, 'Wordsworth's Georgic', 145.
[52] Ibid. 152–3.   [53] Ibid. 150.

what the latter assert—the essential decency and dignity of country people'.[54] Thus she identifies epitaph-making not only with the
culturally stabilizing process of education but with the traditionally stabilizing force of agriculture by way of the labour of grave-
digging.

This suggestion is very appealing. As we have already suggested,
the great imagining of the *Georgics* is the creation of a metaphor
which makes the work of both the ordinary citizen and the poet
congruent with the epic changes around them, a metaphor that
simultaneously confirms the creative potential of those changes
and counteracts their destructive tendencies. Chalker considers the
importance of Virgil's invocation to Octavian and its development
throughout the text as building toward just such a metaphor:
'the thematic greatness of the poem depends very much on its
sense ... of the interplay between the life of the state, and the
activity of the farmer ... the work of the farmer is seen both as
the embodiment of permanence and as a foundation of peace and
prosperity.'[55] Low, too, marks 'Virgilian georgic['s] ... stress on
obscure private individuals who perform small tasks the cumulative
effect of which is to transform society'.[56] If the practice of agriculture no longer supports such a metaphor, the writer of 'georgic'
must look elsewhere for a concrete term.

In the *Excursion*, if we accept Patterson's analysis, the parallel
metaphor is epitaph-making, and yet there are clearly problems
with this choice. Wordsworth himself argues that epitaph-making
is 'not a common or natural employment of men at any time',
while the very point of the farming/cultivation/civilization nexus is
that farming is both natural and common (*PW* v. 451). Nor does
epitaph-making provide, as the labour which is to replace farming,
a non-poetic act of physical economy with which to couple the
essentially poetic act of moral economy and thus complete the
process of true cultivation. The Sexton's appearance is brief, and,
despite the link between his grave-digging and the Pastor's epitaph-making, that single reference remains otherwise isolated, un-
developed by extended discussions or displays of the grave-digger's
labour.

[54] *PW* v. 444; Patterson, 'Wordsworth's Georgic', 151.
[55] John Chalker, *The English Georgic: A Study in the Development of a Form*
(London: Routledge & Kegan Paul, 1969), 9–10.
[56] Low, *Georgic Revolution*, 6.

In fact, the natural, common act of physical economy allied
to poetry, and particularly to epitaph-making, in the *Excursion* is
excursive walking. At a purely formal level the three-day walking
tour undertaken by the narrator, the Wanderer, and the Solitary
leads to the Pastor's epitaphs and, indeed, to all the discourse of the
poem, including the argument for nationalized education. Within
that argument, as we shall briefly see, the primary conflict is that
between the Wanderer and the Solitary, between the sage who gained
his living and his wisdom by pedestrian labour and the morose
hermit who fears to leave his secluded vale. But the crucial conflation of cultivation, walking, and poetry occurs in the two epitaphs
upon which Patterson does not comment, the epitaphs which open
the first book of the *Excursion*: the narrator's characterization of
the Wanderer and the Wanderer's tale of the ruined cottage.

As Book I opens, the narrator 'toil[s] | With languid steps' to-
ward the ruined cottage, where he finds the Wanderer asleep on
a bench (I. 20–1). The narrator then recalls their long friendship,
begun in the narrator's boyhood and renewed just the previous
day by a chance meeting on the road:

> Many a time
> On holidays, we rambled through the woods:
> We sate—we walked; he pleased me with report
> Of things which he had seen; and often touched
> Abstrusest matter, reasonings of the mind
> Turned inward; or at my request would sing
> Old songs, the product of his native hills;
> A skillful distribution of sweet sounds,
> Feeding the soul, and eagerly imbibed
> As cool refreshing water, by the care
> Of the industrious husbandman, diffused
> Through a parched meadow-ground, in time of drought.   (61–72)

The narrator's metaphor likens the Wanderer's walking and sing-
ing to the work of a good farmer; the Wanderer's native songs,
relocated in the boy's memory during their rambles in the woods,
effect a cultivation of the soul.

In fact, the narrator tells us, the Wanderer's own boyhood walks
were taken as a herdsman or on his way to a village school, and
the narrator's account of this time subordinates these two traditionally recognized cultivations to a cultivation of moral sense by
pedestrian action and perspective:

He, many an evening, to his distant home
In solitude returning, saw the hills
Grow larger in the darkness; all alone
Beheld the stars come out above his head,
And travelled through the wood, with no one near
To whom he might confess the things he saw.   (126–31)

For the Wanderer, as for the narrator of the *Prelude*, such experiences 'impressed I So vividly great objects that they lay I Upon
his mind like substances' (136–8). From these impressions, gathered and fixed by walking, the Wanderer gradually gains what the
narrator describes as a capacity to read through nature into the
creative mind, both divine and personal: 'Even in [the rocks'] fixed
and steady lineaments I He traced an ebbing and a flowing mind,
I Expression ever varying' (141–2, 160–3). By these means he
achieves moral perspectives as elevated and broad as those physical
views reached on his walks as 'A Herdsman on the lonely mountain-
tops': 'What wonder if his being thus became I Sublime and
comprehensive!' (219, 233–4).

Actually, of course, there is much to wonder at in this account,
in which certain physical perspectives are translated into enviable
moral security. Like Wordsworth's redefinition of wandering, his
translation of continuous, intimate physical perception into ready
apprehension of a divinity contiguous with human being involves
both sleight of hand and, at some point, a leap of faith. Wordsworth
further enforces our impression that pedestrian perception effects
the Wanderer's moral cultivation by discounting the value of formal
education and emphasizing the need for pedestrian movement.
Given his solitary walks, the narrator tells us, the Wanderer 'had
small need of books' (163). Although he becomes master of the
village school, in fact, the Wanderer is tormented by 'wandering
thoughts', which, in full context, appears to mean 'thoughts of
wandering': he gives up his post and becomes a pedlar (313).

By this narrative move, Wordsworth fully detaches the cultivating effects of walking from the rural labours that created the need
to walk in the first place. The narrator tells us that pedlars' 'hard
service, deemed debasing now, I Gained merited respect in simpler
times' by connecting the isolated inmates of the countryside, and
that 'still no few I Of [the Wanderer's] adventurous countrymen
were led I By perseverance in this track of life I To competence and
ease' (327–8, 333–6). Like the story of the Wanderer's education,

this account obscures a good deal. Although no doubt a settled populace hungry for news did enjoy and anticipate some pedlars' appearances, the idea that in some earlier time their work was more valued, either culturally or economically, does not accord well with what we know of ongoing legal restraint and general suspicion of all travellers and especially of wandering labourers, most of whom could be assumed to be poor and quite probably criminal. A successful pedlar, indeed, would have bought a donkey or a horse or a cart. Yet the Wanderer, working on foot, gains sufficient wealth 'To pass the remnant of his days, untasked | With needless service, from hardship free' (384–5). This carefree retirement contrasts sharply with the poverty-stricken conditions of the Wanderer's childhood and youth 'on a small hereditary farm, | An unproductive slip of rugged ground' (109–10). In Wordsworth's rewrite of a normal pedlar's life, economic labours performed while travelling on foot appear a fruitful, secure alternative to failing agricultural labours, while walking itself retains the capacity for moral and cultural cultivation originally derived from its association with Virgilian cultivation.[57]

Moreover, this pedlar's wandering does not alienate him or threaten the stability of his culture, but draws him into sympathetic human contact from his solitude. His excursive walks now move out into a broader community, mixing close observation of people's 'manners, their enjoyments, and pursuits | Their passions and their feelings; chiefly those | Essential and eternal in the heart' (342–4) with long periods alone in nature where the Wanderer keeps 'In solitude and solitary thought | His mind in a just equipoise of love' (354–5):

> He could *afford* to suffer
> With those whom he saw suffer. Hence it came
> That in our best experience he was rich,
> And in the wisdom of our daily life.
> For hence, minutely, in his various rounds,
> He had observed the progress and decay
> Of many minds, of minds and bodies too;
> The history of many families.   (370–7)

---

[57] See Liu on early 19th-cent. perceptions of pedlars and on Wordsworth's manipulations of these perceptions (*Sense of History*, 341–7). Notice also, in regard to Robert's occupation later in Book I, Liu's comments on weaving in 'The Ruined Cottage' (ibid. 326–31).

The terms of this description enforce our perception of excursive walking as fruitful economic activity: the Wanderer can 'afford' to spend his heart and grows 'rich' with the experience and wisdom earned by his travels. They also attribute the Wanderer's moral stability and perspicuity to his deliberate returns to nature, to human community, to particular locations and people. The values he recollects are 'essential and eternal', but his capacity for vision, his moral poise, is sought in and maintained by movement. For these reasons the Wanderer walks on even after his retirement as a pedlar:

>   still he loved to pace the public roads
> And the wild paths; and, by the summer's warmth
> Invited, often would he leave his home
> And journey far, revisiting the scenes
> That to his memory were most endeared.
> —Vigorous in health, of hopeful spirits, undamped
> By worldly-mindedness or anxious care;
> Observant, studious, thoughtful, and refreshed
> By knowledge gathered up from day to day;
> Thus had he lived a long and innocent life.   (387–96)

The narrator prefaces this account of the Wanderer's life with the assertion that the Wanderer is one of those 'Poets that are sown | By Nature . . . | Yet wanting the accomplishment of verse' whose wisdom is lost when they die, and pledges himself to record 'some small portion of [the Wanderer's] eloquent speech' (77–8, 98). From the Wanderer, then, but through the agency of his pedestrian companion, we hear the story of Margaret's ruined cottage.

The outlines of this epitaph, first composed as 'The Ruined Cottage' in 1797–8, are simple enough: Margaret and her husband, Robert, lose their ability to support themselves; Robert enlists as a soldier, and their once cheerfully sufficient home declines toward abject poverty, its inmates dropping away one by one—Robert never returns, one child is apprenticed and the other dies, and at last Margaret herself succumbs to illness.[58] The details of this

---

[58] For a brief account of the complex composition history of Book I as 'The Ruined Cottage', see Gill, (ed.), *Poems*, 686. James Butler, ed., *The Ruined Cottage and The Pedlar* (Ithaca, NY: Cornell University Press, 1979) and Jonathan Wordsworth, *The Music of Humanity* (London: Thomas Nelson & Sons, 1969) discuss this history in detail.

story echo and reinforce the Wanderer's biography, contrasting the failure of georgic labour with the hope and consolation—in this case, almost entirely philosophic—offered by the peripatetic life.

The Wanderer describes Margaret and Robert when he first knows them as exemplars of georgic industry and fruitfulness. Margaret's 'virtues bloomed beneath this lowly roof (512); her husband, 'Frugal, affectionate, sober and withal | Keenly industrious' (522–3), laboured diligently at his weaving 'ere the mower was abroad' (525) and in the evenings cultivated their small garden:

> They who passed
> At evening, from behind the garden fence
> Might hear his busy spade, which he would ply,
> After his daily work, until the light
> Had failed and every leaf and flower were lost
> In the dark hedges.   (527–32)

The georgic virtue of industry and Virgilian georgic labour have been moved out of the field into a pastoral locus, the garden, with its suggestions of ease and security. But we already know that the garden has 'run wild' and the cottage has been ruined, and the Wanderer's description casts the shadow ahead: already agriculture and its fruits are vanishing, invisible at first to the passers-by and finally becoming so to Robert himself, recoverable only in part by walkers outside the fence who hear and interpret the sounds of cultivation.

As we expect, then, Robert and Margaret's laborious cultivations prove incapable of supporting either comfort or sufficiency. Three economic blows strike the small household: crop failure, war, and debilitating illness. The first two are universally felt—'This happy Land was stricken to the heart!'—while the third, although ostensibly private, follows Famine and War as their familiar, Pestilence (and Death, indeed, is not far behind) (I. 540). The fate of Margaret's household closely resembles that of the female vagrant in 'Salisbury Plain', and as the 'wastes of corn' indicated the failure of the Virgilian solution there, so the decay of Margaret's garden indicates it here.

Even before the Wanderer chooses that image to typify the industry and early prosperity of the cottage, the thirsty narrator climbs a fence that separates the 'public way' from a 'plot | Of

garden ground run wild' where the spring that served the cottage
still flows (460–5). The distance between the well-tended garden
of Margaret's youth and the dismally overgrown yard in which
only the spring—of poetry, as well as hospitality—remains as it
was is not left to the imagination but drawn stage by stage. The
Wanderer's first visit after Robert's departure discovers no outward change; he leaves Margaret comforted, 'busy with her garden tools', as he 'pace[s] along the foot-path way', her labour and
his (for he is still a pedlar at this time) seeming to offer similar
promise (691, 693). In mid-summer after this 'early spring' visit,
however, the Wanderer returns to a different scene. Although the
cottage 'wore its customary look', honeysuckle and stonecrop
encroach upon porch and window, while the garden itself 'appeared
| To lag behind the season, and had lost | Its pride of neatness'
(713, 720–2):

> Daisy-flowers and thrift
> Had broken their trim border-lines, and straggled
> O'er paths they used to deck: carnations, once
> Prized for surpassing beauty, and no less,
> For the peculiar pains they had required,
> Declined their languid heads, wanting support.
> The cumbrous bind-weed, with its wreaths and bells,
> Had twined about her two small rows of peas,
> And dragged them back to earth.   (722–30)

The details of this creeping disarray seem carefully chosen: uncultivated *thrift* obscures the paths, while both beauty and necessity,
carnation and pea, are weighed to earth by forces which georgic
care should mitigate. Such labour has plainly been abandoned, not
from caprice but from a sense of its inefficacy.

It is remarkable, indeed, how little blame the Wanderer attaches
to Margaret. Her neglect of garden and cottage, even the pro-
tracted and pointless wanderings that leave her infant alone in the
cottage for hours at a time, are described not merely with sympathy
but with something like admiration for her tenacity. 'So deeply do
I feel | Her goodness', the Wanderer says,

> that, not seldom, in my walks
> A momentary trance comes over me;
> And to myself I seem to muse on One
> By sorrow laid asleep; or borne away,

> A human being destined to awake
> To human life, or something very near
> To human life, when he shall come again
> For whom she suffered. Yes, it would have grieved
> Your very soul to see her . . .   (782–91)

Any serious culpability plainly lies with the husband and with his failure, for whatever reason, to return. 'Her poor Hut | Sank to decay', we are told, 'for *he* was gone, whose hand' should have repaired it (900–1, emphasis mine).

Whatever we may feel about the justice of the Wanderer's evaluation of Margaret and Robert, it seems clear that the progressive decay of their garden is not displayed as a reprimand to the careless husbandman but as a double image of the failure of that whole way of life of the small freeholder and of the soul-sickness—personal and national—that follows. Margaret's case, we are told plainly, is multiplied many times over; not only her husband but 'shoals of artisans | From ill-requited labour turned adrift' search for charity (or, one imagines, other work) (559–60).

Moreover, it suggests once again that the crucial action here is not Virgilian cultivation, but excursive walking. One of the first manifestations of Robert's despair is that 'he would leave his work—and to the town | Would turn without an errand his slack steps; | Or wander here and there among the fields' (582–4). His enlistment, though purposeful at first, becomes just another of these aimless rambles, for he neither returns himself nor lends any further support, economic or moral, to his family. That failure drives the tragedy: as Luke's return from the city would presumably have saved Michael's freehold, so the Wanderer asserts that Robert's return from soldiering would have halted the ruin of the cottage.

Meanwhile Margaret, who has spoken of 'the misery of that wandering life' which would have been hers as a soldier's wife, finds miserable wandering enough where she is (681). She apologizes to the Wanderer on his second visit after the enlistment for having kept him waiting for some hours near her door:

> 'in good truth, I've wandered much of late;
> And, sometimes—to my shame I speak—have need
> Of my best prayers to bring me back again.
> . . . .

                                to-day
I have been travelling far; and many days
About the fields I wander, knowing this
Only, that what I seek I cannot find;
And so I waste my time: for I am changed;
And to myself,' said she, 'have done much wrong
And to this helpless infant.'   (754–6, 764–9)

When the Wanderer returns a third time the effects of aimless wandering are plain: the cottage, too, is affected, its floors unswept, its hearth 'comfortless', and

                          her small lot of books,
    Which, in the cottage-window, heretofore
    Had been piled up against the corner panes
    In seemly order, now, with straggling leaves
    Lay scattered here and there, open or shut,
    As they had chanced to fall.   (824–9)

Still, as the vegetative image of books overgrown with their own 'straggling leaves' suggests, it is Margaret's garden where the Wanderer sees

                        that poverty and grief
    Were now come nearer to her: weeds defaced
    The hardened soil, and knots of withered grass:
    No ridges there appeared of clear black mould,
    No winter greenness; of her herbs and flowers,
    It seemed the better part were gnawed away
    Or trampled into earth; a chain of straw,
    Which had been twined about the slender stem
    Of a young apple-tree, lay at its root;
    The bark was nibbled round by truant sheep.   (833–42)

In this last vision, neither pastoral ease nor georgic labour remains; the very grazing of the sheep suggests not paradise but its loss, as they too eat of the forbidden tree. What remains of Margaret's story, and of her hope, is rendered in paths and steps rather than in fruits and flowers. After her infant's death she earns her livelihood by spinning hemp, walking back and forth spinning the thread from a hemp belt round her waist:

    There, to and fro, she paced through many a day
    Of the warm summer, from a belt of hemp

> That girt her waist, spinning the long-drawn thread
> With backward steps.   (884–7)

By these tiny excursions that mimic the Wanderer's larger travels she gains some small sustenance and leaves a path that the narrator can still read, though faintly, beneath the encroaching grasses. Her spiritual and emotional livelihood, likewise, is gained from 'that length of road' which she watches in constant hope, questioning wayfarers for news of her husband and waiting for the Wanderer to return (912). But it is too little, too late: Margaret dies in poverty, without word of her husband's fate.

The Wanderer's excursive walking, however, recollects the value of her life in his educative epitaph. Whatever the Wanderer's natural poetic capacity, his repeated walks to her cottage provide the matter of his narrative and the stimulus for its present form, the first deriving from his visits as a pedlar years ago and the second from his current meeting with the narrator at the well-known site. He does not merely remember Margaret's story or mention it in passing, but recollects all his knowledge of her in a narrative so vivid that it moves his auditor to a sense of personal association with Margaret, as if he too remembered her:

> I stood, and leaning o'er the garden wall
> Reviewed that Woman's sufferings; and it seemed
> To comfort me while with a brother's love
> I blessed her in the impotence of grief.   (921–4)

The Wanderer, however, does not wish merely to move the narrator but to teach him. His final recollection asserts the transformation of change and loss into stability and peace:

> I well remember that those very plumes,
> Those weeds, and the high spear-grass on that wall,
> By mist and silent rain-drops silvered o'er,
> As once I passed, into my heart conveyed
> So still an image of tranquillity,
> So calm and still, and looked so beautiful
> Amid the uneasy thoughts which filled my mind
> That what we feel of sorrow and despair
> From ruin and from change, and all the grief
> That passing shows of Being leave behind,
> Appeared an idle dream, that could maintain
> Nowhere, dominion o'er the enlightened spirit

Whose meditative sympathies repose
Upon the breast of Faith. I turned away,
And walked along my road in happiness.   (942–56)

The final line marks excursive walking as an agent of emotional
and moral serenity, a serenity which, like the telling of Margaret's
tale, derives from the Wanderer's repetitive pedestrian travels to
and from the ruined cottage. Moreover, like the end of 'When
first I journeyed hither', this passage juxtaposes the comprehension of flux with movement and points, in its conclusive 'walked
my road in happiness', toward continued motion as the 'end' and
anchor of such comprehension. Thus the Wanderer closes his
recollection of Margaret's life with the assertion that her struggle
and loss, when seen from the correct perspective, become an 'idle
dream'. His own pedestrian wandering, on the other hand, appears
as a cultivating labour that stabilizes the flux of idleness into
tranquillity and faith by creating that proper perspective and
then redrawing the world by discourse. The narrator's actions
underscore the lesson: arriving at these first epitaphs on foot, he
will continue to gather the Wanderer's wisdom as they walk on
together.

In these opening epitaphs, then, we see a full development of
excursive walking as physical economy, as cultivation, as epitaph-
making, and as education—in short, the extension of Virgilian
georgic into Wordsworthian peripatetic. The rest of the *Excursion*
elaborates upon this development, repeating the pattern of excursive
walking producing epitaphs and educative discourse. As the mission
of the narrator is to publish the Wanderer's poetry, opening the
effects of his excursive cultivation into the community of readers,
so the Wanderer's is to draw the Solitary out of harmful seclusion
into human community by involving him in pedestrian excursions
which lead, eventually, to the Pastor's epitaphs and the closing
discussions on national education. And as the narrator and the
Wanderer pursue these joint pedestrian projects, Wordsworth reiterates portions of the peripatetic argument of Book I. Book II,
for instance, opens with the narrator's comparison of the Wanderer to a strolling minstrel. The narrator's idea of a minstrel's life
involves rather less danger than we might expect—he imagines
that a minstrel would be protected from robbers on the road 'By
virtue of that sacred instrument | His harp, suspended at the

traveller's side'—and rather more honour and poetic capacity (II. 14–15). Even this idealized minstrel, the narrator tells us, could not draw

> happier, loftier, more empassioned, thoughts
> From his long journeyings and eventful life,
> Than this obscure Itinerant had skill
> To gather, ranging through the tamer ground
> Of these our unimaginative days;
> Both while he trod the earth in humblest guise
> Accoutred with his burthen and his staff.   (20–6)

The terms of this comparison thus reaffirm (quite unhistorically) the economic security of these pedestrian labourers, and link their poetic capacity with their strolling. Indeed, to ensure that mere travel will not be thought the crucial factor in producing poetic perspectives, the narrator then compares what he learns with the Wanderer in his 'favourite school | ... the fields, the roads, and the rural lanes', with the experiences of swifter travellers:

> The wealthy, the luxurious, by the stress
> Of business roused, or pleasure, ere their time,
> May roll in chariots, or provoke the hoofs
> Of the fleet coursers they bestride...
>   .   .   .   .
> And they, if blest with health and hearts at ease,
> Shall lack not their enjoyment:—but how faint
> Compared with ours! who, pacing side by side,
> Could with an eye of leisure, look on all
> That we beheld; and lend the listening sense
> To every grateful sound of earth and air;
> Pausing at will—our spirits braced, our thoughts
> Pleasant as roses in the thickets blown,
> And pure as dew bathing their crimson leaves.   (97–100, 102–10)

The Solitary, who has chosen to isolate and immobilize himself, describes pedestrian excursion as crucial to the joy and stability of his early married life. He and his wife take daily walks from their cottage through landscapes 'Gay as our spirits, free as our desires; | As our enjoyments, boundless' (III. 543–4). After the birth of their first child, the Solitary walks the old paths alone, 'meditating on follies past' and on his present blessings: 'These acts of mind, and memory, and heart, | And spirit ... Endeared my wanderings; and the mother's kiss I And infant's smile awaited my return' (574–5, 582–3).

And the Pastor, who embodies the virtues possible in a relatively sedentary life, nonetheless chooses excursive walkers for six of his seventeen epitaphs, while two more stories are suggested by nearby paths, the traces of walks. In one epitaph, a fine peripatetic fable, an unrequited lover eases his pain by means of long botanizing walks. When he dies of a sudden fever, he leaves the object of his love a book of pressed plants gathered on those walks, a harvest of recollected emotion—'To her, a monument of faithful love I Conquered, and in tranquillity retained!' (VI. 210–11). In another, a miner's heroic efforts are marked by the 'Path of Perseverance' he wears from his cottage to the mine, a path whose lessons are legible even after riches and idleness have undone the miner (VI. 212–54). Then there is the story of the 'flaming Jacobite I And sullen Hanoverian' whose unlikely friendship takes the form of 'lengthened walks' in life and a common burial in death (VI. 458–9, 475). An unwed mother's lost innocence is remembered by her once light step, 'Caught from the pressure of elastic turf I Upon the mountains gemmed with morning dew, I In the prime hour of sweetest scents and airs', while an adulterer's remorse is expressed in restless wanderings without return (VI. 821–3; VI. 1080–114). Finally, the tale of the arrival of the Pastor's predecessor and his family characterizes them as gypsies or strolling players who excite the suspicion of the 'staid guardian[s] of the public peace' in their 'march' to the church among the mountains—a more likely apprehension of pedestrian wanderers than those the narrator has represented (VII. 63–110).

The Pastor's last epitaph concerns an Elizabethan knight, to whom the Wanderer compares himself as 'doomed' to obsolescence. Book VIII opens with the Solitary's argument, parallel to the narrator's about minstrels, that pedlars still perform those civilizing offices also identified with chivalrous knights, 'Raising, through just gradation, savage life I To rustic, and the rustic to urbane' (70–1). The Wanderer responds that the days of such service are past, altered forever by advances in transport, industry, and commerce:

The foot-path faintly marked, the horse-track wild,
And formidable length of plashy lane . . .

.   .   .   .

Have vanished—swallowed up by stately roads
Easy and bold, that penetrate the gloom
Of Britain's farthest glens. The Earth has lent
Her waters, Air her breezes; and the sail
Of traffic glides with ceaseless intercourse.   (105–6, 109–13)

Nearly thirty lines of praise for industrialization follow, lauding
the rise of cities, the improvement of agriculture, and the improvement of both trade and defence with Britain's growing sea power.

In the discussion that follows, however, the Wanderer's pedestrian endeavours prove necessary after all. Both the narrator and
the Wanderer lament the accompanying loss of 'The old domestic
morals of the land', the depopulation of the rural countryside, and
the impoverishment of the rural labourer:

The Father, if perchance he still retain
His old employments, goes to field or wood,
No longer led or followed by the Sons;
Idlers perchance they were,—but in *his* sight;
Breathing fresh air, and treading the green earth

.   .   .   .

That birthright now is lost.   (276–80, 282)

The performance of old forms of rural labour seems less important
than the loss of companionable pedestrianism which, if maintained,
appears to preserve those 'old domestic morals' despite the loss of
other employment.

When the Solitary challenges the image of an agrarian golden
age implicit in the Wanderer's lament, he too figures the prime
deficiencies of rural life, embodied in this portrait of a 'whistling
plough-boy', as deficiencies in pedestrian capacity:

Stiff are his joints,
Beneath a cumbrous frock, that to the knees
Invests the thriving churl, his legs appear,
Fellows to those that lustily upheld
The wooden stools for everlasting use,
Whereon our fathers sate. And mark his brow!
Under whose shaggy canopy are set
Two eyes—not dim, but of a healthy stare—
Wide, sluggish, blank, and ignorant, and strange—
Proclaiming boldly that they never drew

A look or motion of intelligence
From infant-conning of the Christ-cross-row,
Or puzzling through a primer, line by line,
Till perfect mastery crown the pains at last.   (398, 402–15)

The Solitary characterizes his ploughboy, a practitioner of georgic labour, primarily by the coarseness and stiffness of his legs—by his clumsy walk, in effect—and links that to the educational failure manifested in the boy's equally immobile eyes. When he asks, then, 'What liberty of *mind* is here?', the poem's answer is implied in the metaphorical terms of the problem: liberty of mind accompanies liberty of movement, specifically the liberty of deliberate excursive walking.

Despite what the Wanderer says about his own obsolescence, in fact, the *Excursion* shows his wandering, his excursive walking, supporting the changes he lauds in transport and economy by counteracting their negative effects. The securing of individual economies, the development of poetic perspective, the location and binding of human community, the reappropriation of cultivated lands, the recovery of past value, the affirmation of present change, the education of the individual and his culture—all of these projects, whatever other components they may require, depend in this poem upon peripatetic labour, without which even apparently direct approaches seem of little avail. In Wordsworth's poetry, it appears, the walker has found the place where the sower dwelt and, by returning to it continually, has made it his own.

4

Walking as Ideology

PART of the changing interpretative potential that enabled Wordsworth's replacement of cultivator with pedestrian was the increasing practice of deliberate excursive walking, especially by the relatively well-to-do and educated, throughout the nineteenth century. The conspicuous example set by the Wordsworths and Coleridge, who walked and wrote at the cutting edge of this change, obviously stimulated pedestrian activity among those around them. William Hazlitt, whose first acquaintance with Coleridge in 1798 included walking him part of the way home from a preaching engagement' at Hazlitt's father's church, walked 150 miles to Nether Stowey that spring (having walked to Llangollen by way of training first) to visit Coleridge and Wordsworth and, while there, joined Coleridge on a pedestrian tour to Lynton and the Valley of the Rocks, to which Coleridge and the Wordsworths had walked the previous year.[1] Hazlitt's later pedestrian endeavours included an 1822 walking tour from Glasgow into the Highlands with a friend, Sheridan Knowles, and a walk through Hampshire with Coventry Patmore the following year, the latter affair moving Hazlitt to boast that he was still fully capable of doing 'forty to fifty miles a day'.[2] De Quincey's pedestrian aspirations manifested themselves before he met, but after he had

---

[1] Hazlitt uses this succession of walks as the narrative frame for 'My First Acquaintance with Poets' (in *The Complete Works of William Hazlitt*, ed. P. P. Howe, vol. viii (London and Toronto: J. M. Dent & Sons, 1931), 106–22). In a now-famous passage, he moves from a description of Wordsworth and Coleridge reciting—the former 'lyrical', the latter 'dramatic'—to Coleridge's comment that 'he himself liked to compose in walking over uneven ground, or breaking through the straggling branches of a copse-wood; whereas Wordsworth always wrote (if he could) walking up and down a straight gravel-walk, or in some spot where the continuity of his verse met with no collateral interruption' (pp. 118–19).

[2] Quoted in Marples, *Shanks's Pony*, 54. I am indebted to Marples for much of my information on 19th-cent. pedestrian practice. Marples's full account, which includes more complete descriptions of individual walkers' travels, runs from pp. 41 to 153 of *Shanks's Pony*.

read, Wordsworth: in 1802 he ran away from his grammar school in Manchester by walking the fifty-three miles to his mother's home in Chester, and then convinced his mother to let him take a walking tour—although not through the Lakes, where he had first planned to admire the scenery he associated with Wordsworth's poetry, but in nearby Wales. De Quincey's later association with the Wordsworths and his residence in Grasmere confirmed excursive walking as a lifelong habit, and he 'settled down', as Morris Marples puts it, into 'a tempo of between 70 and 100 miles a week'.[3] And Keats, whose pedestrian meeting with Coleridge at Highgate produced that wonderfully bemused description of Coleridge's ceaseless discourse, walked 642 miles during his 1818 tour of the Lakes and Scotland on the grounds that such 'tramping' would, in the true fashion of Wordsworthian wandering, 'give me more experience, rub off more Prejudice, use [me] to more hardship, identifying finer scenes, load me with grander Mountains, and strengthen more my reach in Poetry, than would stopping at home among Books even though I should read Homer'.[4]

These examples of apparently direct influence, however, must be set in the general wave of pedestrian touring that began in the late eighteenth century, and of which the Wordsworths and Coleridge were themselves part. The extent of such touring can be measured indirectly, Marples suggests, by the popularity of writings about it: 'from about 1800 onwards, it became worth while to publish guidebooks expressly intended for pedestrians, while accounts of pedestrian tours . . . were also popular.'[5] Marples mentions the *Cambrian Directory, or Cursory Sketches of the Welsh Territories* (1800), the Revd Richard Warner's *A Walk through Wales* (1798) and *A Second Walk through Wales* (1799), and William Hutton's *Remarks upon North Wales, being the result of Sixteen tours through that part of the Principality* (1803); from later in the nineteenth century he cites Thomas Roscoe's *Wanderings in North Wales* (1836) and discusses at some length the accounts

[3] Ibid. 59.
[4] For Keats's account of the Highgate meeting, see the 15 Apr. portion of his letter to George and Georgiana Keats of 14 Feb.–3 May 1819. The commentary on walking in Scotland is from the 18–22 July letter to Benjamin Bailey; I have drawn the text from *The Letters of John Keats*, ed. Hyder Rollins (Cambridge, Mass.: Harvard University Press, 1958).
[5] Marples, *Shanks's Pony*, 78.

by George Borrow, Canon Cooper, and Robert Louis Stevenson of their extensive travels on foot.[6]

By the mid-century the very highest echelon of English society regarded pedestrian touring as a valuable educational experience. In the three years spanning 1856–8, Victoria and Albert sent the Prince of Wales on a series of walking tours in Dorset, the Lakes, Germany and Switzerland, and Ireland. Although the Prince's first tutor 'rewarded [him] for good work with afternoon rambles in the countryside', the Prince himself evidently had little liking for these tours, no doubt because his parents and the tutors who accompanied him had such palpable didactic designs on him: his father even sent instructions not to slouch or put his hands in his pockets as he walked.[7] Whether the Prince did in fact stand up straight is not recorded, but he is known to have induged in a certain amount of rebellious mischief, including driving a flock of sheep into Windermere, and a mild debauch with Gladstone's eldest son during the European tour.[8] Certainly he did not then share his mother's enthusiasm for walking (Albert worried about this during her first pregnancy) nor his parents' reliance upon the salutary effects of pedestrian touring.[9]

The establishment of the Commons, Open Spaces and Footpaths Preservation Society in 1865, and the founding of the first walking associations, including the Peak and Northern Footpaths Society, also mark the growing practice of excursive walking and an increasing desire to protect (partly by means of walking, of course) the common lands and public footpaths which gave walkers access to the countryside.[10] Marples infers from scattered evidence in biographies and diaries that there must have been many such walking associations, public and private, as well as 'many unorganized groups of friends and many thousands of individuals' of various classes and degrees of education who undertook pedestrian

---

[6] Ibid. 78–84, 116–32, 140–5, 148–53. Accounts of actual pedestrian travels during this period present the opportunity for much commentary, one which I have reluctantly turned away from in pursuing the philosophical accounts and literary representations of walking.

[7] John Van der Kiste, *Queen Victoria's Children* (Gloucester: Alan Sutton, 1916), 22; Marples, *Shanks's Pony*, 138.

[8] Tyler Whittle, *Victoria and Albert at Home* (London: Routledge & Kegan Paul, 1980), 92.

[9] Van der Kiste, *Queen Victoria's Children*, 9.

[10] Taplin, *English Path*, 38.

excursions, although often under rather greater restrictions than the Prince of Wales.[11] Leslie Stephen's account of Henry Fawcett's long battle against routine enclosure bills through the 1860s, 1870s, and 1880s makes it clear that agricultural labourers offered protests against such bills not only from fear of economic impoverishment but because they would lose access to open spaces in which they wished to walk for recreation.[12] As the testimony of 'Mr. J. Reed, parish clerk of Withypool' to a committee reporting on the 1869 Annual Enclosure Bill suggests, the fact that many of these labourers still depended on walking as their primary transport meant that if they wished to walk recreatively, in the manner Wordsworth recommended in his letter against the Kendal railway, they had to do so within the circle of a day's walk:

When asked how far people would have to go for an open space, the witness replied: 'They could not find one for miles except they did go on the common.' Is there no open common within reach of an ordinary walk? 'No; he would not want any more recreation by the time he came to any other common.—The people say they will be as badly off as in a town.' Are there no fields where they can walk? 'Yes, they can trespass, if they like that.'[13]

Old and new forms of walking, walking as restrictive daily necessity and walking as deliberate educative travel, meet in this account. Philip Bagwell, commenting on 'The Decline of Rural Isolation', reminds us that despite the progressive lifting of physical and economic restrictions on travel, villages where 'children grew up without stirring farther than a few miles from their homes' and where labourers still walked arduous distances to their work 'were by no means freakish exceptions' even in the 1880s.[14] Flora Thompson's Lark Rise was such a place, a hamlet 'connected by a network of paths' where even a bicycle on the road was still a rarity and the nineteen miles to Oxford set that city in misty imagination for village children.[15] Even those who lived in such

[11] Marples, Shanks's Pony, 136.
[12] Leslie Stephen, Life of Henry Fawcett, 3rd edn. (London: Smith, Elder, & Co., 1886), 329.
[13] Ibid. 305–6.
[14] Philip S. Bagwell, 'The Decline of Rural Isolation', in G. E. Mingay (ed.), The Victorian Countryside, 2 vols. (London and Boston, Mass.: Routledge & Kegan Paul, 1981), i. 31, 32.
[15] Flora Thompson, Lark Rise to Candleford: A Trilogy (London and New York: Oxford University Press, 1945), 4.

isolation, Reed's testimony suggests, recognized and pursued deliberate walking as recreation. But in that word 'recreation' lies much difficulty, for it is a word which carries connotations of both labour and leisure, both the remaking of self and world and the sense of relaxation and respite from labour.

Leslie Stephen's comment that 'Walking is among recreations what ploughing and fishing are among industrial labours' illustrates the problem.[16] In this formulation, walking appears allied to and yet removed from the georgics of ploughing and fishing, the alliance lying (so Stephen argues) in their mutual primitive simplicity and naturalness and stimulation of contemplation.[17] Stephen goes on, as we shall see, to portray walking as a making of the self, emphasizing that laboriously creative sense of 'recreation'; plainly fishing, too, is recreative in both the laborious and leisurely senses. Yet he rhetorically sets walking apart from 'labour' as a 'recreation', implying a distinction between work and not-work as well as that between cultivation and industry. In fact, as Reed's testimony also suggests, the free and regular practice of excursive walking, especially at non-local scales, demands that one make a sufficient living to leave leisure, measured in time and/or money, in which to pursue this other, this recreative labour. Varieties of 'labour', rather than coinciding as Wordsworth's poetry asserts, begin to sort themselves out along traditional class lines: walking becomes a sign not only of the deliberate making of self but, to a certain extent, of the freedom from other labours, the leisure, in which to do so.

By the middle of the nineteenth century, deliberate excursive walking had become identified with, although obviously not restricted to, what Marples calls 'the intellectual classes': 'Dons, parsons, public schoolmasters, and higher civil servants, members of that intellectual aristocracy many of whom were related to one another in a complicated network of intermarriages . . . walked, for exercise and relaxation, in the intervals of their work . . . [and] often spent their holidays or vacations on walking tours.'[18] Leslie Stephen exemplifies the type: head of an undergraduate walking

[16] Leslie Stephen, 'In Praise of Walking', in *Studies of a Biographer* (2nd ser.), vol. iii (London: Duckworth & Co., 1902), 254.

[17] The most famous example of the haluetic, or fisherman's georgic, is Izaak Walton's *Compleat Angler*. See Durling, *Georgic Tradition,* for a discussion of this and other examples of the sub-genre.

[18] Marples, *Shanks's Pony,* 133.

club at Cambridge; an original member of the Alpine Club; first
Secretary of the Commons, Open Spaces and Footpaths Preservation Society; and the founder and leader of the Sunday Tramps, a
particularly famous and literary walking club which completed
252 walks, generally about twenty miles in length, undertaken
every other Sunday for about eight months of each year between
1880 and 1895.[19] 'The one pursuit in which I am not contemptible
is walking', he claimed, adding, 'I still think with complacency of
the hot day in which I did my fifty miles from Cambridge to
London in twelve hours to attend a dinner of the Alpine Club.'[20]

These intellectual walkers gave considerable attention to the
regularity and extent of their pedestrian exertion. Marples's specific examples of 'unorganized' individual walkers, which include
an archbishop, two headmasters, a barrister, and a lord, are mostly
'great walkers', people who walked six miles in an hour, or a
steady twenty-five or thirty miles a day for most of their lives.[21]
Yet these pedestrians regarded their excursions as something quite
different from the athletic pedestrianism, also burgeoning in
popularity at this time, of what Stevenson calls 'your athletic men
in purple stockings, who walk their fifty miles a day'.[22] Mountain
climbing fell within the purview of the intelligentsia rather than
the athletes—Stephen regarded 'Alpine walks' as 'the poetry of the
pursuit'—perhaps because of the role of mountains in both picturesque and peripatetic aesthetics.[23] But the intellectual walkers
rejected the production of anything so crass as records or prize
money—or, for that matter, footpaths—in favour of walking done
for its own sake, as 'a reward in itself'.[24]

Yet pride in pedestrian exertion sites the benefits of walking

[19] Frederic William Maitland, *The Life and Letters of Leslie Stephen* (London:
Duckworth & Co., [n.d.]), 357 ff.
[20] Leslie Stephen, *Some Early Impressions* (London: Hogarth Press, 1924), 47.
[21] Marples, *Shanks's Pony*, 136.
[22] Robert Louis Stevenson, 'Walking Tours', in *Virginibus Puerisque*, Biographical Edition (New York: Charles Scribner's Sons, 1914), 238. Further quotations from Stevenson will be noted in the text by page number. For a history of
athletic pedestrianism during this period, see John Cumming's *Runners and
Walkers: A Nineteenth-Century Sports Chronicle* (Chicago: Regnery Gateway, 1981).
Walking and running were indeed lumped together in athletic terminology: a brief
article titled 'Pedestrianism' on p. 15 of *The Times* for 21 June 1897 reports 'one
of the first running performances of the century' in which a Mr F. E. Bacon
covered eleven miles, 1,243 yards in one hour.
[23] Stephen, 'In Praise of Walking', 270.
[24] Stevenson, 'Walking Tours', 232.

in its physical process, a process which insistently calls attention both to walking's original socio-economic content and to its newly enhanced capacity for material appropriation. Again Stephen provides an illustration of the difficulty. His regular advocacy of 'a little judicious trespassing' in the pursuit of rural walks from the environs of London suggests both wandering and reappropriation of lands to common use, and constitutes part of his argument for the preservation of common lands and footpaths so that labourers can walk abroad.[25] Yet that word 'judicious' implies more than good judgement on the part of individual walkers. What, after all, *is* 'judicious'—'soundly judged', with distinct legal overtones—trespassing? Stephen tells us parenthetically that this activity depends on 'the liberality of many private proprietors'— that is, judicious trespassing is trespassing that proceeds with the tacit approval of landowners, according to *their* judgement, not against their will or across their boundaries or (despite the context of Stephen's 'walkers' rights' argument) with the intent of creating public lands. And who is most likely to trespass judiciously, that is, with safety from prosecution? Surely not the labourer, under most circumstances, but the presentable scholar. Thus Stephen's phrase insulates the recreative potential of walking from a portion of the source of that potential, siphoning off the aesthetic advantages of pedestrian perspective from walking's potentially subversive character as appropriation.

The desire of middle- and upper-class walkers to obtain the aesthetic advantages of peripatetic practice without engaging in its socio-economic projects finds expression in several essays, appearing in England and the United States between the writing of the *Excursion* (1814) and Victoria's death (1901), which undertake an account of walking as aesthetic practice: William Hazlitt's 'On Going a Journey' (1821), Henry David Thoreau's 'Walking' (1862), John Burroughs's 'The Exhilarations of the Road' (1872), Robert Louis Stevenson's 'Walking Tours' (1881), and Leslie Stephen's 'In Praise of Walking' (1901).[26] I group these essays under the

[25] Stephen, *Life of Fawcett*, 296.
[26] Given Hazlitt's sometimes biting criticisms of Wordsworth, it is amusing that he should have written this first example of peripatetic theory. For an assessment of Hazlitt's attitude toward Wordsworth and of his review of *The Excursion*, see ch. 4, 'The Egotistical Sublime', in David Bromwich's *Hazlitt: The Mind of a Critic* (Oxford and New York: Oxford University Press, 1983).

rubric 'peripatetic theory', by which I do not mean theory *about* peripatetic, especially in any monolithic sense. Rather, I mean explications of the account of walking implicit in Wordsworthian peripatetic which abstract peripatetic practice from its historical origins, making excursive walking's presumed benefits seem inherent effects of the practice itself rather than expectations derived from particular material and textual conditions.

Hazlitt accomplishes this primarily by rejecting companionable walking, which in Wordsworthian peripatetic helps suggest the possibility of an integrated economic community, in favour of solitary excursion, and by reducing the identification of walking with agricultural labour to the merest suggestion, individualizing and sensualizing peripatetic cultivation so that it appears personal, rather than communal. As Stephen's comment on walking as recreation suggests, the other English essayists follow Hazlitt in this latter tactic. Moreover, peripatetic theorists after Hazlitt present their description of peripatetic practice as a universal description understood by walkers of earlier times and cite great writers who were also great walkers as examples of the effects of excursive walking. Since the theorists do not read literary representations of walking but instead show walking as a 'timeless' authorial activity, peripatetic practice appears to originate text and yet to be free of any origin in text. Thus the historically specific origins of peripatetic theory disappear from view. Under such circumstances walking becomes ideology, its doctrines self-contained and unexaminable, and so comfortably applicable.

Hazlitt's title, 'On Going a Journey', uses 'going' in a sense we no longer recognize easily, although the essay makes it clear in context: 'go' here means specifically 'walk', the first of the *Oxford English Dictionary*'s definitions for 'go' as verb. (The last listed example of such usage comes from 1836, not long after Hazlitt's essay was published.) Thus the title indicates a discussion of walking as travel, and Hazlitt proceeds not only to differentiate walking from other kinds of travel but to tell us how walking should be done to *be* travel in the extended sense of rediscovering and re-making the self.

The essay overtly presents solitude as the crucial element in this process, naming it first and ranging the other qualities and benefits of 'going a journey' around it. Hazlitt chooses to walk alone because he walks in the countryside: 'I can enjoy society in a room; but out of doors, nature is company enough for me. I am then never less alone than when alone.'[27] This is the Wanderer's 'solitude' on his boyhood walks, a strongly felt association and connection with nature enhanced by isolation from other people. The Wanderer, however, grows into a distinct love of pedestrian company and discourse that Hazlitt bluntly rejects: 'I cannot see the wit of walking and talking at the same time. When I am in the country, I wish to vegetate like the country' (181).

That odd word 'vegetate' maps out Hazlitt's multiple responses to Wordsworthian peripatetic. When people are said to 'vegetate', we understand that they approach a merely physical existence involving little or no mental activity. Hazlitt means, in part, just this, for he argues that the great virtue of solitary walking lies in its freedom from conversation or even attempts at sympathy, and in the consequent release from analysis into the direct apprehension of nature: 'You cannot read the book of nature [in the company of other walkers], without being perpetually put to the trouble of translating it for the benefit of others. I am for the synthetical method on a journey, in preference to the analytical. I am content to lay in a stock of ideas then, and to examine and anatomise them afterwards' (182–3). Coleridge, he admits, could walk and talk—compose, actually—at the same time: 'he could go on in the most delightful explanatory way over hill and dale, a summer's day, and convert a landscape into a didactic poem or a Pindaric ode' (183). But Hazlitt himself 'can make nothing out on the spot:—I must have time to collect myself' (184).

On one hand Hazlitt implicitly accepts Wordsworthian assertions about how walking assists the impression of natural objects on the mind, storing feeling and direct apprehension for later recollection and expression. On the other he seems to withdraw, in his insistence on solitude and silence, toward a Rousseauian identification of walking with reverie, pushing his own concept of true walking closer to unrestricted, disconnective wandering: 'The soul of a journey is liberty, perfect liberty, to think, feel, do just as one pleases. We go a journey chiefly to be free of all impediments and of all inconveniences; to leave ourselves behind, much more to get rid of others' (181). One sees in this passage the same

[27] William Hazlitt, 'On Going a Journey', in *The Complete Works of William Hazlitt*, ed. P. P. Howe, vol. viii (London and Toronto: J. M. Dent & Sons, 1931), 181. Further quotations from Hazlitt will be cited in the text by page number only.

element of choice which modifies 'wandering' in *The Excursion* (and, although it was unpublished when Hazlitt wrote, *The Prelude*). There, however, the walker chooses constant movement between solitude and community, so that walking is figured as an instrument of recovered communality. Here the walker appears to choose unbroken solitude, withdrawing even from self.

Yet Hazlitt also shows the solitary walker noisily expressive, 'thinking', and recovering self:

Give me the clear blue sky over my head and the green turf beneath my feet, a winding road before me, and a three hours' march to dinner—and then to thinking! . . . I laugh, I run, I leap, I sing for joy. From the point of yonder cloud, I plunge into my past being, and revel there, as the sunburnt Indian plunges headlong into the wave that wafts him to his native shore. Then long-forgotten things, like 'sunken wrack and sumless treasuries,' burst upon my eager sight, and I begin to feel, think, and be myself again. (182)

This is not the mental recollection of impressions and the 'making out' of something from them, but a direct making of self by walking that seems to involve active thinking—plunging into past being, as the walker runs and leaps and sings. In this representation, Hazlitt develops the other meaning of 'vegetating like the country', the growth and development of plants, here appearing as a deliberate physical/intellectual/emotional cultivation of self.

Hazlitt's digression on the process of recollection (I call it this because he claims to 'return' from it to 'the question [he has] quitted above', namely the value of solitary walking) shows this journey away from and toward the self as departing from quotidian present consciousness and approaching a 'truer' self lodged in memory and thus accessible only to the walker. At first Hazlitt complains that travel reveals 'the short-sightedness or capriciousness of the imagination':

With change of place we change our ideas; nay our opinions and feelings. . . . We cannot enlarge our conceptions; we only shift our point of view. The landscape bares its bosom to the enraptured eye; we take our fill of it; and seem as if we could form no other image of beauty or grandeur. We pass on, and think no more of it: the horizon that shuts it from our sight also blots it from our memory like a dream. (187)

This happens, Hazlitt explains, because 'the mind can form no larger idea of space than the eye can take in at a single glance'.

Thus, 'Things near us are seen of the size of life: things at a distance are diminished to the size of understanding' (187).

This quality of human perception may indeed reduce China to 'An inch of paste-board on a wooden globe' but, Hazlitt says, it also allows us to remember 'an infinity of things and places' as long as we attend to the necessity of recalling them 'in succession':

> One idea recalls another, but it at the same time excludes all others. In trying to renew old recollections, we cannot as it were unfold the whole web of our existence; we must pick out the single threads. So in coming to a place where we have formerly lived and with which we have intimate associations, every one must have found that the feeling grows more vivid the nearer we approach the spot, from the mere anticipation of the actual impression: we remember circumstances, feelings, persons, faces, names, that we had not thought of for years; but for the time all the rest of the world is forgotten! (187–8)

Hazlitt's recollection by travel does not provide 'a growing prospect' but the proportions he assigns to human perception clearly match those of Wordsworth's imaginary foot-traveller whose passage through a landscape, through horizon after horizon of sight, produces 'Something on every side concealed from view, | In every quarter something visible, | Half-seen or wholly, lost and found again' (*Home at Grasmere*, 705–7). Hazlitt does not make the point explicitly, but in this coincidence between the limited, successive views of the pedestrian traveller and the limited, successive nature of recollection must lie his solitary walker's ability to leave behind an analytical, conversational present self and recover a synthetical, 'true' self.

But unlike the avatar of Wordsworth who walks through Grasmere to connect and establish himself in that locale and with its people, Hazlitt walks to abstract himself from the material and social demands of present perception. His language suggests, indeed, that walking will (happily) return him from adult social intercourse—a word he would have used in multiple senses—to the egoistic, unreciprocal receptivity of an infant. Metaphorizing that landscape which 'bares its bosom' to his present perception as a too-seductive female holding his eye 'enraptured', Hazlitt rejects intimate knowledge both of nature and of other people, claiming that this will interfere with his creative ability to 'form . . . other image[s]'. Only his individual and wholly private mind, walking alone along a 'single thread' of memory to a place of 'intimate associations' (and here again he rejects the possibility of a 'web' of existence, insisting on singularity), can achieve increasingly vivid feeling, anticipation capped by creatively renewing recollection.

In remembering his birthday walk to Llangollen, Hazlitt intones Wordsworthian hopes of returning to the inward prospect of 'LIBERTY, GENUIS, LOVE, VIRTUE . . . since faded into the light of common day' that accompanied his view of the Dee valley. But what he describes is no re-entry into a Wordsworthian community of virtue, but regression to the self-involved, self-justified state of infancy:

Still I would return some time or other to this enchanted spot; but I would return to it alone. What other self could I find to share that influx of thoughts, of regret, and delight, the traces of which I could hardly conjure up to myself, so much have they been broken and defaced! I could stand on some tall rock, and overlook the precipice of years that separates me from what I then was. . . . Not only I myself have changed; the world, which was then new to me, has become old and incorrigible. Yet will I turn to thee in thought, O sylvan Dee, as then thou wert, in joy, in youth and gladness; and thou shalt always be to me the river of Paradise, where I will drink of the waters of life freely! (186–7)

Hazlitt's earlier feminization of the landscape now resonates with his characterization of the Dee as an eternally flowing, freely offered source of life to suggest a mother's abundant and undemanding breast: where present perception encounters the constant seduction of transitory forms, memory re-encounters the ideally nuturing past. Moreover, Hazlitt insists that this life-renewing process of peripatetic self-recollection is essentially uncommunicable, even with some 'other self', and therefore (so his logic rather backwardly runs) must be solitary. If what he seeks are gratifying destinations, 'ruins, aqueducts, pictures' and so forth, the walker may wish to join others in a companionable 'party of pleasure', but he cannot then achieve the purely personal recognition of self that Hazlitt sets as the proper goal of walking (188). For the solitary walker, Hazlitt claims, 'the question is what we shall meet with by the way. The mind then is "its own place;" nor are we anxious to arrive at the end of our journey' (188).

Hazlitt's theory of walking is clearly a selective explication of Wordsworthian peripatetic that partially obscures the connections among the walker's creative, economic, and civic labours. Hazlitt retains Wordsworth's assertion that the continuous, successive perspective of the pedestrian connects him with nature (although perhaps only when mediated by recollection) and with his own past, but ignores or denies the concurrent maintenance of human community Wordsworth stresses. He alludes to Wordsworth's association between Virgilian cultivation and walking, but moves very quickly to the metaphorical extension of those activities, the cultivation of self; and although Hazlitt's walker does retain the capacity of placing and appropriation, these now seem to occur almost entirely within the 'place' of mind, while walking approaches wilful wandering. Hazlitt's narrative, indeed, wanders, rambling from point to point along a line with little apparent attempt at unifying commentary or intentional shaping. It comes as something of a shock when he speaks of 'returning' to his main enquiry, for the unwary reader has been led down a bypath step by step. Still, the return is palpable, and the reader experiences the narrative as an excursion which has intentionally departed from and returned to a path.

Elizabeth D. Harvey, in an excellent article on Thoreau's 'Walking', argues that unlike *Walden*, in which 'the extra-vagant . . . is always checked by the surveyor', 'Walking' strives to transgress without return:

As the title promises, the structure of 'Walking' is meandering, almost desultory. . . . The strategy of the essay is to unsettle expectations by providing, instead of a walk between specified locations, a directionless meditation on the activity in its abstract form. As a result, the essay is not an excursion that its readers can enjoy from the safe remove of time and space, but an aimless collection of philosophical remarks, a labyrinth in which Thoreau's readers lose themselves and, in losing themselves, are implicated in the 'truth' of the essay.[28]

To this end, Harvey suggests, Thoreau not only advocates the dissolution of boundaries and the decomposition of the past in his text but engages in these activities through the language of the essay. If, as Harvey thinks (and I agree with her), the essay purports to be 'walking' itself, then Thoreau would seem to propose a non-excursive walking quite distinct from Wordsworth's.

[28] Elizabeth D. Harvey, 'Speaking Without Bounds: The Extra-Vagant Impulse in Thoreau's "Walking"', in *The Dialectic of Discovery: Essays on the Teaching and Interpretation of Literature* (Lexington, Ky.: French Forum, 1984), 179, 180.

Nineteenth-century American practices and representations of walking must, to my way of thinking, diverge in significant ways from British, coinciding as they did with different material and literary conditions. It is not my intention to address those divergences (the subject of another substantial book), although we will inevitably encounter some of them, but to consider how American theories of walking explicated Wordsworthian peripatetic. Thoreau, of course, knew Wordsworth's works well: if his obvious early affinity for Wordworth's cosmology were not sign enough, we know he owned an American typesetting of the 1832 collected poems and a copy of *The Prelude*.[29] Joseph Moldenhauer points out, moreover, that following Wordsworth's death Thoreau was reading and quoting from Christopher Wordsworth's *Memoirs of William Wordsworth* and De Quincey's *Literary Reminiscences*, and was engaged in an active re-evaluation of his previous celebratory treatment of the poet.[30] During this same time (1851 and 1852), Thoreau was giving the first versions of 'Walking' as a lecture.

Such timing notwithstanding, Harvey follows Thoreau's own strongest indications in reading this essay as perpetually transgressive: he opens 'Walking' with an expression of his desire 'to speak a word for Nature, for absolute freedom and wildness, as contrasted with a freedom and culture merely civil'.[31] Yet I would argue that we cannot take Thoreau's word for this, or rather, that we must take all his words on this subject without trying to hold him to any single line, even the line of continual transgression. Thoreau works in radical paradox, countering his own most extreme statements with equally extreme opposites, describing the line of his thought by the movement of boundaries. This is what Harvey notices in *Walden* when, for instance, Thoreau counters his sounding of the pond with a comment on the desirability of a belief in its infinite depth. Near the end of the book, Harvey observes, 'these double and ostensibly antithetical impulses—the wish for defined boundaries and the urge for immeasurability—alternate with increasing frequency and intensity'.[32] *Cape Cod*, too,

[29] Joseph Moldenhauer, 'Walden and Wordsworth's Guide to the English Lake District', *Studies in the American Renaissance* (1990), 261–2.
[30] Ibid. 276 ff.
[31] Henry David Thoreau, 'Walking', in *The Writings of Henry David Thoreau*, vol. v (Boston, Mass. and New York: Houghton Mifflin, 1906), 203. Further quotations from Thoreau's 'Walking' will be cited in the text by page number only.
[32] Harvey, 'Speaking Without Bounds', 179.

displays in the very indeterminateness of the shore a need for mapping and exploration, for remapping and re-exploration, for the constant redefinition of fluctuating boundaries.

In the same way, Thoreau's opening characterization of true walking, of 'the Art of walking', fluctuates between wandering and placement. True walking, Thoreau says, is

> *sauntering*, which word is beautifully derived 'from idle people who roved about the country, in the Middle Ages, and asked charity, under pretense of going *a la Sainte Terre*,' to the Holy Land, till the children exclaimed, 'There goes a *Sainte-Terrer*,' a Saunterer, a Holy-Lander. They who never go to the Holy Land in their walks, as they pretend, are indeed mere idlers and vagabonds; but they who do go there are saunterers in the good sense, such as I mean. Some, however, would derive the word from *sans terre*, without land or a home, which, therefore, in the good sense, will mean, having no particular home, but equally at home everywhere. (205)

Like Wordsworthian peripatetic, this passage constructs an un-wandering wandering. At first sauntering would seem to be idle wandering, the walker a vagabond; but then we learn that it is possible to saunter 'in the good sense' of truly aiming for and reaching the Holy Land. We become aware here, if we have not been before, that walking is not wholly physical, since going to the Promised Land carries a good deal of metaphorical baggage of its own. 'Where', then, is this place that the saunterer aims for? Even if we take Thoreau's Holy Land literally, he immediately destabilizes this settled destination with a new derivation of true walking that leaves the saunterer homeless, without a final destination. And, again, we learn that there is a 'good sense' of this derivation: a saunterer is placed by his displacement, by his movement, through which he makes a home everywhere.

Our perception of this as Wordsworthian walking is seriously challenged by Thoreau's direct assertions about the proper shape and direction of the saunterer's walks. He chastises modern walkers for 'undertak[ing] no persevering, never-ending enterprises':

> Our expeditions are but tours, and come round again at evening to the old hearth-side from which we set out. Half the walk is but retracing our steps. We should go forth on the shortest walk, perchance in the spirit of undying adventure, never to return ... If you are ready to leave father and mother, and brother and sister, and wife and child and friends, and never see them again,—if you have paid your debts, and made your will,

and settled all your affairs, and are a free man, then you are ready for a walk. (206)

One could scarcely imagine a more direct rejection of the ideal of excursive walking—unless, perhaps, it is Thoreau's own later description of the inevitable westering of the true walker, which carries him out beyond the frontier into wilderness without return. This westering Thoreau describes as 'the prevailing tendency of my countrymen' and, indeed, of humanity, away from old culture into the fresh impulse of nature (218). Here would seem to be an American walking owing little to the walks of an English Romantic poet.

Yet, as Thoreau's construction of sauntering indicates, the westering of the true walker is not entirely unrestrained: 'The outline which would bound my walks would be, not a circle, but a parabola, or rather like one of those cometary orbits which have been thought to be non-returning curves, in this case opening westward, in which my house occupies the place of the sun' (217). Again we see the construction of an unwandering wandering which claims to be open yet bounded, moving out yet returning, by focusing on the home from which he departs and to which he will return. Given Thoreau's rejection of excursive intention, we cannot read this as a Wordsworthian excursion. Moreover, the walk's focus on home is complicated by our knowledge that the saunterer can locate his home anywhere. Nonetheless, Thoreau's true walking describes a curve restrained, not an endless linear advance.

Moreover, when Thoreau talks about the difference between east and west, and about moving westward into the future and the wild and the uncultured, it becomes clear that westward movement will eventually carry the walker back to the east, to the old, and to the heroic age in which culture is created. Having crossed the Atlantic and forgotten the old world, he tells us, 'there is perhaps one more chance for the race left before it arrives on the banks of the Styx; and that is in the Lethe of the Pacific, which is three times as wide' (218). That is, if forgetting the old world is not enough, we can cross the next ocean and so arrive—back in the old world again, although transformed and with much forgotten. Seeing a panorama of the Rhine, Thoreau 'go[es] eastward to realize history and study the works of art and literature, retracing the steps of the race'; having 'floated down its historic stream in something more than imagination', he feels 'as if [he] had been transported to an heroic age, and breathed an atmosphere of chivalry' (218, 223, 224). Such is not his prime project in this essay, we know. Here he wishes to 'go westward as into the future, with a spirit of enterprise and adventure' (218). But when he sees a lifesize panorama of the Mississippi, 'work[ing] my way up the river in the light of to-day', he finds himself along the Rhine again:

as I . . . saw the steamboats wooding up, counted the rising cities, gazed on the fresh ruins of Nauvoo, beheld the Indians moving west across the stream, and, as before I had looked up the Moselle, now looked up the Ohio and the Missouri and heard the legends of Dubuque and of Wenona's Cliff,—still thinking more of the future than of the past or present,— I saw that this was a Rhine stream of a different kind; that the foundations of castles were yet to be laid, and the famous bridges were yet to be thrown over the river; and I felt that *this was the heroic age itself* . . . (224)

Clearly Thoreau means to value the west, the wild, the future, the departing intention. From this passage, indeed, he moves directly into the now famous statement that 'in Wildness is the preservation of the World', and talks of consuming wild food with as much relish as he eats the sea-clam on Cape Cod and desires the taste of raw woodchuck by Walden Pond (224). But the westering walker does walk round the world at last; in wildness is the *preservation* of the world, not in its immediate manifestations, but in the original state (as Thoreau imagines it) from which the building of culture commences.

Harvey speaks of Thoreau's 'process of constructing identity, particularly a literary identity', as proceeding from the decomposition of European culture, and her analysis of the process focuses on the swamps Thoreau enters to 'recreate' himself.[33] We must also remain aware that, as sites of decomposition, swamps become sites for agriculture, and that Thoreau, like Wordsworth, links walker, poet, and farmer as cultivators. He seeks recreation by walking in swamps because there he imbibes most directly the tonic of the wild, but he also figures the swamp as a potential farm and his walking as cultivation:

A man's health requires as many acres of meadow to his prospect as his farm does loads of muck. . . . A township where one primitive forest waves

<hr>

[33] Ibid. 185; Thoreau, 'Walking', 228.

above while another primitive forest rots below,—such a town is fitted to raise not only corn and potatoes, but poets and philosophers for the coming ages. In such a soil grew Homer and Confucius and the rest, and out of such a wilderness comes the Reformer eating locusts and wild honey. (228–9)

Walking into the wilderness—and out of it, as Thoreau 'the Reformer' does—cultivates the individual as the farmer fertilizes his land, while an entire community enriched by such prospects of meadow and forest, by inches of both literal and figurative humus, can grow a whole crop of cultivators. Thus Thoreau exemplifies the makers of America, this new westering place, in a farmer preparing to cultivate swampland 'at whose entrance might have been written the words which Dante read over the entrance to the infernal regions, "Leave all hope, ye that enter"', but which the farmer 'would not part with . . . for any consideration, on account of the mud which it contained' (230). 'The weapons with which we have gained our most important victories', Thoreau says, 'are not the sword and the lance, but the bushwack, the turf-cutter, the spade, and the bog hoe'—'the weapons the hardy farmer needs', as Virgil puts it (230; *Georgics*, I. 160).

So, too, when Thoreau asserts that 'In literature it is only the wild that attracts us' and calls for a poet who 'gives expression to Nature', he describes that poet as one who

nailed words to their primitive sense, as farmers drive down stakes in the spring, which the frost has heaved; who derived his words as often as he used them,—transplanted them to his page with earth adhering to their roots; whose words were so true and fresh and natural that they would appear to expand like the buds at the approach of spring, though they lay half smothered between two musty leaves in a library,—aye, to bloom and bear fruit there, after their kind, annually, for the faithful reader, in sympathy with surrounding Nature. (232)

Although Thoreau says that 'you will perceive that I demand something which no Augustan nor Elizabethan age, which no *culture*, in short, can give', it is precisely culture by which he claims this poetry of nature will be accomplished. To make wild poetry, the poet must transplant wild words by deriving their roots—by returning, in fact, to original meanings by means of the books and records of culture he finds so tame. In entering these swamps he not only walks out into the untouched wild but back

into first cultivations. Thoreau makes the movements simultaneous: to walk out *is* to walk back.

The structure of the essay enforces this construction. 'Walking'
closes with Thoreau's description of 'a remarkable sunset one day
last November':

> I was walking in a meadow, the source of a small brook, when the sun
> at last, just before setting, after a cold, gray day, reached a clear stratum
> in the horizon, and the softest, brightest morning sunlight fell on the dry
> grass and on the stems of the trees in the opposite horizon and on the
> leaves of the shrub oaks on the hillside, while our shadows stretched long
> over the meadow eastward, as if we were the only motes in its beams. It
> was such a light as we could not have imagined a moment before, and
> the air also was so warm and serene that nothing was wanting to make
> a paradise of that meadow. When we reflected that this was not a solitary
> phenomenon, never to happen again, but that it would happen forever
> and ever, an infinite number of evenings, and cheer and reassure the latest
> child that walked there, it was more glorious still. . . . The west side of
> every wood and rising ground gleamed like the boundary of Elysium, and
> the sun on our backs seemed like a gentle herdsman driving us home at
> evening.
>   So we saunter toward the Holy Land, till one day the sun shall shine
> more brightly than ever he has done, shall perchance shine into our minds
> and hearts, and light up our whole lives with a great awakening light, as
> warm and serene and golden as on a bankside in autumn. (247–8)

At first the walkers walk west, their shadows pointing eastward,
but then they turn toward home, walking east with the sun on
their backs. Thoreau describes the scene with particular attentions
that make the place itself seem singular, the moment unrecapturable;
yet the meadow is also paradise, the earliest and last home of
humanity, and Thoreau anticipates the perpetual repetition of this
transformation for future walkers. It is sunset, and yet the light
is that of morning. And here again are those saunterers we met
at the beginning of the essay. We now know that they move
westerly, in non-returning curves, intending no return. Yet, as by
homelessness they make their home everywhere, so they walk west
into the Holy Land, into the old east as well as the promised lands
of America, into the 'great awakening light' of dawn. 'Walking'
returns to its beginning.

In Thoreau's essay, as in Hazlitt's, pedestrian perspective proves
essential to the walker's breaking of bounds and to his returns.

For part of his description of this perspective, Thoreau employs the familiar terms of naturally limited proportions which enhance perception. He likens the 'circle of ten miles' radius, or the limits of an afternoon walk' to the natural limits of 'the threescore years and ten of human life': its landscape 'will never become quite familiar to you' (211–12). Thus even the walker bounded by excursive distance can find 'An absolutely new prospect . . . Two or three hours' walking will carry me to as strange a country as I expect ever to see' (211). And if the walker strikes off through such bounds on a walk of 'ten, fifteen, twenty, any number of miles', avoiding the roads 'made for horses and men of business', he can recess civilized, political life to distant views from hilltops or escape it altogether: 'I pass from it as from a bean-field into the forest, and it is forgotten. In one half-hour I can walk off to some portion of the earth's surface where a man does not stand from one year's end to another, and there, consequently, politics are not' (212, 213). Like Hazlitt's walker, Thoreau's profits by natural limitation of his perception. Because the limits are natural, Thoreau asserts, what can be seen within them is inexhaustible. Yet the walker's natural perceptual limits also work to neutralize the unacceptably restricting limits of the 'narrow field, and still narrower highway' of civil, political life, returning the wary walker to absolute nature by shutting out all that is outside his view (213).

Thoreau supplements these familiar visual descriptions of pedestrian perspective with sensual terms originally suggested by Wordsworth. When the narrator of the *Excursion* walks to the cottage, and the narrator of the *Prelude* climbs Snowdon, their approaches to poetic viewpoints are not only visual but tactile. The *Excursion* opens with the narrator's cognizance of hot summer sun and his desire for cooling shade; harassed by clouds of insects, he 'toil[s] | With languid steps that by the slippery turf | Were baffled' toward his meeting with the Wanderer (I. 21–3). The *Prelude*'s narrator struggles up the mountain on 'a close warm night', 'Hemmed round on every side with fog and damp': 'With forehead bent | Earthward, as if in opposition set | Against an enemy, I panted up' (XIII. 10, 16, 29–31). Obviously such representations show the walker labouring, but they also establish that part of pedestrian perception and perspective is tactile contact with the physical conditions of the natural world. For a pleasanter example, we can turn to that passage from Book I of Cowper's

The Task in which the pedestrians sink to their ankles in moss and thyme and green hillocks, suggesting a multitude of tactile sensations: dampness, coolness, softness, fresh odour (I. 266–72). There, too, the passage through, not only of the eye but of the feet and the body, effectively produces the view from a 'speculative height' (I. 288).

Thoreau develops these representations toward an explicit assertion that the pedestrian's tactile continuity with nature constitutes or creates spiritual contact with invigorating wildness. In the process of setting out his definition of true walking, having rejected deliberately excursive and athletic walkers, he invokes Wordsworth as an example of a thinking pedestrian, quoting the now-famous story from Christopher Wordsworth's biography about William's study being out of doors. From this idea of studying out of doors, or of study being out of doors, Thoreau moves into what at first appears to be a digression on how outdoor life—which now includes study and poetry—tans the skin:

Living much out of doors, in the sun and wind, will no doubt produce a certain roughness of character,—will cause a thicker cuticle to grow over some of the finer qualities of our nature, as on the face and hands, or as severe manual labor robs the hands of some of their delicacy of touch. . . . no doubt it is a nice matter to proportion rightly the thick and thin skin. But methinks that is a scurf that will fall off fast enough,— that the natural remedy is to be found in the proportion which the night bears to the day, the winter to the summer, thought to experience. There will be so much the more air and sunshine in our thoughts. The callous palms of the laborer are conversant with finer tissues of self-respect and heroism, whose touch thrills the heart, than the languid fingers of idleness. (210)

Harvey notices that this passage represents skin 'as the organ of translation between the self and the external world': 'Tanned skin presents unmistakable physiological evidence of its communication with the natural, external world, since, while it remains bonded to and obedient to the self, it also expresses its contact with outside phenomena through its alteration in color.'[34] She then comments extensively on the 'astonishing series of conversions' by which Thoreau uses this characterization of skin linguistically to dissolve conventional boundaries, including the boundary between spirit

[34] Harvey, 'Speaking Without Bounds', 182, 181.

and matter: 'the spiritual characteristics of the heart become access-ible to the external touch of a hand'.[35]

This familiar conflation of continuities is accompanied by con-versions from walker to student and poet to labourer that once again suggest the walking/poetry/cultivation nexus generated in Wordsworthian peripatetic. And as Wordsworth's walking nat-urally limits the pedestrian's view, producing the desirable succes-sion of continuous perceptions, Thoreau's walking also ensures the natural proportions of the skin as perceptual organ. With the skin's tactile capacity so proportioned by peripatetic labour, Thoreau asserts, the walker becomes 'the most alive', that is, 'the wildest': 'One who pressed forward incessantly and never rested from his labors, who grew fast and made infinite demands on life, would always find himself in a new country or wilderness, and surrounded by the raw material of life' (226). 'When we walk, we naturally go to the fields and woods . . . In my walks I would fain return to my senses'—Thoreau's true walker is a sensual walker in genuine tactile contact with his surroundings; walking returns the walker to his senses, and so to direct apprehension of wildness (210–11).

John Burroughs opens 'The Exhilarations of the Road' with an even stronger construction of this equivocation on continuity. In language that recalls Hazlitt's figuration of walker and landscape as lovers, Burroughs represents the bare human foot not just as a perceptual organ but as 'a thing sensuous and alive, that seems to take cognizance of whatever it touches or passes': 'That unham-pered, vitally playing piece of anatomy is the type of the pedes-trian, man returned to first principles, in direct contact and intercourse with the earth and the elements, his faculties unsheathed, his mind plastic, his body toughened, his heart light, his soul dilated.'[36]

The intermingling of returns and contacts in this passage occurs by equating juxtaposition: man in direct contact with earth *is* man returned to first principles; the progression of senses, mind, body, heart, and soul, all enhanced in operation by the 'intercourse' of the foot with the ground, unifies matter and spirit in common

[35] Ibid. 182–3.
[36] John Burroughs, 'The Exhilarations of the Road', in *The Writings of John Burroughs*, vol. ii (Boston, Mass. and New York: Houghton Mifflin, 1875), 27–8. Further quotations from Burroughs's 'Exhilarations' will be cited in the text by page number only.

influence and brings them all into the same continuous plane. Burroughs's language suggests, in fact, simultaneous sexual (specifically masculine) and intellectual/spiritual ecstasy—the unsheathed faculties, the dilated soul—rhetorically supporting the Wordsworthian continuities that Hazlitt's metaphorical retreat into infantile sexuality disrupted. Quickly Burroughs transfers the effects of the contact of bare flesh with earth to any pedestrian action, saying that he will not 'advocate the disuse of boots and shoes' but will nonetheless 'brag as lustily as I can on behalf of the pedestrian, and show how all the shining angels second and accompany the man who goes afoot, while all the dark spirits are ever looking out for a chance to ride' (28).

Burroughs continues his seductive mixture of the language of physical sexual fulfilment and spiritual harmony in this no-holds-barred panegyric to the pedestrian:

He looks down upon nobody; he is on the common level. His pores are all open, his circulation is active, his digestion good. His heart is not cold, nor are his faculties asleep. He is the only real traveler; he alone tastes the 'gay, fresh sentiment of the road.' He is not isolated but is at one with things, with the farms and the industries on either hand. The vital, universal currents play through him. He knows the ground is alive; he feels the pulses of the wind, and reads the mute language of things. His sympathies are all aroused; his senses are continually reporting messages to his mind. Wind, frost, rain, heat, cold are something to him. He is not merely a spectator of the panorama of nature, but a participator in it. He experiences the country he passes through,—tastes it, feels it, absorbs it; the traveler in his fine carriage sees it merely. (37)

Again Burroughs translates sensual contact into a variety of other contacts. The walker who 'looks down upon nobody' in the physical sense retains his commonness, his connectedness to other people; the openness of his pores (we may also think of Thoreau here) and awakeness of his senses make him 'one' with all kinds of human endeavour, the ancient way of farming and the new way of industry. When he feels the wind he feels a 'pulse', life itself, 'vital, universal currents' which his senses then pass on as 'messages to his mind', so that feeling becomes knowledge. And Burroughs distinguishes this pansensual 'participator' from the mere 'spectator', the traveller who only sees. In this essay true travel becomes pedestrian travel, its aesthetic wholly shifted from the elevated, framed *view*point of the eighteenth century to the earth-bound, continuously moving, fully sensual perspective of the post-peripatetic pedestrian.

As we would expect, Burroughs ascribes familiar benefits to pedestrian perspective. The pedestrian traveller will 'not only see many things and have adventures that [he] should otherwise miss' in the country he walks through, but will 'come into relations with that country at first hand, and with the men and women in it, in a way that would afford the deepest satisfaction' (38). These first-hand relations, just the sort of intimacy with foreignness that frightened early true travellers, have now become desirable, representing the best sort of education about others and self: 'what characters we should fall in with, and how seasoned and hardy we should arrive at our destination!' (39) If people would even just walk to church and home again on Sunday, Burroughs says, 'it would be tantamount to an astonishing revival of religion': 'Think how the stones would preach to them by the wayside . . . their besetting demons of one kind and another, would drop behind them, unable to keep up or to endure the fresh air . . . for these devils always want to ride, while the simple virtues are never so happy as when on foot' (35–6). Here is Thoreau's saunterer, the true pilgrim risen again as a pedestrian, the process of his journey now more important to salvation than his holy destination. Indeed, Burroughs tells us that the 'capacity to enjoy a walk implies' the walker's 'state of grace', an innocence and simple-heartedness, and that if a person is 'sighing for the golden age', he should 'walk to it. Every step brings him nearer. The youth of the world is but a few days' journey distant' (30, 38).

As we expect, too, Burroughs characterizes the walking that accomplishes all these connections as a superior form of cultivation:

Next to the laborer in the fields, the walker holds the closest relation to the soil; and he holds a closer and more vital relation to nature because he is freer and his mind more at leisure.

Man takes root at his feet, and at best he is no more than a potted plant in his house or carriage till he has established communication with the soil by the loving and magnetic touch of his soles to it. . . . then spring those invisible fibres and rootlets through which character comes to smack of the soil, and which make a man kindred to the spot of earth he inhabits. (43–4)

Like Hazlitt and Thoreau, Burroughs distinguishes the walker's mode of travel/cultivation by its freedom of movement and of mind, its aptitude for wandering, but immediately balances this with a capacity for placement, likening the walker to cultivated plant as well as cultivator. Again Burroughs's rhetorical conflations of sexual and spiritual connection come into play, now in a version of Thoreau's translating skin: the walker plants himself by means of direct physical contact with the earth which is also spiritual contact (I take Burroughs as intending that pun on 'sole/soul'). The walker physically tied to the earth by the action of his feet on it thus comes to have an earth-like character, one that tastes of soil.

Burroughs proceeds to take Americans to task for their indifference to the benefits of walking:

a race that neglects or despises this primitive gift, that fears the touch of the soil, that has no footpaths, no community of ownership in the land which they imply, that warns off the walker as a trespasser, that knows no way but the highway, the carriage-way, that forgets the stile, the footbridge, that even ignores the rights of the pedestrian in the public road, providing no escape for him but in the ditch or up the bank, is in a fair way to far more serious degeneracy. (29)

In this passage Burroughs seems to acknowledge the socio-economic influences on and results of walking, particularly its capacity to appropriate land to community ownership. Yet his initial characterization of walking as a 'primitive gift' undermines the temporal specificity of his recognition; footpaths, community ownership, pedestrian rights of way are identified by juxtaposition as original inalienable rights which Americans have ceased to protect.

Moreover, Burroughs compares American 'degeneracy' with what he represents as ideal pedestrian conditions in England, transforming England into a democratic prototype along the way. One of the reasons he gives for English people's greater regard for and practice of walking is that they 'have plainer tastes, dress plainer, build plainer, speak plainer, keep closer to facts, wear broader shoes and coarser clothes, and place a lower estimate on themselves' than Americans—in short, are more 'common' and democratic than Americans (36). He tells two stories of the establishment of pedestrian rights-of-way that contribute to this picture of egalitarian England, one involving successful protests against a 'surly nobleman' who wants to close a footpath, and the other describing 'the path that connects Stratford-on-Avon with Shottery, Shake-speare's path when he went courting Anne Hathaway':

By the king's highway the distance is some farther, so there is a well-worn path along the hedgerows and through the meadows and turnip patches. The traveler in it has the privilege of crossing the railroad track, an unusual privilege in England, and one denied to the lord in his carriage, who must either go over or under it.   (34)

This description of the situation clearly identifies the instruments of mechanized transport—the highway, the carriage, the railroad—with the aristocracy and then literally crosses them with pedes-trian privilege. Burroughs has accurately described how walking works to appropriate land, but in the process he has also de-scribed England as a democracy without materialism, where footpaths are never closed and the excesses of the nobility and the railroad-builders are held firmly in check by pedestrian action. He represents all English people, children and women and aristocracy included, as avid walkers with—and he puts it just this way—'big feet' (33). And, of course, he mentions Dickens as well as Shake-speare, tying two prime voices of English letters to the love of walking.

In this way, despite his apparent apprehension of the material origins of peripatetic values, Burroughs implies that what he perceives as American antipathy to walking diverges from a prior condition in which walking was naturally revered and universally practised. His location of this condition in England and, for the most part, in his own day mitigates the obscuring effect of such a construction by keeping a relatively small distance between the imagined walker's paradise and the time and place in which peripatetic values developed. But the subtle representation of England as egalitarian increases its attractiveness as a model for American society, while at the same time dehistoricizing English pedestrian practice. The introduction of Shakespeare's path con-firms this dehistoricization, extending ideal English pedestrianism into a hazy, semi-mythological golden age of the arts (including, of course, the art of walking).

Thoreau, too, implies that walking has declined from its ori-ginal practice. True pilgrims to the Holy Land establish a standard to which modern excursive walkers, 'faint-hearted crusaders' that they are, do not measure up. Thoreau speaks of imagining himself a knight 'of a new, or rather an old, order,—not Equestrians or Chevaliers, not Ritters or Riders, but Walkers, a still more ancient and honorable class' (206). And in this class he enrols not only himself but 'the old prophets and poets, Menu, Moses, Homer, Chaucer', who walked in a pathless nature Thoreau re-creates by avoiding roads (214). Thus Thoreau transforms his own true walking, with its obvious debt to Wordsworthian peripatetic and equally obvious expression of a peculiarly American obsession with frontiers, into a perennial form that pre-dates chivalry and crusading and biblical scripture and classical literature.

This process of dehistoricization, universal to peripatetic theorists after Hazlitt, derives logically from the representational strategies of both pre- and post-Wordsworthian texts. At the time when essayists begin to codify selected values of Wordsworthian peripatetic, there are no material histories of walking which might overtly contradict their extension of these values into the past.[37] The old interpretation of walking as dangerous wandering cannot easily be traced in pre-Wordsworthian texts, which suppress the problematic material process of walking by rendering it as true travel or as metaphorical life-journey; nor, given this suppression, is the break in the old interpretation at the beginning of the nineteenth century readily visible. Moreover, the texts which most influentially define the new values assigned to walking, Wordsworth's poems, themselves initiate the extension of this definition back into historical and ideal time. When Wordsworth renovates the reputation of pedlars and identifies the Wanderer with idealized minstrels protected on the road by robbers' recognition of their harps as 'sacred instruments', he not only establishes the socio-economic identity of walking as enriching, stabilizing labour by obscuring walking's older identity as dangerous wandering, but also effaces the role of his own text in constructing such an identity (*Excursion*, I. 327–36, II. 1–26). Disclaiming his own authority in the matter, reconstructing walking as a natural, traditionally venerated mode of moral education, Wordsworth diverts attention from the specific historicity of his

[37] Jusserand's study of medieval wanderers comes as close to a 19th-cent. material history of walking as anything, and does talk about these wanderers as an unrecognized historical force. Clearly, however, Jusserand focuses on wandering rather than its particular mode.

construction. Thus peripatetic theory's account of walking can proceed as an account known and understood from ancient times, intuitively derived from human experiences and natural moral principles, and can assert the positive effects of walking as benefits universally enjoyed by great people in many cultures. Wordsworth becomes just one of these people, one particularly cognizant, perhaps, of the benefits of walking. All textual generation of such values, in fact, recedes into virtual illegibility.

Robert Louis Stevenson's 'Walking Tours' demonstrates this recession of peripatetic values in a highly condensed form. Stevenson follows Hazlitt in his definition of true walking, proposing that walking should be solitary and contemplative, free of impediment (including any too-settled intention, like athletic exertion), so that it becomes 'a reward in itself' (232). He twice quotes Hazlitt on these points, and the second time, after a bit of the 'Give me the clear blue sky' passage, Stevenson says, 'notice how learned [Hazlitt] is . . . in the theory of walking tours' (238). What theory is this, one wonders? In England, at least, Hazlitt appears to be the first essayist to advance anything like an explicit theory of walking tours, and yet Stevenson speaks of Hazlitt's ideas as if they were particularly eloquent expressions of accepted concepts. This impression is heightened, I think, by Stevenson's later injunction to the walker to carry no timepiece with him: 'You may dally as long as you like by the roadside. It is almost as if the millennium were arrived, when we shall throw our clocks and watches over the housetop, and remember time and seasons no more' (241). True walking becomes literally timeless, an activity unmeasured by any count of years and unbounded by history, a condition of the idyllic past before mechanized time-keeping and of humanity's future redemption.[38]

Clearly this removal of peripatetic from historical time and literary antecedent hardens peripatetic into aesthetic theory by hiding its material origins: if those origins cannot be located, they cannot

[38] At the beginning of 'Walking Tours', Stevenson actually rejects the notion that walking offers a superior perspective for the viewing of landscape. In 'Roads', however, he argues for winding roads and natural footpaths on the grounds that they limit the traveller's view, developing anticipation by continuous but successive perceptions of the landscape (in *Essays of Travel and in the Art of Writing*, Biographical Edition (New York: Charles Scribner's Sons, 1905), 98–107).

be examined and perhaps challenged. This is one of the reasons Wordsworthian peripatetic has remained unrecognized. Readings of walking in literary texts would reveal and possibly undermine the assertions upon which peripatetic itself rests—Wordsworth's rhetorical smoothing of wandering into placement, for instance, and the hypothetical continuity of nature, humanity, and divinity that permits walking to act as a physical recovery of moral value. Peripatetic theory encourages us to see walking as text and text as walking by its rambling narrative structures and examples of pedestrian composition without acknowledging literature's representations of walking. Thus readers of peripatetic remain unable to perceive the significance of walking in literary texts and unaware of how their expectations of walking's effects are generated.

Moreover, as peripatetic theory's account of its origins becomes ahistorical, the community of walkers figured in the Wanderer, Wordsworth's fusion of vagrant and poet, begins to split into two separate classes. More specifically, the common walker virtually disappears, leaving the scholar/philosopher in apparent possession of the road. Burroughs, whose walkers' paradise is decidedly democratic, writes of the walker being 'on the common level', and happily imagines meeting all sorts of tramps as he walks. But although Stevenson speaks eloquently of common pleasures and plain living, he devotes a single sharp phrase to distinguishing the 'strange mechanical bearing of the common tramp' from the demeanour of the poet-walker who goes along 'talking, laughing, and gesticulating to himself . . . composing articles, delivering orations, and conducting the most impassioned interviews, by the way' (237, 236). This estrangement of tramp from poet also operates to solidify the assertions of peripatetic theory by making the most subversive socio-economic claim for Wordsworth's excursive walking, the connection and equalization of the labouring and educated classes, far less visible.

Near the beginning of 'In Praise of Walking', Leslie Stephen speaks jokingly of an eccentric German innkeeper who looks at Stephen, who has just finished a thirty-mile hike and is still in his tramping clothes, 'as possibly a capitalist in (very deep) disguise'.[39]

---

[39] Stephen, 'In Praise of Walking', 260. Further quotations from this essay will be cited in the text by page number.

But the disguise is not very deep at all. The closest we come to seeing a common pedestrian in this essay is 'a kind of scholar-gipsy of the fens' whose family pays up his public-house bills rather than trusting him with money. Even he is no Old Cumberland Beggar, however, or even a poet-pedlar, but a leisured 'gentleman' who composes poetry and quotes it to those he meets on the towpath (fortunately Stephen claims to have forgotten it all) (273). Indeed, Stephen's real project seems to be not disguising the wealthy as vagrants, but disguising walkers as gentlemen-scholars.

For instance, Stephen worries that the 'professional pedestrian'—that is, one who might get paid for his pedestrian labours—may develop his skills because of 'vanity' and 'lower motives which may lead to [walking's] degeneration' (256, 255). 'The true walker', he says, is 'one to whom the pursuit is in itself delightful; who is not indeed priggish enough to be above a certain complacency in the physical prowess required for his pursuit, but to whom the muscular effort of the legs is subsidiary to the "cerebration" stimulated by the effort . . . the true pedestrian loves walking because, so far from distracting his mind, it is favourable to the equable and abundant flow of tranquil and half-conscious medi-tation' (256). Although Stephen does not reject physical process completely, he clearly subordinates it to the mental experiences of the walker. The intellectual work becomes the highest labour of the pedestrian. Even that, indeed, is described as 'tranquil and half-conscious', essentially without effort, so that the Wordsworthian identification of walking as labour recedes into the leisure of 'meditation'.

Stephen none the less claims the aesthetic advantages of success-ive yet continuous pedestrian perspective for his true walker. The *raison d'être* of 'In Praise' is Stephen's desire to recall what parts of his life have been 'well spent', and while he remarks that 'any part in which I thoroughly enjoyed myself' might fall into this category, in fact what he remembers most clearly are 'old walks':

The memories of walks . . . are all localised and dated; they are hitched on to particular times and places; they spontaneously form a kind of calen-dar or connecting thread upon which other memories may be strung. . . . The labour of scribbling books happily leaves no distinct im-pression, and I would forget that it had ever been undergone; but the picture of some delightful ramble includes incidentally a reference to the nightmare of literary toil from which it relieved me. The author is but the accidental appendage of the tramp. My days are bound each to each not by 'natural piety' (or not, let me say, by natural piety alone) but by pedestrian enthusiasm. (254, 257–8)

Stephen thus makes walking the agent of most vivid impression and most ready recollection, its memorial records overriding others 'of incomparably greater instrinsic value' because those more valuable memories 'coalesce into wholes' (257). Walking, however, places and dates events, connecting them and yet maintaining their distinctness and the order of their succession. More specifically, the 'memories of old walks' do this to themselves 'spontaneously', suggesting an effortless assimilation quite different from, and preferred to, the 'labour of scribbling books'. Stephen claims, in fact, that the memorial narratives he makes by walking supersede the narratives he makes by writing and implicitly supersede others' written texts too, as the subordination of Wordsworth's phrase to Stephen's suggests. 'The author is but the accidental appendage of the tramp' thus carries several senses: walking preserves writing, making the process of writing recallable (the literal meaning in context); the author arises from the tramp, writing from walking; writing is less important than walking, being a merely 'accidental' effect.

Stephen's validation of walking actually depends to a certain extent upon the opposite logical construction—that is, he gives walking value by comparing it to writing, which his readers 'know' is important: 'Walking tours . . . play in one's personal recollections the part of those historical passages in which Carlyle is an unequalled master; the little islands of light in the midst of the darkening gloom of the past . . . walks are the unobtrusive connecting thread of other memories, and yet each walk is a little drama in itself, with a definite plot with episodes and catastrophes, according to the requirements of Aristotle' (261). Plainly Stephen values walking by its capacity to be like writing, to function in the individual memory as Carlyle's texts do in historical memory, to conform to the requirements of Aristotelian dramatic theory. But then both Carlyle and Aristotle, the first explicitly and the second implicitly in Stephen's invocation of the word 'peripatetic', appear later in the essay as examples of philosophers who walk, so that their pedestrian and literary capacities become inextricably tangled. Stephen concludes a description of Carlyle's walk from Glasgow to Drumclog with Washington Irving with these consecutive clauses: 'the next day Carlyle took his longest walk, fifty-four miles. Carlyle is unsurpassable in his descriptions of scenery' (268). The ordered juxtaposition is nearly irresistible: Carlyle walks fifty-four miles in a day; (therefore) Carlyle writes superb descriptions of scenery.

The middle third of 'In Praise', in fact, is given over to continuous repetition of this argument. As Thomas Nugent lists great travellers of the past (some of them mythical) to support his contention that travel is a 'noble and ancient custom' universally understood to improve the traveller,[40] so Stephen unfurls a list of writers and thinkers and spiritual leaders who were also walkers: Shakespeare, Ben Jonson, Will Kemp (whose name Stephen cannot remember), Coryate, Swift, Wesley, Richardson, Samuel Johnson, Wordsworth, De Quincey, Coleridge, Walter Scott, Hobbes, Bentham, James and John Stuart Mill, Carlyle, and Ruskin. This is an odd lot, really, oddly arrayed. Kemp danced his course, while Swift was extremely nervous about travel; Scott appears contrasted with Byron to show what the 'wholesome influence' of 'walking under difficulties' (both men were lame) can do to develop a 'manly nature' (266). The list itself goes back no farther than Elizabethan times, but the variety of its members suggests once again that the effects of walking on writing are universal. Stephen prefaces his list, in fact, with the comment that 'All great men of letters have ... been enthusiastic walkers', and although he adds the parenthetic qualification 'exceptions, of course, excepted', the immediate countering weight of Shakespeare's name (the first in the list) and the gradual effect of some eight pages identifying great writers who were walkers enforces those parentheses, dropping the lightly phrased qualification out of the text (262).

Stephen closes this part of the essay by remarking that these walkers/writers 'have inclined to ignore the true source of their impulse. Even when they speak of the beauties of nature, they would give us to understand that they might have been disembodied spirits, taking aerial flights among mountain solitudes, and independent of the physical machinery of legs and stomachs' (268). Yet he simply dismisses his own recognition of these writers' selection of a determinedly non-pedestrian aesthetic, asserting that

[40] Nugent, *The Grand Tour*, p. xi.

the writers' walking is the 'true source' of their texts. His handling of Wordsworth as walker/writer relies on the same assertion, ascribing the 'literary movement at the end of the eighteenth century'—the development of Romanticism, in short—'in great part, if not mainly, to the renewed practice of walking':

Wordsworth's poetical autobiography shows how every stage in his early mental development was connected with some walk in the Lakes. The sunrise which startled him on a walk after a night spent in dancing first set him apart as a 'dedicated spirit.' His walking tour in the Alps—then a novel performance—roused him to his first considerable poem. His chief performance is the record of an excursion on foot. He kept up the practice ... (265)

At every point in this account walking precedes writing, generates text, while text appears to generate nothing at all, certainly not ideas about the walking it represents. 'Walking' becomes pure aesthetic practice, an a priori cause of certain predictable effects, itself unaffected by time and text.

Thus, when Stephen does show walking functioning as cultivation, he does so only in the extended senses of cultivation and not in Wordsworth's more basic sense of labour. Stephen describes the rambles of two pedestrians who, evading the 'vast octopus arms' of London and moving 'between the great lines of railway', come to a farmhouse where the mistress feeds them lunch and refuses payment. Stephen remarks that her generosity 'suggested an idyllic state of society which, it is true, one must not count upon discovering' (277). Yet these walkers, in fact, do rediscover 'hospitality, the virtue of primitive regions' (277). As the travellers go on from this idyllic place, they make 'time run back for a couple of centuries' in another sense by walking to William Penn's grave, a bench where John Milton sat and discussed *Paradise Regained*, a monument to Captain Cook, and the site of one of George III's stag hunts (278).

In this story walkers connect London and the surrounding countryside, recover ideal rural virtue in the form of hospitality, and relocate English history. But they do not labour at their mediations. Indeed, Stephen tells us, such 'association[s]' should arise 'spontaneously and unobtrusively', not as 'the avowed goal but [as] the accidental addition to the interest of a walk; and it is then pleasant to think of one's ancestors as sharers in the pleasures'

(278–9). No deliberate recollection of past value is intended; no vagrants appear along the way, much less tell their stories; all is accomplished, as by a dilettante, with ease and unintentional elegance.

Along with a few later essays (notably Hilaire Belloc's introduction to *The Footpath Way* (1911) and G. M. Trevelyan's 'Walking' (1913)), these five works have anchored anthologies celebrating walking, from Belloc's, through Mitchell's *The Pleasures of Walking* (1934), to Susman and Goode's *The Magic of Walking* (1967). The stability of peripatetic theory, it seems to me, derives from its careful decontextualization of the expectations generated by Wordsworthian peripatetic, a decontextualization which defuses the most unsettling of those expectations and discourages close examination of the theory's origins. As we shall see, some Victorian literary peripatetics handle the strain in Wordsworth's radically continuous universe with similar suppressions and disappearances. Some, however, confront that strain and explore the possibility of peripatetic failure.

5
Walking at All Risks

HOW conscious Victorian writers were of the specific connection
between Wordsworth's poetry and the essays which work out
peripatetic theory, or of peripatetic as a literary mode, cannot, of
course, be fully known. Certainly Wordsworth was not a past but
a present literary force, continuing to write, revise, and publish
through the early Victorian period: the fifth collected edition of his
Poems appeared in 1836–7 (with an additional volume, *Poems,
Chiefly of Early and Late Years*, published in 1842), to be followed by sixth and seventh editions in 1845 and 1849–50 and by
the posthumous publication of the *Prelude* in July of 1850. Despite the dearth of newly composed peripatetics after 1835—'Airey-
Force Valley' was really the last of Wordsworth's sustained
peripatetics—the poems we have discussed in previous chapters
were repeatedly available as contemporary publications, and the
Prelude, with an extended narrative and symbolic reliance upon
walking rivalled only by the *Excursion*, was new to the general
reading public of 1850. Although Matthew Arnold notes a decline
in Wordsworth's popularity after 'Tennyson's decisive appearance'
in 1842, Arnold also says that by the same year 'the verdict of
posterity . . . had already been pronounced, and Wordsworth's
English fame was secure', his continuing influence publicly marked
by his position as Poet Laureate of England from 1843 until the
end of his life.[1]

On the other hand, these manifestations of Wordsworth's influential position—successive standard editions, critical affirmation,
official political elevation—also suggest the thorough appropriation
of Wordsworth's writings to Victorian uses and the consequent
(I think necessary) unconsciousness of the extent to which
Wordsworthianism suffused Victorian culture. The peripatetic
theorists, who assume prominent features of Wordsworth's redefinition of walking as timeless truths, and represent Wordsworth

[1] Matthew Arnold, 'Wordsworth', in *English Literature and Irish Politics*, ed.
R. H. Super (Ann Arbor: University of Michigan Press, 1973), 36.

himself only as an exemplar of those truths, demonstrate the paradox. Although these essayists make selective use of Wordsworthian peripatetic's claims, they uncritically assimilate those selected claims as normative expectations and appear not merely not to acknowledge, but not to recognize, their specific source. Wordsworth's literary success, the broad dissemination and acceptance of his writings, helped accomplish exactly the effect he promoted: his representations and precepts now seemed 'natural', obvious, not constructed by Wordsworth but fundamental to human experience. Victorian readers, whether reading him in his own voice or in others', pausing perhaps to question certain details, nonetheless passed over much in unconscious approbation. (Only recently, indeed, since Jerome McGann's challenge to our twentieth-century perpetuations of *The Romantic Ideology* (1983), have the extent and significance of the critical and philosophical silences generated by institutionalized Romanticism become clearer.)

Whatever their degree of consciousness about its origins, however, Victorian writers used peripatetic convention fluently, embedding bits of theory and walking episodes in narratives that do not otherwise function as peripatetic, as well as producing full-fledged peripatetic novels and poems. The philosophical essays, as we have seen, uniformly celebrate Wordsworthian walking, asserting that proper peripatetic practice always yields certain salutary results. In peripatetic episodes, the kinds of suppressions practised by the theorists produce similar results: as long as the peripatetic effort remains brief, or can be privatized or aestheticized, it seems to succeed. In sustained peripatetics, however, mediation of the tensions suspended in Wordsworthian peripatetic becomes anxious and forced; walkers retreat toward purely personal resolutions, offering little hope for similar renovation of the world outside self, only to find that their peripatetic efforts fail even in that small sphere. Thus, in Victorian literary peripatetics, the increasingly frequent disappointment of peripatetic expectations maps growing doubt about the writer's, and the reader's, ability effectively to counter the disconnective tendencies of technologized life.

George Eliot and Elizabeth Gaskell introduce walking as a sign or agent of continuity with an imagined English past, a more rural and more communal way of life, at crucial moments in their pastoral (or what I would term pastoral/georgic) and 'industrial' novels, relying on these conventional associations to outline the conflict

between this past and the industrialized present/future, and to
suggest the possibility of some mediation between the two.[2] None
of the three novels I will look at—*Adam Bede* (1859), *Felix Holt*
(1866), and *Mary Barton* (1848)—fully supports the weight of its
brief peripatetic assertions, but by means of these assertions each
still seriously proposes idyllic possibilities. So, too, do the walking
episodes in *David Copperfield* (1849–50) and *Aurora Leigh* (1857),
which outline the recreative possibilities of deliberate life-journeys
in the same brief fashion.

Raymond Williams talks about the general movement toward
such private solutions in George Eliot's novels, and in the 'whole
literary tradition' she 'shaped and trained', as a 'withdrawal from
any full response to an existing society. Value inheres in the past,
as a general retrospective condition, and exists in the present only
as a particular and private sensibility, the individual moral action.'[3]
Interestingly, Williams's supporting analysis focuses on the two
overtly peripatetic commentaries/episodes in *Adam Bede* and *Felix
Holt*, the first novel's narrative aside on the merits of 'Old Leisure', a personification of late eighteenth-century country manners
and mores, and the second's introductory coach-ride through the
English countryside. Reading these passages as peripatetic reveals
both their appeal to excursive action and truncations of that action,
complicating Williams's picture of a retreat into the private.

The 'Old Leisure' section which closes Chapter LII of *Adam Bede*
argues that 'Surely all other leisure is hurry compared with a
sunny walk through the fields from "afternoon church"—as such
walks used to be in those old leisurely times, when the boat,
gliding sleepily along the canal, was the newest locomotive wonder',
and presents Old Leisure himself as a 'contemplative, rather stout
gentleman, of excellent digestion . . . fond of sauntering by the fruit-
tree wall and scenting the apricots when they were warmed by the
morning sunshine'.[4] As Williams says, this digression is 'lightly

---

[2] 'Industrial novel' is Raymond Williams's term for a group of novels 'written
at the middle of the century, which not only provide some of the most vivid
descriptions of life in an unsettled industrial society, but also illustrate certain
common assumptions within which [the response to industrialism] was undertaken' (*Culture and Society, 1780–1950* (New York: Columbia University Press,
1983), 87). Williams includes both *Felix Holt* and *Mary Barton* in this group.

[3] Williams, *Country and City*, 180.

[4] George Eliot, *Adam Bede*, ed. John Paterson (Boston, Mass.: Houghton Mifflin,
1968), 428, 429.

enough written', and disarms itself by gently chiding old and new alike: Old Leisure has 'an easy, jolly conscience, broad-backed like himself', and is not to be judged by 'our modern standard,' for 'He never went to Exeter Hall, or heard a popular preacher, or read *Tracts for the Times* or *Sartor Resartus*'.[5] Moreover, this walking Leisure is, as Williams points out, 'a class figure who can afford to saunter, who has leisure precisely in the sweat of other men's work'.[6] Yet Eliot's irony is not inattentive to these problems of generalized nostalgia—otherwise, obviously, we would perceive no irony—nor does it completely empty the idealization of virtue of its potential value or force. Hetty Sorrel, too, embodies unrealized virtue in a foolish prettiness; her easy thoughtlessness and sensuality open her to narrative criticism; and yet we are plainly directed to experience the loss of the potential good in her as a truly grievous loss.

Moreover, peripatetic proposes that the ideal possibilities of the past can be actuated in the present by the individually willed, connecting action represented by walking. Eliot figures the ideal virtue of the past and its imaginative recovery in a leisurely afternoon walk, a saunter in a sunlit garden, not only in the terms of the digression but in the digression's narrative setting: Adam and Dinah walking out to meet the homecoming churchgoers after Adam's first declaration of love. The lovers must walk together once more before Dinah can pledge herself to Adam and the two can begin to create the peaceful rural community of their family. But such work comes naturally to a hero who 'can walk forty mile a-day', and a heroine who is a sometime itinerant preacher.[7] Adam and Dinah are not leisurely, well-to-do walkers but excursive walkers whose pedestrianism is an everyday part of their labour and love, and who succeed in establishing a self-sufficient, stable home.

I do not disagree with Williams about Eliot's essential withdrawal of value into the past and/or the individual. One sign of this withdrawal, indeed, is that Eliot does not make much more of walking in *Adam Bede* than what I have displayed above; it remains just one element of the broadly pastoral/georgic pattern of the novel, its own renovative tendencies subordinated, in general,

[5] Williams, *Country and City*, 178; Eliot, *Adam Bede*, 429.
[6] Williams, *Country and City*, 178.   [7] Eliot, *Adam Bede*, 15.

to retrospective. But the presence of the peripatetic commentary, its context in Adam and Dinah's full story, and the deeper context of that story in Wordsworthian peripatetic, indicate to me that her withdrawal is complicated by a continuing excursive impulse. By using walking as a recurring reference point by which the ebb and flow of ideal rural life can be measured, Eliot's narrative continues to assert the possibility of some recovery of past value into an 'existing society'.

Felix Holt initially relies upon the same point of reference, although in a curious translation that obscures the physical act of walking. The narrative introduction to the novel sets the story in the mid-1830s, when 'the glory had not yet departed from the old coach-roads':

Posterity may be shot, like a bullet through a tube, by atmospheric pressure from Winchester to Newcastle . . . but the slow old-fashioned way of getting from one end of our country to the other is the better thing to have in the memory. The tube-journey can never lend much to picture and narrative; it is as barren as an exclamatory O! Whereas the happy outside passenger seated on the box from the dawn to the gloaming gathered enough stories of English life, enough of English labours in town and country, enough aspects of earth and sky, to make episodes for a modern Odyssey.[8]

The terms of this assertion are familiar enough: the quality of memory and narrative depend upon the mode of perception, upon speed and position, which is deemed superior, because more intimate and natural, in older, slower modes of transport. Sure enough, when the reader has passed through the following descriptions of English countryside, he finds that although his ideal guide is a coachman, that coachman is none the less a species of pedestrian: '[The coachman] could tell the names of sites and persons, and explain the meaning of groups, as well as the shade of Virgil in a more memorable journey; he had as many stories about parishes, and the men and women in them, as the Wanderer in the "Excursion," only his style was different' (9). Naturally his style would be different, since he travels in a different way; naturally,

---

[8] George Eliot, *Felix Holt, the Radical*, ed. Fred C. Thomson (Oxford: Clarendon Press, 1980), 5. Following quotations from *Felix Holt* will be cited in the text by page number.

too, the proper points of reference for assessing the coachman's perspective are Dante's Virgil and Wordsworth's Wanderer, poet-walkers both. Even from the vantage-point of a coach, apparently, pedestrian perception and expression form the baseline from which memorial and narrative excellence are measured. And when the imagined outrider sees for us, he sees the alternation of 'trim cheerful villages' with the dirt and smoke of the new manufacturing towns not so much with a sense of rushing change as with a sense of the old agrarian ways preserved, 'as if Time itself were pausing': 'The busy scenes of the shuttle and the wheel, of the roaring furnace, of the shaft and the pulley, seemed to make but crowded nests in the midst of the large-spaced, slow-moving life of homesteads and far-away cottages and oak-sheltered parks' (7, 8). This is five-and-thirty years ago, to be sure, and yet the rural life is preserved, the industrial contained, in the memory and narrative of Eliot's outrider-Wanderer.

Williams speaks of this introduction as showing 'even more clearly [than the 'Old Leisure' digression] the structure of feeling which was being laid over the country': by 'placing' both industrialization and labour unrest 'after the country idyll', Williams suggests, Eliot essentially devalues both 'suffering and, crucially . . . protest against suffering'.[9] But I would lay stress equally on both acts of placing, recomplicating the processes of overlaying and containing which I think Williams tends to simplify into a kind of bourgeois domination by idealization. As the coachman's perspective depends upon the pedestrian's, so the placement of labour unrest 'after' country idyll depends upon the placement of industrialization itself after that idyll. That is, by invoking peripatetic, Eliot necessarily invokes the containment of a dominant industrial economic system by the action of the poor labourer, rural or otherwise. That her 'walker' is a coachman speaks to Williams's point, and there is no doubt that this transformation indicates a growing discomfort with the socio-economic implications of renovative peripatetic action, the potential metaphorical equivalent of labour unrest; but that her coachman sees with pedestrian eyes suggests an appeal to that action which once again asserts the possibility of recovering older rural perceptions and values into the industrialized world by means specifically identified with labour and poverty.

[9] Williams, *Country and City*, 178, 179, 180.

The unmediated peripatetic at the beginning of Gaskell's *Mary Barton* makes this appeal directly. Opening with an epigraph identified as a 'Manchester Song' (probably written by Gaskell's husband for the novel) which sets the hardships of factory labour against a family's holiday ramble through the fields, the first chapter then describes '"Green Heys Fields," through which runs a public footpath to a little village about two miles distant'.[10] The real emphasis of this description falls on the path: what we see we see from the path, both in the early general rendering of the fields as enjoyed by workers from the city (who get there by walking on the path) and in the later detailed look at 'the charm of one particular stile' (2). Moreover, although the epigraph seems to set up a Clare-like opposition between work and the leisure of walking, the recreative value of Green Heys Fields resides to a great extent in the remnants of old rural labours, 'of other times and other occupations', which the Fields still harbour: 'Here in their seasons may be seen the country business of hay-making, ploughing, etc., which are such pleasant mysteries for townspeople to watch, and here the artisan, deafened with noise of tongues and engines', can hear instead the sounds of georgic industry, 'the lowing of cattle, the milkmaid's call, the clatter and cackle of poultry in the old farmyards' (1–2). At the stile, too, along with the semi-natural beauties of a pond and trees and flowers, the walkers see a farmhouse, a farmyard, and a garden of medicinal herbs and flowers now 'allowed to grow in scrambling and wild luxuriance' (2). Walking the footpath through Green Heys Fields restores the workers not only through relaxed, leisurely wandering and the appreciation of natural beauty, but through contact with cultivating labours, some ongoing, some (like the apparently abandoned farm garden) charmingly decayed. Past or present, the 'pleasant mysteries' of cultivation become available to Manchester's workers by means of walking the footpath.

Of course, this passage is idealized. We are reading, after all, an expression of ideas, of values: 'nature', 'labour', 'cultivation'. But this idealization not only imposes upper-middle-class values upon a working-class world, seeking to abate or contain the force of

---

[10] Elizabeth Gaskell, *Mary Barton*, ed. Edgar Wright (Oxford and New York: Oxford University Press, 1987), 1. Further quotations from *Mary Barton* will be cited in the text by page number.

labour unrest with pretty pictures of a light that never was (and I do grant that as an unvoiced part of its project). Because it is framed as peripatetic, it also promotes unrest, action, wandering, by representing labourers as potential transformers of their material world. Gaskell's labouring walkers, not red-cheeked rustics but sallow and bony, intelligent and restive, recreate themselves in a way which *labourers* saw as a real mitigation of the hardships of industrialized life (and if we have any doubt of that we can return to the statistics on holiday tickets that carried workers into the countryside). Peripatetic functions precisely to advocate material action that will realize the ideal; its fundamental metaphor insists, moreover, that such action, if carried forward by middle- and upper-class scholars, arises from the labouring classes; and the writer who uses the convention carries all that baggage, willingly or no, into her work. Recognizing the appearance, or absence, or degree of truncation of peripatetic thus becomes of some importance to a full and sufficiently complex assessment of a text's attitude toward industrialization.

Eliot and Gaskell deliberately appeal to peripatetic precisely because it does carry such baggage and so can both set the terms of the conflict between old and new, rural and industrial, and suggest that some mediation of the two can be imagined. Yet equally obviously they are not entirely comfortable with all that even their brief reliance on the convention implies. Eliot distances pedestrian action in various ways, through irony, temporal distance, and that odd substitution of coach-rider for walker, and in *Felix Holt* indeed retreats into private rather than public resolution. Gaskell seems both more hopeful and less afraid of the economic implications of her walking labourers, but her novel finally relies on one of Dickens's favourite methods of resolving thorny social problems: she has Mary and Jem emigrate, giving them that pastoral retreat they seek but apparently cannot find in England. These novels do not wholeheartedly demonstrate that resolution—*that* resolution, in the terms of mediative renovation—implied in their appeals to peripatetic convention.[11]

[11] Deirdre David describes these endgames, in which 'the tension between representation of social actuality and desire for difference is mythically resolved', as 'fictions of resolution'. See her *Fictions of Resolution in Three Victorian Novels: 'North and South', 'Our Mutual Friend' and 'Daniel Deronda'* (New York: Columbia University Press, 1981).

Wordsworthian peripatetic is, after all, a *concordia discors* designed to integrate and solve opposites, and response to the full range of its implied demands for such resolution, ongoing textual faith in the recovery of personal and national origins and values by everyday material means, proves extremely difficult for Victorian writers to maintain. The area of greatest difficulty does seem to be resolution of economic, particularly class, differences: when Victorian writers use peripatetic episodes rapidly to sketch individual development and renovation, emphasizing the life-journey aspect of the convention rather than its socio-economic aspect, they seem much less uncomfortable than Eliot and Gaskell. David Copperfield's walk from London to Dover, through which he escapes the meanness of a future with Murdstone and Grinby and makes a new life out of old connections, functions in this way, as a condensed life-journey which shows the walker successfully renovating his life by returning to his origins—in this case, to the last living connection with his mother and father, Betsey Trotwood. The long penniless wandering itself pronounces the reality and dangers of class distinction, as David's beggary threatens to keep him from his goal. But he succeeds in walking back into the class of gentleman, and as soon as he gains his aunt's house, his economic movement returns to its place as one part of an effort of self-making that includes artistic, moral, and emotional movements of at least equal importance. Because Dickens mutes walking's economic implications in this way, I think, his peripatetic episode seems more fully realized in his novel's progress than Eliot's and Gaskell's brief uses of the convention are in theirs.

A similar episode occurs in the second book of *Aurora Leigh* (1857), where, as Ellen Moers indicates, Elizabeth Barrett Browning figures Aurora Leigh's artistic sensibilities and her determination to develop them in Aurora's independent walking.[12] Aurora's early obedience to her demanding aunt, during which she 'walked

---

[12] I am indebted to Moers for her extremely suggestive discussion of 'Traveling Heroinism: Gothic for Heroines' in her book *Literary Women* (New York: Oxford University Press, 1977). She opens her brief comments on Aurora Leigh with the remark that '[a] whole history of literary feminism might be told in terms of the metaphor of walking' (p. 130)—a remark I hope to expand upon someday. For a current example of the possibilities, see 'A Dialogue of Self and Soul: Plain Jane's Progress', in Sandra M. Gilbert and Susan Gubar, *The Madwoman in the Attic* (New Haven, Conn. and London: Yale University Press, 1979), 336–71.

| Demurely in [the aunt's] carpeted low rooms',[13] gives way in time to a need to

> escape
> As a soul from the body, out of doors,
> Glide through the shrubberies, drop into the lane,
> And wander on the hills an hour or two,
> Then back again before the house should stir.   (I. 693–7)

The second book opens with such a walk on the morning of Aurora's twentieth birthday as she contemplates herself 'Woman and artist,—either incomplete, | Both credulous of completion' (II. 4–5). In this mood of memory and resolution, rejecting bay as overweening and myrtle, 'which means chiefly love', she crowns herself with ivy as a sign and promise of her potential poetic achievement, but is surprised in the act by her disapproving cousin and suitor Romney, who regards her seriousness about poetry as dangerous (II. 40).

In the conversations on art and love and sexual identity which follow, first with Romney and then with her aunt, Aurora returns again and again to walking as an emblem of her commitment to her work. Unlike Jane Austen's Elizabeth Bennet, whose walking is immediately ratified by Mr Darcy as a sign of her true gentility and functions as a path toward marriage, Aurora must vigorously defend her pedestrian practice and the vocation it asserts. When Romney advises her to keep her aspirations in bounds since 'even dreaming' of great or lasting fame 'Brings headaches, pretty cousin, and defiles | The clean white morning dresses' (II. 94–6), she vehemently replies:

> I would rather take my part
> With God's Dead, who afford to walk in white
> Yet spread His glory, than keep quiet here
> And gather up my feet from even a step
> For fear to soil my gown in so much dust.
> I choose to walk at all risks.   (II. 101–6)

Again, when her aunt chides her for not accepting Romney's proposal, Aurora responds, 'But I am born . . . | To walk another way

---

[13] Elizabeth Barrett Browning, *Aurora Leigh and Other Poems*, introd. Cora Kaplan (London: The Women's Press, 1978), Book I, lines 488–9. Further quotations from Barrett Browning will be cited in the text by book and line numbers.

than his' (II. 580–1). Her aunt takes up the metaphor, first attack-
ing her as no more capable of walking unaided than 'A babe at
thirteen months', and then asking if Aurora thinks herself 'rich
and free to choose a way to walk' (II. 582, 588). This turn of phrase
sets out explicitly, and for the first time, the economic dimension
of the figure Aurora conceives in spiritual and artistic terms:
Aurora's insistence on walking means that she insists on choice,
independence, and freedom, in the economic as well as the personal sphere. Admirable goals, one might suppose—but of course
Aurora is a woman and, as we would expect, given the special
stigma attached to women wanderers, both Romney and her aunt
make it quite clear that her desires for walking, artistry, and an
independent life are as unladylike as a soiled dress. At the end of
the second book Romney is still trying (with consciously noble
intentions, it is true) to support Aurora with his money and to
convince her not to labour at poetry, both of which proposals she
firmly rejects.

Although Barrett Browning does not sustain her peripatetic, it
does provide the crucial terms of Aurora's consecration to poetry
and her rejection of economic dependence. By not sustaining it, in
fact, Barrett Browning partially isolates the episode from the poem's
later socio-economic concerns: Romney's involvement with Marian,
the sacking of Leigh Hall, the whole question of the efficacy of
social action. Like her protagonist, the author cannot completely
avoid mention of the economic implications of peripatetic; the
convention's linkage of walking and art and labour does not permit
evasion of the materiality of 'making a living'. But Barrett Browning
can and does insist most strongly on the personal, spiritual dimension of the figure, retaining its material force but limiting it to
a small rhetorical space within which it can then function as full
Wordsworthian peripatetic.

In such brief episodes, especially when the life-journey aspect
of peripatetic is emphasized, the suppression of the uneasiness
generated by the convention's demand for mediation and continuity remains relatively subtle. In a sustained peripatetic like
George Meredith's The Egoist (1879), however, any truncation
of the mode's mediative project becomes more palpable and more
disturbing.

Meredith was one of Leslie Stephen's Sunday Tramps, and his
version of the Wanderer reflects Meredith's own participation in

that athletic, intermittent, theoretical brand of walking and writing. Vernon Whitfield is a 'lean long-walking scholar' with little admixture of gypsy and little, if any, aimless roaming in him. He measures his walks by time rather than distance or landmarks— 'nine and a half hours today'—and mostly takes them for quite distinct purposes, as part of his training for Alpine climbing, or to 'walk off [his] temper' or his fancy.[14] As he says to Clara Middleton, 'the secret of good work' is 'to plod on and still keep the passion fresh'; and when she counters, 'Yes, when we have an aim in view,' he responds, 'We always have one' (158).

From the beginning of the novel, both in narrative voice and in the commentary of his other characters, Meredith presents this intent pedestrianism as the primary signifier of Vernon's virtues, rhetorically inseparable from his intellectual accomplishments and sympathetic if unsociable disposition. In fact Meredith characterizes each of his prime players by pedestrian attitudes or images. The astute Mrs Mountstuart's 'word' on Willoughby Patterne is that 'he has a leg'—as the narrative voice continues, 'the leg of the born cavalier', formed for dancing and riding and dalliance (although poor Willoughby 'has the leg without the naughtiness') and not for the 'leg-work' of less aristocratic mortals (44, 45). Predictably, he finds pedestrianism 'a sour business', and loves to see Vernon on horseback, where the scholar is at a noticeable disadvantage (62). Both Laetitia Dale and Clara, on the other hand, prefer walking to riding—although, it must be noted, theirs are for the most part the companionable, ambling walks permitted ladies. Young Crossjay is astonished when Clara shows talent for 'hare and hounds', and both Laetitia and Willoughby take Clara to task when she walks alone, the genuine basis of their shock obviously embodied in Clara's eventual pedestrian flight from Willoughby's house (206, 218). Even Vernon, in admiring Clara's pedestrian ability, 'groan[s] to think that of all the girls of the earth this one should have been chosen for the position of fine lady' (157).

Meredith himself succumbs at times to this exclusion of women from the league of walkers, describing Clara's gait as 'glid[ing]

[14] George Meredith, *The Egoist*, ed. George Woodcock (Harmondsworth: Penguin, 1968), 42, 109, 156–7). Further quotations from Meredith's *Egoist* will be cited in the text by page number.

along easily' or (as she runs with Crossjay) 'as though a hundred little feet were bearing her onward smooth as water over the lawn and the sweeps of grass of the park, so swiftly did the hidden pair multiply one another to speed her' (157, 104). Despite such precious description, which makes Clara seem as limbless as a skirted piano, the morning when Clara sets out on foot to escape her unhappy engagement to Willoughby constitutes the dramatic climax of the novel: the crisis of Clara's character, the measure of Vernon and Willoughby's capacities for sympathy and action, the test even of Crossjay's loyalty and common sense. Although we are told at one point, and through no less interested a perspective than Clara's, that Vernon's 'pedestrian vigour . . . means one who walks away from the sex', his literal pursuit of Clara when she flees Patterne Hall succeeds in rescuing her both physically and psychologically, throwing everything into a state of confrontation that eventually resolves into his own successful bid for Clara's heart, precisely because of his extraordinary skill and speed at walking (111).

With the characters thus aligned into walking and non-walking nations, and with the central conflicts of the novel—those within Clara, and the more externalized social struggle between Willoughby and Vernon—embodied and resolved in walking, that action becomes the concrete metaphorical term in *The Egoist*. Non-walking *is* egoism, humourlessness, self-satisfaction, lack of exertion and sympathy, all the voids of Willoughby's character. And although Vernon is indeed an ascetic Apollo, stiff and graceless and difficult at times, his mindful, striving, spare yet loving character promises a different future, 'a new kind of thing' standing—or walking—against Willoughby's eternal 'English gentleman' (58). Meredith's title might, with some truth, have run *The Egoist and the Pedestrian*.

Meredith sustains his peripatetic, using walking as action and plot and metaphor and narrative and symbol, with an optimism quite comparable to that of Wordsworth's *Excursion*. But the optimism depends, I think, on the suppression of the more radical social and economic effects asserted by Wordsworthian peripatetic. *The Egoist* takes place in an Austenish world of country houses—more than Austenish, indeed, for despite Williams's depreciating comment that Austen's 'country is weather or a place for a walk', her walks at least strike out across fields and take to public roads.[15] Vernon may walk such ways but we do not see him. With the exception of the path to the village, all the walks we read are within Patterne Park or the house gardens. Clara complains, in fact, that 'The prettiness' of her walks 'is overwhelming . . . I would rather have fields, commons.' And when Laetitia defends the 'delightful green walks' of private parks, Clara responds that such things are good 'If there is a right-of-way for the public':

I chafe at restraint: hedges and palings everywhere! I should have to travel ten years to sit down contented among these fortifications. Of course I can read of this rich kind of English country with pleasure in poetry. But it seems to me to require poetry. (199–200)

Much of Clara's sense of restraint comes from her special status as a woman walker and yet the terms of her complaint suggest that the walking in the world of this novel does not unenclose land, that rights of way are not continually reasserted by pedestrian action, that the barriers isolating Patterne Hall remain in place because walking is not sufficiently 'travel' to break them down. Even the renovating perception of rural life and cultivation thins to a poetic appreciation of natural beauty—if we hear Clara's objection, to a very limited poetry at that.

The intensity of Clara and Vernon's long rainy walk, indeed, reflects the fact that the path they follow is the only public path in the novel, the only connection between private English walks and the railroad, the only place where Vernon can meet a tramp to put him on the right track. Only along this single line does pedestrian action materially, if briefly, connect Willoughby's old England with industrialization, with the wandering poor, with the movement and change and struggle that is Vernon's new England; beyond this path, enveloping the sharp contacts of excursive walking, is the cotton wool of Patterne Hall and its private walks— hundreds of pages of cotton wool, indeed, on each side of the crucially public path. Despite Meredith's rhetorical emphasis on laborious, aimful walking, he mutes the mediation of old and new, country and city, private and public such walking conventionally accomplishes to an astonishing extent—hence, I think, the purity of light and laughter and genuine comedy in this peripatetic.

Matthew Arnold's peripatetics, on the other hand, insist on the effectuality of connective pedestrian labour with a desperate

[15] Williams, *Country and City*, 166.

fervour that seems itself a sign of the strain in the mode. Arnold's literary and experiential roots in walking were a good deal less distant and Victorianized than Meredith's, for Arnold met Wordsworth in 1831 when he was 9, lived in Wordsworth's old residence, Allan Bank, the summer he was 11, and after the Arnolds opened Fox How, near Loughrigg Fell, as their holiday home in 1834, had continuing contact with the older poet until Wordsworth's death in 1850.[16] And Arnold spent a good deal of time, both as a boy and as a man, walking in the same locale that Wordsworth had for so many years been walking in and writing about, sometimes walking with Wordsworth himself, and sometimes discussing and reciting poetry with others.[17]

For Arnold, indeed, the physical act of walking may have had more significance than it did for Wordsworth, not only because Arnold had Wordsworth's poetry working in him and so providing an implicit ideological construct for its meaning, but because Arnold suffered with a crooked, steel-braced leg at the very time when he would have been learning to toddle. Park Honan suggests that the trials 'of being clamped into irons in a family of romping children and of needing years afterward to learn to walk properly' contributed significantly to Arnold's 'strenuous exertion in maturity, his lethally effective critical manner, and his deep, fierce pride'.[18] Certainly Arnold's poetry often associates walking not merely with labour but with heroic exertion, presenting the walker or mountain climber as moral and intellectual guide, even as saviour. In 'Rugby Chapel', for example, those not content thoughtlessly to 'eat and drink, | Chatter and love and hate, | Gather and squander', are described as those who

> have chosen our path—
> Path to a clear-purposed goal,
> Path of advance!—but it leads
> A long steep journey, through sunk
> Gorges, o'er mountains in snow.[19]

---

[16] I have drawn my information on Arnold's association with Wordsworth and other aspects of Arnold's life from Park Honan's *Matthew Arnold* (New York: McGraw-Hill, 1981). See esp. pp. 23–5, 38–9, and 95–7.

[17] Ibid. 39, 104.   [18] Ibid. 92, 12.

[19] Matthew Arnold, 'Rugby Chapel', in *Matthew Arnold*, ed. Miriam Allott and Robert H. Super (Oxford and New York: Oxford University Press, 1986), lines 61–3, 84–8. All quotations from Arnold's poetry are drawn from this edition, and are cited in the text by title and line numbers.

In this already select and striving company Thomas Arnold appears as one of the very few who will turn back to comfort and assist others toward the final goal, a 'faithful shepherd' to whom 'it was given | Many to save with thyself' (143, 140–1). In the presence of such guides, 'the host of mankind, | A feeble, wavering line' of wanderers long lost in the wilderness, re-form their ranks,

> Strengthen the wavering line,
> Stablish, continue our march,
> On, to the bound of the waste,
> On, to the City of God.   (205–8)

Although a touch less grandiose in its terms, Arnold's 'Epilogue to Lessing's "Laocoon"', too, pictures the mass of humanity as wandering, in the bad old sense of being aimless and lost, in the wilderness of life. As the speaker of the poem walks through Hyde Park with a friend, debating the relation of painting and the other arts to poetry, he represents the guide and saviour of this lost tribe as a pedestrian-poet like himself. Unlike painters or musicians, the speaker argues, the poet cannot merely express the impulses of a moment but 'must life's *movement* tell' (140),

> Its pain and pleasure, rest and strife;
> His eye must travel down, at full,
> The long, unpausing spectacle
>   .   .   .   .
> From change to change and year to year.   (144–6, 149)

Like Schiller's writer of idyll, Arnold's poet must somehow 'tell' movement and change without losing his own stability, and to the end of stabilizing his culture; and, as in Wordsworth's poetry, peripatetic action represents the successful solution of change and stability. Those whom 'Life's movement fascinates, controls' remain, for the most part, lost in the wilderness 'In pain, in terror, in distress', unable to perceive or represent the flow of life with any accuracy because they cannot stabilize transient value (164, 175). 'Only a few'—the poets, the speaker of this poem—'the life-stream's shore | With safe unwandering feet explore', expressing what they see of life's changes with such 'pathos' and 'power' that their words encourage and comfort 'their thankful race' (188–9, 200, 207). In short, these few walk truly, wander without wandering, engage in excursus that incorporates both departure and return, both movement and stability.

Arnold most memorably represents the unwandering wanderer as the Scholar-Gipsy, whose presence links two poems. 'The Scholar-Gipsy' itself retells a story from Joseph Glanvill's *The Vanity of Dogmatising* (1661) about an Oxford student who, becoming too poor to continue his studies, joins a band of gypsies and becomes an adherent of their traditional knowledge. Arnold transforms this tale into Wordsworthian peripatetic by setting it in a georgic frame and by granting the Scholar-Gipsy eternal life so that, like a supernatural version of the Wanderer, he continues to walk the paths near Oxford long after he could be presumed to have died. The poem opens with an address to a shepherd apparently returning to his work after a brief rest, admonishing him to 'Come . . . and again begin the quest' once 'the fields are still, | And the tired men and dogs all gone to rest' (10, 7–8). The speaker himself is resting in a shaded corner of a 'high, half-reaped field', 'where the reaper was at work of late', looking down on Oxford and reading Glanvill (21, 11). The 'quest' thus allied with cultivation, interrupted but to be taken up again, appears to be both the quest for and the quest of the Scholar-Gipsy, and although the specific shepherd of the invocation vanishes into a more generalized listener, the procession of rural and scholarly labourers and wanderers who glimpse the Scholar-Gipsy maintain the parallels among the herders' and reapers' labours, the poet-speaker's searching and speaking, and the Scholar-Gipsy's own single-minded pursuit of the full extent of the gypsies' learning and art.

It is indeed the focused and singular will of the Scholar-Gipsy that keeps him immune to 'this strange disease of modern life, | With its sick hurry, its divided aims', and so preserves him: 'Thou hadst *one* aim, *one* business, *one* desire; | Else wert thou long since number'd with the dead!' (203–5, 152–3). He expresses that will through continued pedestrian wandering, which then becomes both agent and emblem of his saving dedication to knowledge:

Thou through the fields and through the woods dost stray,
Roaming the country-side, a truant boy,
Nursing thy project in unclouded joy,
And every doubt long blown by time away.   (197–200)

'Stray', 'roaming', and 'truant' imply aimlessness or unlawfulness, and so seem to identify the Scholar-Gipsy as a wanderer in the old sense. Immediately, however, we read not only his aim—to 'nurse his project'—but his steadfast, undoubting pursuit of that aim, an unwandering wandering indeed. For the speaker, the Scholar-Gipsy's pursuit has become his goal, the preserving, knowing action that counteracts the fevers of speed and uncertainty and divided hearts, and that must be continued: 'fly our paths', the speaker warns, urging the Scholar-Gipsy to follow his 'free, onward impulse' away from all contact with the modern infection.

In 'Thyrsis', in fact, although the speaker obviously regards the Scholar-Gipsy's survival as crucial to the success of his own elegiac work, he must trace that survival through an intermediary sign, the 'signal-elm' which the speaker and Thyrsis associated with the mythical wanderer: 'while it stood, we said, | Our friend, the Gipsy-Scholar, was not dead; | While the tree lived, he in these fields lived on' (14, 28–30). This intervention intensifies both the extremities and the fusion of unwandering and wandering originally represented by the Scholar-Gipsy alone. On one hand, the Scholar-Gipsy disappears into the forest, 'out of the heed of mortals', so that his wandering does indeed seem to have successfully taken him away into survival, away from all those maidens and shepherds and scholars and housewives who glimpsed him before (208). On the other hand, he has metaphorically taken root, has become the forest, so that he can now easily be seen as a single, stable, unmoving object which *means* 'wandering'. The speaker himself moves very deliberately toward this sign, anxiously checking landmarks against memory, a bit uncertain about the way, wandering but successfully directed. And when the speaker finally sees the tree, he reads not only the Scholar-Gipsy's survival but that of his friend Thyrsis, now bodilessly mobile in death and rooted in the grave, whose voice the speaker's quest recovers and preserves as a help 'To chase fatigue and fear': '*Roam on! The light we sought is shining still.* | . . . *Our tree yet crowns the hill,* | *Our Scholar travels yet the loved hill-side*' (236, 238–40). The aim of wandering is wandering itself, the courage to wander, the purpose of wandering, from which derive the forms and rewards of the poem itself. By unwandering wandering, by excursive walking, 'Thyrsis' recovers the specific landscape of a physical path, at least partly imagined but actualized by successive detail, changed but continuous in memory, and so recovers the associated memorial path, reviving youth, friendship, the poetic impulse, images of rural labour and leisure.

Yet peripatetic survives in Arnold's poetry under obvious strain. Perhaps the clearest sign of this is the rhetorical shift from the 'Wanderer' to the 'Scholar-Gipsy'. Wordsworth's Wanderer is scholar and pedlar, wandering and unwandering in one. Only one name names all: walker, thinker, vagrant, poet, pedlar, priest. As the pressures which engendered this unity grow, however, they unknit it. Now there are two terms, scholar and gypsy, tenuously joined by a thin line; now the Scholar-Gipsy becomes the unseen moving spirit, bodiless and unapproachable, and the signal-elm— two parts, each signing the other but no longer whole, and neither visibly walking. Arnold forces his anxiety, the sense of strain in his heroic walkers and of uncertainty and fear of change in the speakers of 'The Scholar-Gipsy' and 'Thyrsis', toward Wordsworthian assertions of success, but there is no ease, little sense of that 'soothing voice' and 'healing power' for which Arnold praises Wordsworth's poetry ('Memorial Verses, April 1850', 35, 63).

What I read here is a struggle to keep Wordsworth's Wanderer on his unwandering path, as the poet peels away from the vagrant. On Victorian literary roads we find not Wordsworth's philosophical beggars but scholars *and* gypsies, Vernon and the tramp, a population once again gaping in the middle and vacant at the top; we find walking not as a universal or universalizing choice but as the resource of a second restricted class, defined in this case by special understanding. Because of Wordsworthian peripatetic, we know this gap symbolizes economic, temporal, personal, and artistic gaps, suggesting a loss of confidence in the possibility of shaping material change, and in artistic ability to imagine such beneficial shaping. In many of the texts discussed above, as we have seen, the walker struggles to keep whole and directed, and to keep his world so. In the works of Dickens and Hardy this struggle intensifies: although their pedestrians retain their belief in Wordsworthian walking, the effort toward continuity produces mixed or negligible or even destructive effects, suggesting that even intentional, aimful walkers wander.

In Dickens this disintegration surfaces in the identification of the countryside with death and crime, the prominence of nocturnal city walking, and an emphasis on women walkers whose 'straying' may signify not only their own difficulties but those of Dickens's texts. Kim Taplin notes that although Dickens figures the countryside as a refuge and place of peace, that peace is too often deathly. She points to a number of instances of death or disappointment after a walk into the rural world where renewal is expected: Little Nell's long journey in *The Old Curiosity Shop*, which takes her to both peace of mind and death; Sissy and Rachael's discovery, while taking a theoretically reviving Sunday walk in the fields, of the mortally injured Stephen Blackpool in Old Hell Shaft, where he has fallen while walking home to clear his name (*Hard Times*); and Arthur Clennam's walks to the Meagles', the most beautiful of which concludes in his rejection by Pet and his premature but heartfelt resignation of a 'dying hope' that he will love a woman as wife (*Little Dorrit*). To these I would add the many instances of walks into the country associated with crime, particularly with murder, also noticed by Robert Newsom in *Dickens on the Romantic Side of Familiar Things* and (implicitly) by Laurie Langbauer in her article on 'Dickens's Streetwalkers: Women and the Form of Romance'.[20] Bill Sikes (*Oliver Twist*), Jonas Chuzzlewit (*Martin Chuzzlewit*), and Bradley Headstone (*Our Mutual Friend*) all walk into the country before or after they commit murder, Sikes in an attempt to escape recognition after the fact, and Chuzzlewit and Headstone as part of their disguises as rural characters; Hortense walks barefoot over dew-laden fields because she wishes to remember her ultimately murderous anger against Lady Dedlock (*Bleak House*); and Lady Dedlock herself, suspected of murder and guilty of much else, walks out into the country to find her disguise and cover her tracks, and so, in fact, seals her own fate in the delay of a false trail. Little wonder Taplin concludes that the 'connecting thread' of the footpath has been broken: 'For Dickens the countryside was clean, quiet, good, beautiful *and dead.* . . . the process of urbanisation and industrialisation has gone so far that people are not now any longer joined to their rural past, nor able to draw reviving strength from the countryside.'[21]

Dickens's city walks also suggest gaps between rural and urban, past and present, that cannot be wholly bridged. Drawing one of his first examples from Book VII of the *Prelude*, 'Residence in

---

[20] A revised version of Langbauer's argument appears in her book *Women and Romance: The Consolations of Gender in the English Novel* (Ithaca, NY and London: Cornell University Press, 1990).

[21] Taplin, *English Path*, 38.

London', Williams points out that 'perception of the new qualities of the modern city had been associated from the beginning with a man walking, as if alone, in its streets' and comments on the walker's simultaneous, equally intense contact with and isolation from other humans.[22] As Williams observes, such an experience 'could go either way: into an affirmation of common humanity ... or into an emphasis of isolation, of mystery—an ordinary feeling that can become a terror', and nineteenth-century literature, he feels, explores both directions.[23] The flow of his argument, however, seems to show the sense of isolation hardening into a standard vision of the city as the city of death, as the wasteland, a vision 'as relentless and as conventional as pastoral' which is broken only when 'there is no longer a city ... only a man walking through it'.[24] Then (and here Williams turns to Joyce's Bloom walking in Dublin) the individual can reconnect with others by means of a collective mythological consciousness for which the exterior forms, 'cities, towns, villages', become 'signs ... material ... agents' of communication.[25]

I suspect that one reason for this passage through the city of death before the recognition of the city as community is the original model of perception—that is, because the city is perceived/represented through walking, and walking is at the same time conventionalized as a fundamentally rural, past, unmechanized mode of perception, the city is necessarily seen as alien and alienating. Wordsworthian walkers in the country encounter the Old Cumberland Beggar, the Wanderer, the Leech-Gatherer, other walkers not wholly conscious, perhaps, of their own meaning but 'speaking' to the narrators in ways that close gaps, that establish continuities. Wordsworth's persona walking in London experiences that familiar knowing, expressive drive, the creative energy and desire of the country walker. But his final image of the city, the one that takes on the force of the fell rising into sight as his youthful self rows out in the stolen boat, is that of

---

[22] Williams, *Country and City*, 233.
[23] Ibid. 234.   [24] Ibid. 240, 243.
[25] Ibid. 246. Peter Barta's 1986 dissertation on 'The Structural and Thematic Function of Walking in the Modernist European Urban Novel' develops Williams' argument in readings of Bely's *Peterburg*, Joyce's *Ulysses*, and Doblin's *Berlin Alexanderplatz* (DAI 48/02A, 384).

a blind Beggar, who, with upright face,
Stood, propped against a wall ...
    .   .   .   .
                          a type,
Or emblem of the utmost that we know,
Both of ourselves and of the universe ...
And on the shape of the unmoving man,
His fixed face and sightless eyes, I looked,
As if admonished from another world. (*Prelude*, VII. 639–40, 644–9)

I do not argue that Wordsworth 'sets' our view of the city *per se*, but that his proposal of walking as the true mode of perception *because* it is rural, natural, laborious, and cyclical generates instant incongruence when 'true perception' enters the city. The Beggar stops moving altogether, stops expressing and seeing; he becomes an emblem of death and unknowing and disconnection, speaking to the narrator only 'from another world'. Walking in the city is thus a perilous business which, in striving to connect in country fashion, may discover only city fashions—and so, in the language of the country, disconnection. We shall see in our discussion of Dickens's 'Night Walks', and of Dickens's own walking, the terrible conflict between expectations and results in city walking.[26]

Langbauer joins Ellen Moers[27] in recognizing that Dickens's walking women embody his worries about wandering, both the wandering from the domestic stability he ideally envisions as women's special creation and his own textual wanderings.

---

[26] There is, of course, a Continental tradition of city walking, partly deriving from imaginative flight (see Ch. 2, n. 7, above) and reaching its fullest expression in Baudelaire. For an account of the rise and fall of the *flâneur*, 'who goes botanizing on the asphalt', and flourishes in the interior space of the arcade, see 'The *Flâneur*' in Walter Benjamin's *Charles Baudelaire: A Lyric Poet in the Era of High Capitalism*, trans. Harry Zohn (London: New Left Books, 1973), 35–66. See also Ned Lukacher's compelling reading of Benjamin, Dickens, and Freud in *Primal Scenes: Literature, Philosophy, Psychoanalysis* (Ithaca, NY and London: Cornell University Press, 1986), especially the section on Benjamin's linking of compulsive walking and literary creativity in both Baudelaire and Dickens (pp. 291–7). The prime images in Benjamin's and Lukacher's accounts are interiors—dark passages, labyrinths, no thoroughfares—arrived at/passed through in walking, suggesting the distinct material origins of this urban walking and its possible cross-fertilization (which I do not explore here) with the Wordsworthian walking I am tracing in my study.

[27] Ellen Moers, '*Bleak House*: The Agitating Women', *The Dickensian*, 69/1 (Jan. 1973), 13–24.

Langbauer focuses on 'random walking', in *The Old Curiosity Shop* in particular, as a literalization of Dickens's disruptive (or so she feels he perceived them) tendencies toward romance; Moers discusses possible historical sources for a concern with the encroachment of women into male spheres in general and novel-writing in particular. To their arguments I would add peripatetic's identification of walking and writing—which really clinches the connections they make through genre and history, I think—and also the peculiar intensity of walking women as 'symbol[s] of straying, lawless desire', as Langbauer puts it, in an age when walking men have been idealized as the orderers and redeemers of society.[28] This latter element highlights, once again, the presence of unbridgeable gaps in the socio-economic structure: it is precisely a pre-peripatetic concept of walking as lower class and criminal and sexually free which dictates that *ladies*, upper-class women, should not walk. That is, the distance between poor and rich supposedly bridged in peripatetic action has been preserved all this time in a distance between genders, and now surfaces to disrupt imagined continuities. Moreover, if by walking the women write, and if indeed Dickens, as Langbauer suggests happens in *David Copperfield* and clearly happens in *Bleak House* as well, enters into storytelling by 'putting himself'—as David or Esther— 'into a woman's place', then he is indeed 'aligning himself with the illicitness and indirection' of his walking women, and so sliding back into the gap, as it were, away from aimfulness and toward wandering.[29]

As is obvious from this brief discussion, peripatetic episodes intervene at crucial junctures in many of Dickens's novels. However, I would only call *The Old Curiosity Shop* (1841) a sustained peripatetic. Nell's long walk away from London with her grandfather forms the primary narrative axis of the novel and, as in Wordsworthian peripatetic, is undertaken with hopes of renewal and renovation. On the first morning of their travels Nell explicitly compares their situation with that of Christian in the *Pilgrim's*

---

[28] Laurie Langbauer, 'Dickens's Streetwalkers: Women and the Form of Romance', *ELH* 53 (1986), 412.

[29] Ibid. 428. See also Cheri Larson's unpublished paper on 'Dickens' Twisted Heroine: A Study of Oliver's Role as a Female', delivered at the conference *Dickens and Others*, 21–23 Feb. 1986, at the University of California–Santa Barbara.

Progress, a text 'over which she had often pored whole evenings' in their old home.[30] But Nell's description of her own historical model for their pilgrimage, her remembrance of the walks she and her grandfather took 'in the fields and among the green trees', shows that her implicit model is Wordsworthian peripatetic: 'when we came home at night, we liked it better for being tired, and said what a happy place it was. And if it was dark and rather dull, we used to say, what did it matter to us, for it only made us remember our last walk with greater pleasure, and look forward to our next one' (98). From these reviving memories of rural walks that illuminated present and future, Nell projects their flight from London into a Wordsworthian paradise of rural simplicity and community:

She saw in this [plan of action], but a return of the simple pleasures they had once enjoyed, a relief from the gloomy solitude in which she had lived, an escape from the heartless people by whom she had been surrounded in her late time of trial, the restoration of the old man's health and peace, and a life of tranquil happiness. Sun, and stream, and meadow, and summer days, shone brightly in her view, and there was no dark tint at all in the sparkling picture. (148)

In Nell's mind, indeed, even the fact that they must go as beggars will be resolved by their countryward walking. 'I have no fear but we shall have enough, I am sure we shall,' she says to her grandfather, and pictures an idyllic Wordsworthian vagrancy ' "through country places" where they can "thank God together" ' (124).

True to convention, these passages suggest that Nell's reliance on walking is the product of experience and memory; we do not see her with a volume of Wordsworth in her old home. Nor, apparently, is any explication of how or why walking should work like this necessarily. Nell's expectations are evidently those of Dickens's imagined audience and to a certain extent, as we shall see, of Dickens himself. But at the same time that Nell voices the hopes embodied in pedestrian action, the narrative implicitly questions these idealized expectations, introducing her bright picture

---

[30] Charles Dickens, *The Old Curiosity Shop*, ed. Angus Easson, introd. Malcolm Andrews (Harmondsworth: Penguin, 1972), 175. Further quotations from *The Old Curiosity Shop* will be cited in the text by page number.

of the future with the remark that 'She had no thought of hunger or cold, or thirst, or suffering' (148). When, on the night of their departure, she dreams 'of rambling through light and sunny places, but with some vague object unattained', the vagueness of her aim, and its characterization as 'unattained', combine with this narrative alertness to hardship and with Nell's sex to suggest that the walk she is about to embark on will contain some tincture of that bad old wandering of hardship, poverty, criminality, and death (149).

In fact, her journey as a whole is much closer to the *Pilgrim's Progress* than to the *Excursion*, but with the extra complication of Wordsworthian expectations which, uncomfortably, both sustain and disappoint. As Nell and her grandfather set out from London, for instance, their idealization of the foot journey transforms the city into Nell's rural paradise:

It was the beginning of a day in June; the deep blue sky unsullied by a cloud, and teeming with brilliant light. . . . the healthful air of morning fell like breath from angels on the sleeping town.

The old man and the child passed on through the glad silence elate with hope and pleasure. . . . every object was bright and fresh; nothing reminded them, otherwise than by contrast, of the monotony and constraint they had left behind; church towers and steeples, frowning and dark at other times, now shone and dazzled in the sun; each humble nook and corner rejoiced in light; and the sky, dimmed by excessive distance, shed its placid smile on everything beneath. (150–1)

But, as we are immediately reminded, these are 'two poor adventurers, wandering they knew not whither', and even as the light rises, they enter the company of the dead and the criminal (151). The empty streets become 'like bodies without souls [from which] all habitual character and expression had departed, leaving but one dead uniform repose . . . the few pale people whom they met seemed as much unsuited to the scene, as the sickly lamp which been here and there left burning was powerless and faint in the full glory of the sun' (171). As the streets become less deserted and the 'citiness' of London reasserts itself in the bustle of business and traffic, the old man 'pressed his finger on his lip, and drew the child along by narrow courts and winding ways . . . murmuring that ruin and self-murder were crouching in every street, and would follow if they scented them; and that they could

not fly too fast' (172). In so short a time, in the bare course of half
a morning, the travellers walk from hope to fear, from Nell's bright
visions to the old man's guilt, and from the reflections of these
emotions and characters in Wordsworth's natural light to the same
dark London streets through which Oliver Twist and Bill Sikes
fled from their pursuers.

Again and again Dickens repeats this pattern of Wordsworthian
expectation—now clearly, as his manipulation shows, Dickens's
vision of readers' as well as characters' expectations—giving way
to death, disappointment, and hardship. With each fresh setback
walking is sought as a remedy, and each new journey leads to the
same mixed or unhappy results. Near the end of their first day of
travel, for instance, the walkers press on from a hospitable country farm to find rest near the graves of a country churchyard.
There Nell does indeed hear a tale much like the epitaphs of the
Pastor in Wordsworth's 'Churchyard in the Mountains', but also
meets the strolling players who lead them to the Vanity Fair of the
races and threaten to give them up to Quilp. Langbauer points to
a particular incident at the races that marks their path as wandering
in the bad sense: an obviously 'fallen' woman in a carriage, apparently recognizing the vulnerability of the pretty girl begging as the
prelude to fortunes like her own, gives Nell money and tells her
to 'go home and keep at home for God's sake'.[31] From farm to
churchyard—a mixed site, involving both memory and death—
to races describes a downward path from comfortable domesticity
toward tawdry wandering.

Fleeing the races and the Punch players' watchful eyes, Nell and
her grandfather walk down a beautiful rural footpath to find refuge with a kind schoolmaster. There are lessons to be learned at
his side, but these lessons derive from the death of the master's
favourite pupil, with whom Nell identifies and whose place in the
master's heart she eventually fills (261–2, 434–5). Again, while
they are staying with Mrs Jarley, Nell finds comfort in shadowing
two loving sisters, 'follow[ing] them at a distance in their walks
and rambles, stopping when they stopped, sitting on the grass
when they sat down, rising when they went on, and feeling it a
companionship and delight to be so near them' (316). Her mar-
ginal participation suggests that, although these walks become

[31] Ibid. 214; Langbauer, 'Streetwalkers', 421–2.

'her only pleasure or relief from care', such pleasure and relief must be relative indeed. In fact her last walk with them results in the terrible knowledge that her grandfather is gambling once again and may steal to continue his vice (396–8).

Yet again Nell turns to walking as a remedy for her cares. 'Flying from disgrace and crime', the two pedestrians travel (for a brief while by boat, but mostly on foot) from the country into and through a terrifyingly, magnificently envisioned manufacturing hell, 'where nothing green could live but on the surface of the stagnant pools', and where, tended by ragged people of all ages and sexes and founded on ashes, 'strange engines spun and writhed like tortured creatures; clanking their iron chains, shrieking in their rapid whirl from time to time as though in torment unendurable' (423, 424). Nell and her grandfather do emerge, although weakened nearly to death, from this most terrible failure of peripatetic expectations. They meet the schoolmaster, who has 'determined to walk' to his new post as schoolmaster and clerk in a nearby village, and who takes them under his wing and finds a home for them in—of course—the village churchyard (434). Briefly it seems that their expectations may be met after all: we are shown views of the old and peaceful precincts of the church and of 'the brown thatched roofs of cottage, barn, and homestead, peeping from among the trees; the stream that rippled by the distant watermill; the blue Welch mountains far away', and are told that 'It was for such a spot the child had wearied in the dense, dark, miserable haunts of labour' (438). Even the graveyard, the sexton tells her, is also a garden—and here the figures of the *Excursion*, with its 'georgic of the grave', are very near.

But the peace and rest of this place, as Taplin tells us, are indeed the peace and rest of death. The churchyard is an 'aged, ghostly place', full of

arches in ruins, remains of oriel windows, and fragments of blackened walls . . . other portions of the old building, which had crumbled away and fallen down, were mingled with the churchyard earth and overgrown with grass, as if they too claimed a burying place and sought to mix their ashes with the dust of men. Hard by these gravestones of dead years, and forming a part of the ruin . . . were two small dwellings . . . fast hastening to decay, empty and desolate. (440)

Nell and her grandfather are to live in one of these ruined houses and, not at all surprisingly, Nell will die here. It is as if the fires of the manufacturing hell burned out and left the unlit, unmoving shells of its life behind, as if Nell had walked not from old life through adversity to new life, but from fear through disease to death, her only possible resurrection being into the next world.

Yet to her very death, and beyond, Nell's hopes and those of her loved ones take the shape of peripatetic memory and expectation. In her last hours she dreams 'of her journeying with the old man . . . of no painful scenes, but of those who had helped and used them kindly' (655). Her grandfather preserves the shoes she wore on their journey (was Dickens thinking of Thomas Coryate's shoes, which hung in the Odcombe parish church until the eighteenth century?); he sits by her grave imagining 'new journeys over pleasant country, of resting places under the free broad sky, of rambles in the fields and woods, and paths not often trod . . . visions of what had been and what he hoped was yet to be' when she returns, as he wildly believes she will, to join him (661).

And the story does allow peripatetic triumphs. Nell's last days of peace and relative happiness are no small accomplishment; the multiple searches for the travelling pair result in Quilp's death and Brass's imprisonment, certainly a palpable renovation of London; and the single gentleman takes up the peripatetic standard, finding it his 'chief delight to travel in the steps of the old man and the child . . . to halt where they had halted, sympathise where they had suffered, and rejoice where they had been made glad', and making it his business to reward and comfort all those who helped the walkers on their way (670).

Despite these successes, however, we are faced with the incontrovertible fact of Nell's death as a conclusion to her journey, and with the repeated pattern of that journey from hope to loss. As Malcolm Andrews notes in the introduction to the Penguin edition of *The Old Curiosity Shop*:

the novel has continually demonstrated that the death of a loved one does not do its 'blessed work on earth in those that loved it here.' The widow in the graveyard, the orphan man by the furnace, and even the grandfather are paralysed beings through their experience of the death of husband, father, and granddaughter respectively. Finally, Dickens admits to Forster, 'I can't preach to myself the schoolmaster's consolation [that good people live on through their deeds], though I try.' (28–9)

Moreover, even if we accept the schoolmaster's (and Dickens's) intended comfort and assert the importance of Nell's spiritual resurrection, the novel confronts us with further complications of the Wordsworthian recreative walk. In the portion of the original frame for the novel in *Master Humphrey's Clock* retained in its publication as a book, walking with decidedly un-Wordsworthian elements—nocturnal, urban, wandering walking—problematizes peripatetic's creative dimension. Master Humphrey opens the novel by telling us that, 'Night is generally my time for walking. In the summer I often leave home early in the morning, and roam about fields and lanes all day, or even escape for days or weeks together, but saving in the country I seldom go out until after dark' (43). He prefers the night not only because it hides his unspecified 'infirmity' but because it leaves the faces and scenes of the city partially veiled in darkness, freeing his imagination to work on them. But he also imagines the creative task of speculation on the unseen as the affliction of a diseased man:

Think of a sick man in such a place as Saint Martin's Court, listening to the footsteps, and in the midst of pain and weariness obliged, despite himself (as though it were a task he must perform) to detect the child's step from the man's, the slipshod beggar from the booted exquisite, the lounging from the busy, the dull heel of the sauntering outcast from the quick tread of an expectant pleasure-seeker—think of the hum and noise being always present to his senses, and of the stream of life that will not stop, pouring on, on, on, through all his restless dreams, as if he were condemned to lie dead but conscious, in a noisy churchyard, and had no hope of rest for centuries to come. (43)

By the end of this passage the illness has become mortal, and we find ourselves for the first time in that churchyard we will visit with Nell so many times in this novel, hearing always the tales of the dead, finding death and ruin so mixed with consolation that the tales seem to kill teller and listener alike. The narrator then shows us the crowds his hypothetical sick man must imagine moving down with the river to the sea, heavily laden and dreaming of rest, dreaming of Dickens's favourite self-murder, drowning. And 'out of one of these rambles'—a night walk? a rambling of the imagination? a walk down life's river to the sea of eternity?—Nell's story springs: Master Humphrey comes upon her when she is lost and takes her home, but by a circuitous route, delaying by misdirection her recognition of the territory (and the end of her 'lostness') so that he can see her home and learn her tale (44).

Thus in *The Old Curiosity Shop* Wordsworthian peripatetic,

although revered and partially realized, is enclosed and generated by a very different kind of walking, a fevered, haunted, misdirecting, unilluminated, and unilluminating walking, still the emblem and agent of creative work but now of work that often falls short of its desire for renewal and connection. At the heart of the novel, in the midst of hell, we encounter a man 'both swift and sure of foot' and yet untravelled who embodies this dark urban creativity (416). He shelters and directs Nell and her grandfather, caring for them by the industrial furnace by which he was born and from which he has never been parted for even a night:

'It's like a book to me,' he said, 'the only book I ever learned to read; and many an old story it tells me. It's music, for I should know its voice among a thousand, and there are other voices in its roar. It has its pictures too. You don't know how many strange faces and different scenes I trace in the red-hot coals. It's my memory, that fire, and shows me all my life.' (419–20)[32]

Here clearly is a keeper of the creative flame, one who recollects the past not in the green country but in the fires of industry, one whose capacity to read the truths of that past depend once more not upon excursive but upon purely local walking/knowledge. Here, I feel, is one of the visions Dickens had of himself, his own swift and surefooted excursive capacity somehow circumscribed by the massive flame of his creativity: sending his pilgrims out into the world, he hopes to enable the future but sees only the ashes of the past.

In accounts of Dickens's walking and its connections to his creative and emotional life, we observe that same strange combination of explosive power and containment, and of walking/writing as both antidote and illness, as both creative and destructive or ineffectual. He was a regular, determined, vigorous pedestrian with a 'constant daily habit of taking long walks in all weathers'.[33] These walks ran anywhere from seven to fifteen miles, depending on whose account one follows, and all accounts agree that Dickens's deliberate pace was a stiff four miles an hour (purposeful walkers

[32] Again, see Lukacher on Benjamin's reading of the relation between creativity and a specifically urban variety of walking (n. 26 above). In *Our Mutual Friend* Lizzie Hexam is also able to see not just stories but the story of her own life in her kitchen fire.

[33] Marcus Stone, in Philip Collins, ed., *Dickens: Interviews and Recollections*, 2 vols. (Totowa, NJ: Barnes & Noble, 1981), 182.

generally average about three, or maybe three and a half).[34] Edgar Johnson offers this description of 'the usual' as experienced by visitors to Gad's Hill:

When everything had been seen [on the afternoon tour of stables, grounds, etc.], Dickens suggested a walk, but of those who had walked with him before only the bravest dared face the gruelling ordeal again. To Chatham and Fort Pitt, over Cooling Marsh, or even, skirting Cobham Wood and Park, to Chalk and Gravesend, Dickens maintained a relentless pace of four miles an hour, swinging his blackthorn stick and talking cheerfully all the while. . . . Sometimes his perspiring companions gave way to blisters and breathlessness. 'I have now in my mind's eye,' wrote Edmund Yates, 'a portly American gentleman in varnished boots, who started with us full of courage, but whom we left panting by the wayside, and for whom the basket-carriage had to be sent.' On their return, tired and dripping, Dickens saluted the energetic survivors: '"Well done! Twelve miles in three hours."'[35]

The relation of these athletic excursions to Dickens's work is complex. His walking tended to mirror his writing in extent and quality, functioning both as an antidote or safety valve for the pressure of mental work, and as a site for observation and composition. His deliberate, measured exertion reflected his recognition of the former function, as George Augustus Sala tells us in discussing his 'self-appointed pedestrianism': 'It was one of Mr. Dickens's maxims that a given amount of mental exertion should be counteracted by a commensurate amount of bodily fatigue; and for a length of years his physical labours were measured exactly by the duration of his intellectual work.'[36] Grace Greenwood, too, reports Dickens's own comment that when his usual time for walking arrived, he went 'at once . . . hardly waiting to complete a sentence', fearing for his health if he should miss his 'tramp'. In that same interview with Greenwood, Dickens speaks both of composing and of gathering materials and observations to use in

[34] Some estimates of the length of Dickens's daily constitutionals, ascending from shortest to longest, can be found in Edgar Johnson, *Charles Dickens: His Tragedy and Triumph*, 2 vols. (London: Victor Gollancz, 1953), 209–10, and in these recollections in Collins, *Interviews*: Henry Burnett (p. 24), Mary Boyle (p. 86), Charles Dickens, Jun. (p. 140), and Marcus Stone (p. 182).

[35] Johnson, *Tragedy and Triumph*, 1055–6.

[36] George Augustas Sala, in Collins, *Interviews*, 199.

his writing as he walks.[37] Both Charles Junior and Henry Dickens remember walking long distances with their father while he silently composed, 'striding along with his regular four-miles-an-hour swing; his eyes looking straight before him, his lips slightly working as they generally did when he sat thinking and writing'.[38] Others observed Dickens acting out his characters, as he habitually did both in composition and as an entertainment, while walking.[39]

All of this suggests that Dickens used walking in conventional Wordsworthian fashion, seeking it out as a restorative, as a preferred mode of collecting impressions and as an expressive mode of composition. But, as in Arnold's poetry, the elements of labour and purpose intensify to the point of anxiety—even, when the creative and economic pressures on Dickens rose, to the point of obsession. In times of stress his walks lengthened through their upper range of fifteen, on to twenty, or even thirty miles; they became night walks that took the place of sleep, or took on the aspect of illness, blocking or replacing creative activity; and, as even Yates's description of a 'normal' walk suggests, they began to damage the people around Dickens. Johnson records a number of instances of creative or emotional upset linked with intense, frequently destructive walking. At Broadstairs in 1843, angry at Chapman and Hall over a financial demand triggered by the relative unpopularity of *Martin Chuzzlewit*, Dickens set out on what he himself calls 'an insane match against time', walking eighteen miles in four and a half hours. That night he could not sleep and the next day found himself as ready to 'eat the cliffs as write about anything'.[40] During the composition of *A Christmas Carol*, Dickens became so overexcited that he reportedly 'walked about the black streets of London fifteen and twenty miles a night'.[41] On two separate occasions, one in 1847 and one ten years later, his holiday after theatrical endeavours took the form of walks so long and difficult that he lamed his companions (Wilkie Collins actually sprained his ankle in Cumberland in 1857); and late in his life, during the extraordinary effort of the American reading tour,

---

[37] Grace Greenwood and Dickens, in Collins, *Interviews*, 235.
[38] Charles Dickens, Jun., in Collins, *Interviews*, 121. See also Henry's account in ibid. 159.
[39] John J. Sharp, and James and Annie Fields, in Collins, *Interviews*, 274, 310–11.
[40] Johnson, *Tragedy and Triumph*, 458.   [41] Ibid. 466.

Dickens walked so much that he lamed himself.[42] The longest,
strangest walk of which I have seen a record was a response to
a domestic disturbance, part of the upset of his failing marriage:
a 2 a.m., thirty-mile hike from Tavistock House to Gad's Hill,
essentially a walk away from his wife.[43] Marcus Stone may
overstate the case when he cites Dickens's 'mania for walking
long distances, which almost assumed the form of a disease', as
one of the prime causes of his death—the other being 'the ex-
haustion and excitement caused by his "dramatic readings" '—but
he accurately perceives the destructive, disabling aspect of Dickens's pedestrianism and, by implication, its parallel in Dickens's
literary work.[44]

Robert Newsom speculates that the essay 'Night Walks' in *The
Uncommercial Traveller* records another instance of walking as a
creative response to Dickens's sense of dissolution, and one in
which walking/writing palpably fails to resolve the difficulties
of experience/text. Citing the particular mention of the month
of March, the narrator's third-person references to himself as
'Houselessness'—a condition Newsom links with parent/child role
difficulties in Dickens's fiction—and the setting of emotional crisis,
Newsom suggests that Dickens's father's illness and death in March
1851 precipitated both the attacks of insomnia and, eventually,
'Night Walks' itself.[45] Although the first publication of 'Night
Walks' was in the 21 July 1860 issue of *All the Year Round*,
Newsom argues that there is no 'other March in Dickens's life
before the writing of the essay that fits the circumstances so well'.[46]

Whatever the actual or imagined cause of the narrator's insomnia, his walking leaves him 'almost as much a prey to his own
unpleasant imaginings as he is when lying awake'.[47] His initial
assumption of the character of 'Houselessness' certainly does not
suggest that his walks foster any sense of belonging in the city or
of connection with others or even of connection with himself, the
use of the third person putting some further distance between
the rhetorical observer and the author. In all guises the narrator

[42] Ibid. 619, 879; George Dolby, in Collins, *Interviews*, 263.
[43] Johnson, *Tragedy and Triumph*, 912.
[44] Stone, in Collins, *Interviews*, 220, 223.
[45] Robert Newsom, *Dickens on the Romantic Side of Familiar Things* (New York:
Columbia University Press, 1977), 106–7.
[46] Ibid. 161.   [47] Ibid. 111.

perceives the city as dead or dying, in the violent modes of murder and suicide. From Waterloo Bridge he observes that

the river had an awful look, the buildings on the banks were muffled in black shrouds, and the reflected lights seemed to originate deep in the water, as if the spectres of suicides were holding them to show where they went down. The wild moon and clouds were as restless as an evil conscience in a tumbled bed, and the very shadow of the immensity of London seemed to lie oppressively upon the river.[48]

That 'evil conscience in a tumbled bed' might be the narrator's own: his insomnia resonates with Macbeth's and, like Dickens's own murderers, the quality of the narrator's perceptions suggests a terrible guilt manifesting itself through the environment. From the bridge, indeed, he takes us to dark theatres reminiscent of Yorick's skull and orchestra pits like graves, views of Newgate as 'Death's Door', insane asylums and cemeteries, until finally the whole becomes a Thomsonian city housing 'vast armies of dead' that, if raised, 'would overflow the hills and valleys beyond the city . . . God knows how far' (152, 156).

This terrible vision of individual guilt and social disease spilling out from the city into the countryside, of the dead displacing the living, remains essentially unmitigated. Immediately after this perception the narrator meets a genuinely homeless person, a member of the very class with which the narrator has tried to associate himself in sympathy and condition, one of the displaced urban poor, still alive in this huge graveyard. But the narrator can make no contact: he refers to this person as a 'creature', as 'it', and likens him to 'a worried dog', so that the man rhetorically becomes inhuman and so fundamentally separate from the narrator (156). Even when the narrator touches him in reassurance, intending to give him money, the poor man slips out of his coat and flees. Briefly, too, the narrator makes some positive contact through a place that serves early morning coffee, but this is quickly disrupted by a man in a snuff-coloured coat who dispatches a meat pudding, metaphorically associated with the man's mother's corpse and finally with the man himself, with an uncomfortably

[48] Charles Dickens, 'Night Walks', in *The Uncommercial Traveller* (London and New York: Chapman & Hall, and Charles Scribner's Sons, 1898), 151. Further quotations from this and other essays in *The Uncommercial Traveller* will be cited in the text by page number.

long knife. After two encounters with this regular customer, the
narrator says, 'the pudding seemed an unwholesome pudding
... and I put myself in its way no more' (158). At last the narrator
is left in that condition Williams describes, a man wandering
without any city at all, utterly disconnected in 'the real desert
region of the night', avoiding even the presence of 'Vice and
Misfortune': 'my houselessness had many miles upon miles of streets
in which it could, and did, have its own solitary way' ('Night
Walks', 159).

'Night Walks' is the culmination of a series of essays in the
Uncommercial Traveller in which walking, although often sought
as a connective and recreative activity, fails to foster the continuities the narrator seeks. Roughly a third of the *Uncommercial*'s
travels (mostly in the early essays) are pedestrian, and most of
these lead to observations tinged with the same darkness that
overwhelms 'Night Walks', portraits of workhouses and dying
suburban churches and morgues in London and Paris. Moreover,
the premiss of the collection detaches the narrator who perceives
these things from material economy, setting him up as a metaphorical traveller 'for the great house of Human Interest Brothers',
a move which may seem to disconnect him from the source of
many of the evils he sees but which also leaves him an isolated and
immaterial ghost of a traveller, presumably as unable to intervene
for good as he is for ill in human affairs (2).

The three essays which precede 'Night Walks' develop this
condition of detachment as creative, socio-economic, and temporal. 'Shy Neighbourhoods' opens with the narrator's rapidly
transforming characterizations of himself as a sporting pedestrian,
a sleepwalker, and an Alpine climber, with sleepwalking as the
literal and dominant mode, and the one in which he experiences
extraordinary fluency in poetry and 'forgotten' languages. He then
goes on to distinguish between 'two kinds' of walking he does,
'one, straight on end to a definite goal at a round pace; one,
objectless, loitering, and purely vagabond'. As one might expect
from the connection between poetry and the semi-conscious mode
of sleepwalking, it is 'in a vagabond course' that the narrator's
observations of 'Shy Neighbourhoods' take place (110–11). Thus,
in a reflection of the *Uncommercial*'s premiss, fluent observation
and expression become associated with purposelessness and wandering rather than with the heroic exertion of aimful walking,

stripping creative work of much sense of conscious shaping will and so, I think, of certain claims to effectuality.

'Tramps' then expands the division between the labourer and the vagrant implied in 'Shy Neighbourhoods', with somewhat confusing results. This essay catalogues the variety of tramps one might expect to meet in the summer on the country roads, arranging them from the several types of able-bodied shirkers through the companionable young adventurers to the genuinely labouring wanderers who, like Wordsworth's, actually live by travelling. The narrator renders most of his observations in the first or, more usually, second person singular, the 'I' or 'you' being firmly distinguished from the distastefully lazy beggars in the early part of the essay. Then, as he begins to describe the labouring tramps, he seems to suggest his (and our) solidarity with them by speaking in the first-person plural. '*We*' now enjoy an idyllic countryside, taking pride in our labours under conditions superior to those experienced by writer and reader: lamenting the absence of the admiring glances a chair-mender gathers, the narrator complains, 'No one looks at us while we plait and weave these words' (130). By the end of the essay, however, the narrator has moved back into a firm first-person-singular stance from which he represents the camps of the vagrants as landscape and the vagrants themselves as picturesque additions to that landscape. One wonders how to reconcile the different accounts of walking as labour in this essay and in its predecessor. Is not the inspired writer a semi-conscious, loitering vagrant? Not here, it seems, and yet the brief association of the narrator, foisted on the reader also, with the 'deserving poor' seems an unconvincing ploy. As in the Old Curiosity Shop, disconnection frames the flash of Wordsworthian idyll, disrupting peripatetic expectations of continuity.

Finally, in 'Dullborough Town', the narrator attempts to walk back into his childhood. Predictably he finds his old home ground damaged by the encroachments of the railroad, his playing field 'disfigured' and 'swallowed up' by the station (137). Predictably, too, the narrator walks into the town in search of familiar faces and sensations, but he can find no one to recognize him and can scarcely recognize the perceptually shrunken and altered landmarks of the town himself. At last, when he encounters a boyhood friend, 'the air filled with the scent of trodden grass, and the perspective of years opened'; he and his friend sit down to drink and reminisce

(145). Yet even this recovered companionship offers no true re-creation, no genuinely reviving recollection of the past: the two friends 'spoke of our old selves as though our old selves were dead and gone, and indeed indeed they were—dead and gone as the playingfield that had become a wilderness of rusty iron, and the property of S.E.R.' (147). Walking takes the narrator into memory, into companionship, but cannot heal the losses of the past or undo the damages of the present or offer much hope for the future. The narrator's past and present selves, his relatively rural boyhood and his industrialized present, remain sundered. Even the essay as re-collection—that is, the essay itself seen as a peripatetic triumph recovering the past—is darkened by its primary focus on wrongful transformation and loss, and by its thematic insistence that the past is, finally, unrecoverable.

These three essays disrupt or deny much of what Wordsworth asserts—what Dickens himself so often hoped for—as peripatetic effect: the connection of material and creative labours, of city and country, of past and present, of self and other. And after them, not surprisingly, comes 'Night Walks', desperately applying the sovereign remedy to a fearful combination of personal and societal guilt, fear, alienation, and loss, and watching that remedy fail. 'Night Walks' does achieve tremendous hallucinogenic clarity, the clarity of mortal fever, as if the very exercise of creative artistic power, embodied in the act of walking, intensifies the horror of the urban labyrinth. Such nightmare beauty is, at least, compelling—that, perhaps, can be set to peripatetic credit—for the threat lurking beneath all these texts, in all Dickens's walks, visible in their anxiety and fervour, and sometimes embodied in their results, is the fear that finally walking/writing is wholly in-effectual.

In Hardy's works Dickens's intermittently successful struggle to maintain peripatetic hope by greater effort, harder walking, gives way to an explicit reduction of walking's effects to not merely local but purely personal knowledge and renovation. Hardy's poems include what appear to be direct refutations of peripatetic ex-pectations in general, and of Arnold's heroic assertions in particu-lar; his novels amplify Dickens's representations of semi-conscious, nocturnal, deathly, or ineffectual walks with direct commentary on the narrow limits Hardy assigns to peripatetic effect. Thus, using the mode's form to question its assertions, Hardy resolves the desperate tension of Victorian literary peripatetic into conscious subversion.

Hardy might be thought of as a slightly more affluent and psychologically successful version of John Clare. His father, a master mason (also, Hardy tells us, 'a great walker'), belonged to that class of artisans and freeholders just above the rural labourers, and his family maintained its self-sufficiency by means of an extensive garden and the keeping of bees, chickens and an annual pig.[49] Thus Hardy himself first became a walker in the old localizing style of the born countryman: 'Travelling everywhere on foot—or at best on a wagon drawn by a slow-paced horse—he became familiar with the occupants of every cottage, the name of every field and every gate, the profile of every tree, the depth and temperament of every pond and stream'.[50] Even when he first began to draw away from his childhood, during the years of school and apprenticeship and first loves from 1850 on into the early 1860s, he 'continued to walk back and forth between the rural isolation of Higher Bockhampton and the comparative bustle of Dorchester'.[51] What must have begun as necessity grew into a part of his artistic process, as when, in 1887, having completed *The Woodlanders* and preparing for *Tess of the D'Urbervilles*, Hardy took a series of walks in south-western England which Millgate describes as 'part of a deliberate process of thinking himself into the social as well as the emotional texture of his new story, of invoking that sense of historical time and visitable place which provided the essential underpinning for his most ambitious imaginative enterprises'.[52]

Hardy's life provides, in short, the perfect setting for Wordsworthian peripatetic. Clearly, in fact, that is how Millgate reads both Hardy's 1887 excursions and his earlier walking. But Hardy represented walking quite differently from Wordsworth, primarily because Hardy found the gap between his past and present, and all the different values those broad territories encompassed, to be essentially, and perhaps in some senses happily, unbridgeable.

---

[49] Michael Millgate, *Thomas Hardy* (Oxford and New York: Oxford University Press, 1985), 19, 26–7.
[50] Ibid. 30.   [51] Ibid. 61.   [52] Ibid. 293.

Discussing Hardy's tribute to William Barnes in 'The Last Signal', and the contrast of Hardy's literary methods with Barnes's deliberately maintained simplicity and dialectism, Millgate argues:

Simple as [Hardy's] taste and even his personal habits remained, profoundly sympathetic as he was to the fundamental truths (in a Wordsworthian sense) of his earliest experience, Hardy had learned through years of deliberate self education and of London living that there were other, more sophisticated, and in some respects better ways of thinking and acting ... He was able as an artist to articulate the thoughts and feelings of country people precisely because he could look back upon his own early self from the vantage point provided by a much altered set of attitudes and beliefs.[53]

If this perspective enhanced Hardy's artistic expressions, it also darkened them. Peter Casagrande argues convincingly that a series of disappointments first figured as departure and return—'his departure from and return to his native Dorset ... his loss of religious faith ... his disillusionment with his work as a restorer of Gothic churches ... and his disappointment with love and marriage'—shaped Hardy's vision of 'the world as a spectacle of thwarted efforts of regeneration'.[54] Casagrande divides the major novels into novels of return and novels of restoration, the former showing 'the attempt—always painful—to return to one's native place after long absence', and the latter 'The struggle—always futile—to atone for error or mend defect', and concludes that 'The theme in both is the same—there is no return, no restoration.'[55] What is possible, or at least conceivable, as Casagrande's eloquent discussion of Tess and Jude the Obscure shows, is 'redemption', a term he initally defines as 'the traditional Christian belief in regeneration through a supernatural agency', but finally modifies to redemption by 'human means'.[56] Casagrande further modifies even that possibility, which is rather marginally (in my opinion) indicated by Tess's brief reunion with Angel Clare and its possible extension in a union between Clare and Tess's sister Liza-Lu, by requiring that we read neither Tess nor Jude alone: 'Hardy's view of things', he insists, 'is a truly dichotomous one; it rests somewhere inside the extraordinary dialogue he carried on through the two

---

[53] Ibid. 276–7.
[54] Peter Casagrande, Unity in Hardy's Novels: 'Repetitive Symmetries' (Lawrence, Kan.: The Regents Press of Kansas, 1982), 12–13, 12.
[55] Ibid. 2.   [56] Ibid. 3, 217.

halves of the magnificent diptych with which he chose to end his career as a writer of novels'.[57] Thus hopes for redemption and despair of it continually speak against each other, each only momentarily 'separated'.

Peripatetic, with its proposal of a universal human means not only of redemption but of return and renewal, offers an appealing ground upon which to work out the nuances of this dialogue, particularly when combined with walking's natural association with Hardy's childhood and its continued part in his later life. In fact, walking as narration and action, and characters with peripatetic expectations and endeavours, are virtually as common in Hardy's work as in Wordsworth's.[58] But when Hardy's walkers succeed, they succeed in utterly personal ways that have little or no exterior effect. And when they fail, which is often, the result is error or destruction or (most horrible) nothing at all. This subversion of convention enables peripatetic as one of the sites for Casagrande's 'extraordinary dialogue', both permitting and questioning redemptive hopes, and finally limiting them, I think, to a very personal sphere of influence.

Consider, for instance, 'The Supplanter', in which a particularly nasty version of Angel Clare returns to the grave of his sweetheart to lay a wreath. A young woman whose birthday party he joins seduces him first to dance and then, pointing to his wreath of 'white flowers upon the floor | Betrodden to a clot' as a sign of common forgetfulness, to bed.[59] He wakes in remorse and disgust, and abandons his new lover. But sure enough he returns again, not to the young woman who has now borne his child, but to the grave of the first lover, and when his child's mother pleads with him for recognition and love, responds,

---

[57] Ibid. 218.

[58] I am indebted to Simon Gatrell's suggestive essay on Hardy as 'Travelling Man' (in *The Poetry of Thomas Hardy*, ed. Patricia Clements and Juliet Grindle (n.p.: Vision, 1980), 155–71) for pointing to a number of poems in which walking is the mode of travel. Among the novels, *The Woodlanders*, *The Mayor of Casterbridge*, and *Tess of the D'Urbervilles* open with peripatetic incidents. Without considering the ubiquity of walking in Hardy's pictures of rural life, one might remember Fanny Robin's walk to the Casterbridge Union in *Far From the Madding Crowd*, and Jude's journey to Christminster in *Jude the Obscure*.

[59] Thomas Hardy, 'The Supplanter', in *The Variorum Edition of the Complete Poems of Thomas Hardy*, ed. James Gibson (New York: Macmillan, 1978), lines 49–50. Further quotations from Hardy's poetry are drawn from this edition, and are noted in the text by title and line numbers.

'I know you not ...
'Nor know your child. I knew this maid,
  But she's in Paradise!'
And he has vanished in the shade
  From her beseeching eyes.   (92–6)

His walking, which first accomplishes precisely the opposite of what he intends, literally trampling on his first love's memory as embodied in the white wreath, finally returns him only to an inaccessibly personal and materially unrecoverable past which, rather than connecting him with others and with the best part of himself, injures and alienates his new lover and effectually obliterates him from sight. Any redemption here must be limited to an utterly personal—and, from anyone else's perspective, pretty sadistic—satisfaction.

If 'The Supplanter' functions as a refutation of peripatetic by showing walking as destructive, 'Middle-Age Enthusiasms' simply empties peripatetic of its anticipated value. Here Hardy's companionable pedestrians (lovers?) express, in successive stanzas, perception of some deeper meaning in the landscape, intentions to return to the spot and to re-create it elsewhere, and belief that their recollection of the spot will unite their thoughts after death. Each of the four stanzas, however, closes with an abrupt denial of its possibilities, contrasting the initially ecstatic expressions stimulated by the walkers' movement through the landscape with their final sense of impotence. The contrast is particularly palpable in the last stanza:

'So sweet the place,' we said,
'Its tacit tales so dear,
Our thoughts, when breath has sped,
Will meet and mingle here!' ...
'Words!' mused we. 'Passed the mortal door,
Our thoughts will reach this nook no more.'   (19–24)

The closing lines annihilate the effect not only of the place itself and the walk that has taken them there but of the expressive words the place and act have stimulated: the tales of the woodland remain tacit, any expression of them blown with breath into mortal and ineffectual silence.

'The Pedestrian' and 'The Last Signal', which appear to answer directly Arnold's assertions of peripatetic effect in 'The

Scholar-Gipsy' and 'Thyrsis', enlarge upon this possible silencing of the reader/writer. The narrator of 'The Pedestrian'—not a pedestrian, but a coach-rider—meets a man who, like the Scholar-Gipsy, walks to preserve his life: his doctors have told him he has only six months to live 'Unless I vamp my sturdiest' (21). Hardy makes the strain between scholar and gypsy visible in the pedestrian's dress, oddly compounded of beggar and gentleman:

> He wore but a thin
> Wind-thridded suit,
> Yet well-shaped shoes for walking in,
> Artistic beaver, cane gold-topped.   (11–14)

But, as the speaker's mode of travel suggests, this solution of opposites does little good. Here neither the scholar's desire for knowledge nor the gypsy's walking can save his life: although we do not absolutely know the outcome of the pedestrian's efforts, the speaker remembers his 'short breath, | His aspect, marked for early death, | As he dropped into the night for ever' with his studies in philosophy and poetry uncompleted (36–8).

Nor does the pedestrian-poet's voice survive him in 'The Last Signal'. Like 'Thyrsis', Hardy's poem is dedicated to a dead poet friend, and takes as its 'plot' the narrative of a walk in which the speaker remembers the earlier pedestrian rambles of that friend, William Barnes.[60] Arnold's poem, however, saturates the speaker's present walk with a lush compound of personal recollection and classical allusion, while 'The Last Signal' concentrates upon its own brief and vivid present, permitting just one retrospective of Barnes, 'who in his prime | Trudged so many a time from that gate athwart the land!' (13–14). Nor is there any hope here, as there is in 'Thyrsis', of the friend's voice raised again to ease the speaker's grief and draw him back to the scenes and senses of their poetic rambles: this is the *last* signal, a chance gleam of light in an east darkened by cloud and abandoned by the setting sun.

---

[60] Barnes, a Dorset schoolmaster and clergyman, wrote much of his poetry in Dorset dialect. Taplin offers a brief biography of him in her first chapter, selecting Barnes and Hardy as two of the six writers 'who stand out for their frequent mention of paths, who attach importance to them for their own sakes and endue them with literary significance' (*English Path*, 7). (The other four are John Clare, Richard Jeffries, John Cowper Powys, and Edward Thomas.)

It meant the west mirrored by the coffin of my friend there,
Turning to the road from his green,
To take his last journey forth
· · · · · · · · · · ·
Thus a farewell to me he signaled on his grave-way,
As with a wave of his hand.

(11–13, 15–16)

The silence of this last signal, its singular and irreplicable form,
matches the poem's insistent focus upon a single walk and its near
refusal to recall any other—none other taken by the speaker—or
to suggest future recollections of this one. 'The Last Signal' does
function for the reader as a creative recollection, as a preservation
of its own time and place, and, if ever so briefly, as a memorial
of things outside its own present, all cast in the shape of a walk.
But its images and themes rhetorically involute the peripatetic
conventions, looping their excursive intentions more and more
tightly within the singularity of the text so that the past remains
within the past—beautiful, vivid, but a memory, preserved without hope of extension beyond itself.

Only, in fact, in the preservation of personal memory does
walking sometimes function in Hardy as it does in Wordsworth.
Hardy's first poem, 'Domicilium', builds a picture of his boyhood
home as a garden overlooking fields around the memory of a walk
during which his grandmother recalled even earlier, less cultivated
conditions at the site; in 'After the Journey', the speaker follows
the peripatetic ghost of his love to the scenes they once walked
together, finally imploring her, 'bring me here again! I I am just
the same as when I Our days were a joy, and our paths through
flowers' (30–2). 'The Roman Road' suggests that such recoveries
of the past succeed because they are entirely personal: the speaker
knows and recounts the road's history, but he *sees* 'no tall brass-
helmed legionnaire', just '[a] mother's form . . . I Guiding my infant steps' (10, 12–13). By comparison the pedestrian speaker of
Wordsworth's 'The Pass of Kirkstone', in a frenzy of visionary
capability undeterred by historical gaps, seems to apprehend Ro-
mans and Druids and Egyptians, all who have ever 'panted up the
hill I Of duty with reluctant will' (55–6).

Tess of the D'Urbervilles (1891) explicitly sets out reasons for
this confined effect. In this novel, as in his poetry, Hardy sets up
the forms of peripatetic and then subverts them with disastrous or

ineffectual consequences. Both Wordsworthian aspiration and Victorian discomfort are evident in the casting of the principals as pedestrians: Tess is an accomplished rural walker who knows her own ground thoroughly and can also step out 'across country without much regard to roads', while Angel first appears as the type of the scholarly gentleman out on tour with his books, taking his walks purposely as Tess does hers necessarily.[61] Together, as the saying goes, they make a considerable pedestrian, but the union that might have healed the Scholar-Gipsy into the Wanderer is a signal failure. Every walk they take after their marriage, from the walk of the first morning after Tess's revelation to the Dickensian walk away from Tess's murder of Alec D'Urberville, disappoints their hopes for forgiveness and reconciliation and healing. Even Angel's episode of sleepwalking, during which he reveals both his love for Tess and the divisive fears he has hidden from his conscious mind, remains ineffectual because he does not remember it and Tess does not tell it, once again marking personal memory as the largest possible bounds of peripatetic effect.[62] During the course of two solo walks, one by Tess and one by Angel, it becomes clear that this boundary is enforced by fundamental disconnection from or absence of both natural moral law and human community.

The narrative voice reveals the first of these gaps in the process of describing Tess's regular twilight walks during her pregnancy. 'At times', we are told, '[Tess's] whimsical fancy would intensify natural process around her till they seemed a part of her own story', as indeed they are in the argument of the narrative, 'for the world is only a psychological phenomenon' (134). But by this Tess does not half-create, half-perceive divine meaning in nature, nor does her own moral condition seem, as that of Dickens's characters often does, to alter the fabric of her environment. The whole thing, her feeling that a wet day expressed divine sorrow over her plight or her sense of herself as 'a figure of Guilt intruding into the haunts of Innocence', is 'a sorry and mistaken creation of Tess's fancy', for 'all the while she was making a distinction where there

---

[61] Thomas Hardy, *Tess of the D'Urbervilles*, ed. David Skilton (Harmondsworth: Penguin, 1978), 483. Further quotations from *Tess* are noted in the text by page number.

[62] For an extraordinary development of the walking/sleepwalking contrast, see Charles Brockden Brown's *Edgar Huntley, or, The Sleepwalker*. This late 18th-cent. American novel offers post-Hardy representations of walking by way of Hume's sceptical empiricism.

was no difference ... She had been made to break an accepted
social law, but no law known to the environment in which she
fancied herself such an anomaly' (135). Hardy's narrator perceives
in Tess the same error Raymond Williams perceives in
Wordsworth's account of London: it is not that Wordsworth is
out of touch with natural laws but that there are no laws which
inform seeing, only conventions, and Wordsworth's convention
is somehow inappropriate to the city.[63] In Tess's case, too, the
peripatetic convention of moral connection through pedestrian
intimacy with nature fails because the convention does not fit the
reality: she cannot read either divine or human moral values in the
natural world because such laws are not there to read. Her identification with nature and consequent capacity for renewal depend
not on conscious action/perception that discovers morality in natural
forms, but on the unconscious, undirectable and unrecallable forces
of instinct that permit her spirits to rise 'as automatically as the
sap in the twigs' (151). Walking as willed, knowing action adds
nothing to this instinctual renewal. Indeed, the narrative directly
contrasts the natural effects of time on youth to 'long wandering',
which 'often unfits us for further travel, and of what use is our
experience to us then?' (149).

Moreover, as Angel discovers when he walks to the Durbeyfields'
old house in search of Tess after his return from Brazil, conscious
peripatetic recollection cannot link disparate consciousnesses into
community, for each set of memories remains locked in its individual, wholly personal context. Not only does Angel not find
Tess at her old home but he sees that 'The new residents ...
walked about the garden-paths with thoughts of their own concerns entirely uppermost, bringing their actions at every moment
into jarring collision with the dim figures behind them, talking as
though the time when Tess lived there were not one whit intenser
in story than now' (459). *He* remembers her there, raising the ghosts
of former times to his own sight, but the memories remain insub-
stantial, ineffectual shades, incommunicable to the present of other
people. So, too, his journey does not take him back to Tess
Durbeyfield but to Tess D'Urberville. Like his memories, the recreation of their marriage during their brief reunion at Bramshurst
Manor is limited to a small interior unconnected to the rest of

---

[63] Williams, *Country and City*, 242.

humanity: 'within was affection, union, error forgiven; outside was the inexorable', the social but uncommunal instrument of Tess's death (481).

Thus Hardy's peripatetic reduces the excursive effect to a tiny, wholly personal circle of influence, beyond which the conscious exercise of will has little or no effect. If *Tess* demonstrates, as Casagrande suggests, hope for this personal redemption, *The Return of the Native* (1878) demonstrates the frequent futility of this hope, and the nearly certain futility of any re-creative effort beyond that—including that of creative labour.

The Return of the Native is filled with accomplished and purposeful pedestrians: Diggory Venn's profession demands travel, much of it plainly on foot; Clym Yeobright, who, like Tess, can walk home across the heath 'without attending to paths', becomes in turn a furze-cutter (and thus a heath-walker) and an itinerant preacher; even Eustacia, with her decidedly urban tastes, inclines to midnight rambles.[64] Indeed, so much of the action of *The Return of the Native* occurs on the paths and roads of Egdon Heath that the elusive narrator himself can be imagined, as he does imagine various 'lookers-on' who serve as his proxies, walking beside his characters or waiting at some convenient tree or stile for them to pass.

Yet in this novel the walker's signal characteristic is sheer inefficacy: his perceptions are without distinction, his efforts to remake the world, whether for good or ill, overwhelmed by accident and hindered by his own failed vision. Clym's resolution to 'keep a school as near Egdon as possible, so as to be able to walk over there and have a night-school in my mother's house', perfectly embodies the heroic will of the scholar-gypsy, which should theoretically enable him to naturalize his foreign knowledge and educate the other natives of the heath (227). Yet rather than expanding his vision from his own past into the future, his efforts provoke semi-blindness; his subsequent heath-walking and furze-cutting contribute to Eustacia's discontent and, ultimately, to the deaths of both his wife and his mother. At last Clym's dreams of a natural life ennobled decline to the wanderings of an itinerant preacher, 'kindly received' not for the wisdom of his words but

---

[64] Thomas Hardy, *The Return of the Native*, ed. George Woodcock (Harmondsworth: Penguin, 1978), 231. Further quotations from *The Return of the Native* are cited in the text by page number.

because 'the story of his life had become generally known'—not, that is, because of his effectual pedestrian/verbal intervention in the world but because of the narrow failures of his personal life (474).

The deaths of Clym's mother and wife, moreover, take place at the end of walks undertaken to clear their vision and reshape their lives. Mrs Yeobright's fatal walk, in particular, demonstrates the inefficacy of such peripatetic effort. She sets out, on Diggory Venn's advice, to attempt a reconciliation with Clym and Eustacia. Not knowing the precise way to her son's house, she 'tried one ascending path and another, and found they led her astray' (338). She then follows a furze-cutter who, according to a nearby labourer, is 'going to the same place', but does not recognize her guide as Clym until she realizes that '[his] walk is exactly as [her] husband's walk used to be' (338, 339). Later, she watches Wildeve circumambulate the cottage in a 'peculiar, hesitating' manner and does not recognize him at all, although part of Venn's argument for her journey is that she can 'make Wildeve walk straighter than he is inclined to do' (333). In short, Mrs Yeobright's peripatetic perspective remains distanced and disjointed, uncertain of paths and persons and motives; even that doubly pedestrian moment of illumination, her walking recognition of her son's walk, contributes to her erroneous supposition that Clym has wilfully shut her out of his life. Far from clearing her vision and renewing her life, as she had hoped it would, the walk to Clym's house leaves her disoriented and unsure, prey to error not pernicious but merely accidental.

Mrs Yeobright's fate is that of all of the novel's pedestrian seekers of vision and power: she sees, but without resolution; she acts, but with meagre effect for either good or ill. Even Diggory Venn, whose fate is at least conventionally happy, becomes a suitable aspirant to Thomasin's hand only by giving up his peripatetic profession. Nor is the frequently peripatetic narrator excepted: his vision, like Clym's, may be sufficient 'for walking about' but is unequal to 'being strained upon any definite object' (310). The narrative thus obtained flickers like the firelight on Rainbarrow, the very multiplicity and mobility of its perspectives suggesting that same 'unstable' and 'evanescent' light which makes 'the permanent moral expression of each face . . . impossible to discover' (67). Thus many incidents are told and retold from several perspectives, as if to mitigate the uncertainty of a single view, and yet key details are often lost. The exact import of Eustacia's death, for instance, remains unclear—did she leap, or fall?—for the narrative records only the circumstances around it: her despair on Rainbarrow, a splash in the darkness, and the recovery of the bodies. At one point Hardy abdicates narrative authority altogether, adding a note to the penultimate chapter which explains that the 'ending' we are about to read is not the original or even necessarily the most desirable ending, and concluding: 'Readers can therefore choose between the endings, and those with an austere artistic code can assume the more consistent conclusion to be the true. one' (464).

In Hardy the suppressed anxieties of Victorian peripatetic surface into conscious recognition. Pedestrian effort, all that that effort encompasses after Wordsworth—the effort to tell life's movement into a solution of stability and growth, to temper the future with the past, to connect the rural with the urban and the common labourer with the intellectual, to safeguard public rights and to freehold our own paths, to connect childhood and mature endeavour, to read the moral in the natural—all these efforts falter or fail. 'The inexorable' rushes on outside, nature and society equally indifferent to fervent memory and striving. When the native returns to find his playing fields overrun by the railway, his education useless or irreconcilable with his origins, what avails a memorial walk, even for himself? The cottage is not merely ruined but effaced as if it had not been. The risks of walking become huge; the poet-pedestrian, asked to guide others, shakes his head and points back at them.

Hardy's lifting of such despair into conscious view does not signal the death of peripatetic. For twentieth-century writers, peripatetic remains a mode in which, by the degree to which conventional expectations are fulfilled, or by a combination of fulfilments and disappointments, the writer can develop the text's attitude toward a wide range of issues—industrialization, free will, artistic creation, class conflict, and so forth. For instance, in the familiar poem by Robert Frost, 'Acquainted with the Night', the pedestrian narrator extends his night walk beyond 'the furthest city light', presumably out of the city itself, and moves in proper excursive fashion, walking 'out in rain—and back in rain'. But nothing happens. The walker cannot explain what he's doing to

the one person he meets; he hears voices but they do not 'call
[him] back or say good-by'; the clock tells him that 'the time was
neither wrong nor right'. City and country (the latter rhetorically
absent from the poem) remain unconnnected, past and present are
out of the question, and the narrator makes no human contact.
The poem comes round to its first line again, but now, exploding
the possibilities of knowledge and community it first generated,
that line tells us that the narrator has come to know only the
night, the darkness of his own uncertainty and wandering. The
darkness is made more terrible, indeed, if we recognize that the
narrator has fulfilled all of the formal demands of excursive walking, a process which should accomplish the connections he obviously
wants. Now pedestrian excursion, the human effort to achieve
community and to shape the world, becomes an empty (if beautiful) form that generates only itself.[65]

Wendell Berry, however, uses peripatetic to assert the efficacy of
such effort. In 'Setting Out', he tells us that

> Even love must pass through loneliness,
> the husbandman become again
> the Long Hunter . . .
> He can no longer be at home,
> he cannot return, unless he begin
> the circle that first will carry him away.[66]

There is something of Thoreau's walker in this husbandman, who
must go into 'the forest of the night, | the true wilderness' before

---

[65] I have used the text of 'Acquainted with the Night' in *Complete Poems of
Robert Frost: 1949* (New York: Henry Hall & Co., 1949). Roger Gilbert reads
'Acquainted with the Night' as a poem in which Frost 'represent[s] knowledge less
as discovery than as confirmation': 'A kind of detached neutrality, an impassive-
ness that can be achieved only from an "unearthly height," is the reward of the
speaker's acquaintance with the night' (*Walks in the World: Representation and
Experience in Modern American Poetry* (Princeton, NJ: Princeton University Press,
1991), 64, 65). Despite Gilbert's recognition of the speaker's 'labor' as 'wholly
negative', he asserts that what we are reading is nonetheless the attainment of a
species of wisdom, a conclusion I believe derives from Gilbert's implicit acceptance
of peripatetic theory. Gilbert does offer extensive readings of Frost, Stevens, Williams,
Roethke, Bishop, O'Hara, Snyder, Ammons, and Ashbery, potentially mapping out
the variety of uses of peripatetic in 20th-cent. American poetry. Interestingly, he
does not consider Wendell Berry, surely one of the most regular writers about/
through walking.
[66] Wendell Berry, 'Setting Out', in *Collected Poems* (San Francisco: North Point
Press, 1985), 248. Other quotations from Berry's poetry will be from this edition,
and will be cited in the text by title and page number.

he can effect his return, and we do not see him achieve that return
here. But in 'Returning', a pedestrian narrator relocates his home
after travel, walking up out of 'a dark valley' into 'morning light'

> until my head emerged,
> my shoulders were mantled with the light,
> and my whole body came up
> out of the darkness, and stood
> on the new shore of the day.
> Where I had come was home,
> for my own house stood white
> where the dark river wore the earth.
> The sheen of bounty was on the grass,
> and the spring of the year had come.   (252)

Returning out of the dark wilderness, the walker comes upon
himself reborn, a new day, his 'own house', and the fresh growth
of spring. If we understand walking also as husbandry and realize
what might happen to a walker into wilderness—that he might
share the fate of Frost's narrator in 'Acquainted'—then we understand that Berry is telling us, once again, about the need to place
one's care in the land, to 'serve the earth', and about the potential
rewards of that placing ('The Morning's News', 110). And by
figuring placement as walking, he asserts that the return to localized,
agrarian life is not a radical conservative withdrawal into the past
but an action recovering the value of the past for present use, an
action that must move out and forward as well as in and back.

It is time, I think, to read such texts consciously, with a clear
understanding of all that it may mean to walk out and to return,
of where and how peripatetic appeared and of how it functions in
literature. To ignore such a rich and broadly significant mode
limits our understanding, not just of literature, but of life as those
of us in technologically developed areas of the world live it, and
limits also our ability to respond to that kind of life and to its
conflicts of value.

Select Bibliography

ABRAMS, M. H., *Natural Supernaturalism: Tradition and Revolution in Romantic Literature* (New York: Norton, 1971).

—— 'Structure and Style in the Greater Romantic Lyric', in Harold Bloom *et al.* (ed.), *From Sensibility to Romanticism* (New York: Oxford University Press, 1965).

ALDCROFT, D. H., and DYOS, H. J., *British Transport* (Leicester: Leicester University Press, 1969).

ALEXANDER, MEENA, *Women in Romanticism: Mary Wollstonecraft, Dorothy Wordsworth and Mary Shelley* (Savage, Md.: Barnes & Noble, 1989).

ARNOLD, MATTHEW, *English Literature and Irish Politics*, ed. R. H. Super (Ann Arbor: University of Michigan Press, 1973).

—— *Matthew Arnold*, ed. Miriam Allott and Robert H. Super (Oxford and New York: Oxford University Press, 1986).

AUSTEN, JANE, *Emma*, ed. Ronald Blythe (Harmondsworth: Penguin, 1966).

—— *Northanger Abbey*, in *The Novels of Jane Austen*, ed. R. W. Chapman, vol. v (Oxford and New York: Oxford University Press, 1969).

—— *Pride and Prejudice*, in *The Novels of Jane Austen*, ed. R. W. Chapman, vol. ii (Oxford and New York: Oxford University Press, 1965).

BACON, FRANCIS, 'Of Travaile', in *The Essayes or Counsels, Civill and Morall*, ed. Michael Kiernan (Cambridge, Mass.: Harvard University Press, 1985).

BAGWELL, PHILIP S., *The Transport Revolution from 1770* (London: B. T. Batsford, 1974).

BARRELL, JOHN, *The Idea of Landscape and the Sense of Place, 1730–1840* (Cambridge: Cambridge University Press, 1972).

—— *Poetry, Language and Politics* (New York: Manchester University Press, 1988).

—— and BULL, JOHN, ed., *A Book of English Pastoral Verse* (New York: Oxford University Press, 1975).

BARRETT BROWNING, ELIZABETH, *Aurora Leigh and Other Poems*, introd. Cora Kaplan (London: The Women's Press, 1978).

BARTA, PETER I., 'The Structural and Thematic Function of Walking in the Modernist European Urban Novel', *DAI* 48/02A (1986), 384.

BAYNE-POWELL, ROSAMOND, *Travellers in Eighteenth-Century England* (London: John Murray, 1951).

BENJAMIN, WALTER, *Charles Baudelaire: A Lyric Poet in the Era of High Capitalism*, trans. Harry Zohn (London: New Left Books, 1973).

BERMINGHAM, ANN, *Landscape and Ideology: The English Rustic Tradition, 1740–1860* (Berkeley: University of California Press, 1986).

BERRY, WENDELL, *Collected Poems* (San Francisco: North Point Press, 1985).

BICKNELL, PETER, and WOOF, ROBERT, *The Discovery of the Lake District, 1750–1810: A Context for Wordsworth* (Grasmere: Trustees of Dove Cottage, 1982).

BLEYLE, PATRICIA EDWARDS, 'Heavenly Gait', *Ms.* (July 1988), 24–5.

BROMLEY, WILLIAM, *Remarks made in Travels through France and Italy* (London: Thomas Basset, 1693).

BROMWICH, DAVID, 'The Egotistical Sublime: Wordsworth and Rousseau', in *Hazlitt: The Mind of a Critic* (Oxford and New York: Oxford University Press, 1983).

BROUGHTON, LESLIE NATHAN, *The Theocritean Element in the Works of William Wordsworth* (n.p.: Halle, 1920).

BUNYAN, JOHN, *The Pilgrim's Progress*, ed. Roger Sharrock (Harmondsworth: Penguin, 1965).

BURROUGHS, JOHN, 'The Exhilarations of the Road', in *The Writings of John Burroughs*, vol. ii (Boston, Mass. and New York: Houghton Mifflin, 1875), 27–45.

BUSHNELL, NELSON S., *A Walk after John Keats* (New York: Farrar & Rinehart, 1936).

CANTOR, PAUL A., *Creature and Creator: Myth-Making and English Romanticism* (Cambridge: Cambridge University Press, 1984).

CARNOCHAN, W. B., *Confinement and Flight: An Essay on English Literature of the Eighteenth Century* (Berkeley: University of California Press, 1977).

CASAGRANDE, PETER, *Unity in Hardy's Novels: 'Repetitive Symmetries'* (Lawrence, Kan.: The Regents Press of Kansas, 1982).

CAVALIERO, GLEN, *The Rural Tradition in the English Novel, 1900–1939* (Plymouth: The Bowering Press, 1977).

CHALKER, JOHN, *The English Georgic: A Study in the Development of a Form* (London: Routledge & Kegan Paul, 1969).

CHANDLER, JAMES K., *Wordsworth's Second Nature: A Study of the Poetry and Politics* (Chicago and London: University of Chicago Press, 1984).

CLARE, JOHN, *John Clare*, ed. Eric Robinson and David Powell (Oxford and New York: Oxford University Press, 1984).

——*John Clare: Selected Poetry and Prose*, ed. Merryn and Raymond Williams (London and New York: Methuen, 1986).

CLARK, THOMAS A., *In Praise of Walking* (n.p.: Cairn Gallery, 1988).

COHEN, JON S., and WEITZMAN, MARTIN L., 'Enclosures and Depopulation: A Marxian Analysis', in William N. Parker and Eric L. Jones (ed.),

European Peasants and their Markets: Essays in Agrarian Economic History (Princeton, NJ: Princeton University Press, 1975).

COLLINS, PHILIP, ed., *Dickens: Interviews and Recollections,* 2 vols. (Totowa, NJ: Barnes & Noble, 1981).

CONGLETON, J. E., *Theories of Pastoral Poetry in England, 1684–1798* (Gainesville: University of Florida Press, 1952).

CORYAT[E], THOMAS, *Coryat's Crudities: Hastily gobled up in five Moneths travells in France, Italy, etc.,* 2 vols. (Glasgow: James MacLehose & Sons, 1905).

COWPER, WILLIAM, *The Task,* in *The Poetical Works of William Cowper,* ed. William Benham, Globe Edition (London: Macmillan, 1908).

COX, EDWARD GODFREY, *A Reference Guide to the Literature of Travel,* vol. i (Seattle: University of Washington Press, 1935).

CUMMINGS, JOHN, *Runners and Walkers: A Nineteenth-Century Sports Chronicle* (Chicago: Regnery Gateway, 1981).

DAHLMAN, CARL J., *The Open Field System and Beyond* (Cambridge: Cambridge University Press, 1980).

DAVID, DEIRDRE, *Fictions of Resolution in Three Victorian Novels: 'North and South', 'Our Mutual Friend' and 'Daniel Deronda'* (New York: Columbia University Press, 1981).

DEFOE, DANIEL, *The Life and Strange Surprizing Adventures of Robinson Crusoe of York, Mariner, and The Farther Adventures of Robinson Crusoe,* 3 vols. (Oxford: Basil Blackwell, 1927).

DE QUINCEY, THOMAS, *Recollections of the Lakes and the Lake Poets,* ed. David Wright (Harmondsworth: Penguin, 1970).

—— 'Travelling in England in the Old Days', in *The Collected Writings of Thomas De Quincey,* ed. David Masson (London: A. & C. Black, 1896).

DICKENS, CHARLES, *The Old Curiosity Shop,* ed. Angus Easson, introd. Malcolm Andrews (Harmondsworth: Penguin, 1972).

—— *The Uncommercial Traveller* (London and New York: Chapman & Hall, and Charles Scribner's Sons, 1898).

DRUMMOND, WILLIAM, *Ben Jonson's Conversations with William Drummond of Hawthornden,* ed. R. F. Patterson (London: Blackie & Son, 1924).

DURLING, DWIGHT L., *Georgic Tradition in English Poetry* (New York: Columbia University Press, 1935).

Edinburgh: The Grand Panorama of Edinburgh as seen in a Walk round the Calton Hill in 1847 (1847; repr. Edinburgh: Paul Harris Publishing, 1982).

ELDER, JOHN, *Imagining the Earth: Poetry and the Vision of Nature* (Urbana and Chicago: University of Illinois Press, 1985).

ELIOT, GEORGE, *Adam Bede,* ed. John Paterson (Boston, Mass.: Houghton Mifflin, 1968).

—— *Felix Holt, the Radical*, ed. Fred C. Thomson (Oxford: Clarendon Press, 1980).

EMERSON, RALPH WALDO, *Selected Writings of Emerson*, ed. Donald McQuade (New York: Modern Library, 1981).

Farther Excursions of the Observant Pedestrian (London: R. Dutton, 1801).

FEINGOLD, RICHARD, *Nature and Society: Later Eighteenth-Century Uses of the Pastoral and Georgic* (New Brunswick, NJ: Rutgers University Press, 1978).

FERGUSON, FRANCES, 'Historicism, Deconstruction, and Wordsworth', *Diacritics* 17/4 (Winter 1987), 32–43.

FRANTZ, R. W., *The English Traveller and the Movement of Ideas*, University Studies, vol. 32 (Lincoln: University of Nebraska Press, 1934).

FROST, ROBERT, *Complete Poems of Robert Frost: 1949* (New York: Henry Hall & Co., 1949).

FUSSELL, PAUL, JR., 'Patrick Brydone: The Eighteenth-Century Traveler as Representative Man', in Warner G. Rice (ed.), *Literature as a Mode of Travel* (New York: New York Public Library, 1963).

GALPERIN, WILLIAM H., *Revision and Authority in Wordsworth: The Interpretation of a Career* (Philadelphia: University of Pennsylvania Press, 1989).

GASKELL, ELIZABETH, *Mary Barton*, ed. Edgar Wright (Oxford and New York: Oxford University Press, 1987).

GATRELL, SIMON, 'Travelling Man', in Patricia Clements and Juliet Grindle (ed.), *The Poetry of Thomas Hardy* (n.p.: Vision, 1980), 155–71.

GAY, JOHN, *Trivia; or, the Art of Walking the Streets of London*, introd. W. H. Williams (London: Daniel O'Connor, 1922).

GILBERT, ROGER, *Walks in the World: Representation and Experience in Modern American Poetry* (Princeton, NJ: Princeton University Press, 1991).

GILBERT, SANDRA M., and GUBAR, SUSAN, *The Madwoman in the Attic* (New Haven, Conn. and London: Yale University Press, 1979).

GILL, STEPHEN, *Wordsworth: A Life* (Oxford: Clarendon Press, 1989).

GILPIN, WILLIAM, *Three Essays: On Picturesque Beauty; on Picturesque Travel; and on Sketching Landscape: To which is added a poem, On Landscape Painting* (London: R. Blamire, 1792).

GISBORNE, THOMAS, *Walks in a Forest: or, Poems Descriptive of Scenery and Incidents Characteristic of a Forest at Different Seasons of the Year*, 9th edn., corrected (London: T. Cadell & W. Davies, 1814).

GOLDMARK, PAULINE, and HOPKINS, MARY, *The Gypsy Trail: An Anthology for Campers*, 2nd edn. (Garden City, New York: Doubleday, Doran & Co., 1930).

GRAHAM, STEPHEN, *The Gentle Art of Tramping* (New York: D. Appleton & Co., 1926).

GRAY, HOWARD LEVI, *English Field Systems* (Cambridge, Mass.: Harvard University Press, 1915).

GROSART, ALEXANDER B., *The Prose Works of William Wordsworth*, vol. iii (London: Edward Moxon, Son, & Co., 1876).

GROVE, NOEL, 'A Tunnel Through Time: The Appalachian Trail', *National Geographic*, 171 (1987), 216–43.

GURR, ANDREW, *The Shakespearean Stage, 1574–1642* (Cambridge: Cambridge University Press, 1980).

HALL, TOM S., *Walking Tours in Scotland: Thirty Itineraries with Maps* (Edinburgh and London: The Moroy Press, 1935).

HARDY, THOMAS, *The Return of the Native*, ed. George Woodcock (Harmondsworth: Penguin, 1978).

—— *Tess of the D'Urbervilles*, ed. David Skilton (Harmondsworth: Penguin, 1978).

—— *The Variorum Edition of the Complete Poems of Thomas Hardy*, ed. James Gibson (New York: Macmillan, 1978).

HARTMAN, GEOFFREY H., *Wordsworth's Poetry, 1787–1814* (Cambridge, Mass. and London: Harvard University Press, 1987).

HARTMANN, CYRIL HUGHES, *The Story of the Roads* (London: George Routledge & Sons, 1927).

HARVEY, ELIZABETH D., 'Speaking Without Bounds: The Extra-Vagant Impulse in Thoreau's "Walking" ', in *The Dialectic of Discovery: Essays on the Teaching and Interpretation of Literature* (Lexington, Ky.: French Forum, 1984), 178–89.

HAULTAIN, ARNOLD, *Of Walks and Walking Tours: An Attempt to Find a Philosophy and a Creed* (London: T. Werner Laurie, 1914).

HAVENS, RAYMOND DEXTER, *The Mind of a Poet*, 2 vols. (Baltimore: The Johns Hopkins Press, 1941).

HAZLITT, WILLIAM, 'My First Acquaintance with Poets' and 'On Going a Journey', in *The Complete Works of William Hazlitt*, ed. P. P. Howe, vol. viii (London and Toronto: J. M. Dent & Sons, 1931), 106–22, 181–9.

HEINZELMAN, KURT, *The Economics of the Imagination* (Amherst: University of Massachusetts Press, 1980).

—— ' "Crossing the Wye"—Or, Why Value Landscape?', *The Maine Scholar*, 1 (1988), 171–91.

—— 'The Cult of Domesticity: Dorothy and William Wordsworth at Grasmere', in Anne Mellor (ed.), *Romanticism and Feminism* (Bloomington: Indiana University Press, 1987).

—— 'Self-Interest and the Politics of Composition in Keats's *Isabella*', *ELH* 55 (1988), 159–93.

HOLLIDAY, ROBERT CORTES, *Walking-Stick Papers* (New York: George H. Doran Co., 1918).

Honan, Park, *Matthew Arnold* (New York: McGraw-Hill, 1981).

Hoskins, W. G., *The Making of the English Landscape* (Harmondsworth: Penguin, 1955).

Howell, James, *Instructions and Directions for Forren Travell* ... (London: Humphrey Mosley, 1650).

Hudson, W. H., *Afoot in England* (Oxford and New York: Oxford University Press, 1982).

Hughson, David, *Walks through London, Including Westminster and the Borough of Southwark ... forming a complete guide to the British Metropolis*, 2 vols. (London: Sherwood, Neely & Jones, 1817).

Jameson, Fredric, *The Political Unconscious: Narrative as a Socially Symbolic Act* (Ithaca, NY: Cornell University Press, 1981).

Johnson, Edgar, *Charles Dickens: His Tragedy and Triumph*, 2 vols. (London: Victor Gollancz, 1953).

Johnson, Samuel, *Rasselas, Poems, and Selected Prose*, 3rd edn. enlarged, ed. Bertrand H. Bronson (New York: Holt, Rinehart & Winston, 1958).

—— and Boswell, James, *Journey to the Western Islands of Scotland and Journal of a Tour to the Hebrides with Samuel Johnson, L.L.D*, ed. R. W. Chapman (Oxford: Oxford University Press, 1924).

Johnston, Kenneth, *Wordsworth and The Recluse* (New Haven, Conn. and London: Yale University Press, 1984).

Joyce, James, *Dubliners* (Harmondsworth: Penguin, 1967).

Jusserand, J. J., *English Wayfaring Life in the Middle Ages* (London: T. Fisher Unwin, 1888).

Kermode, Frank, *English Pastoral Poetry: From the Beginnings to Marvell* (London: George G. Harrap & Co., 1952).

Kroeber, Karl, *Romantic Landscape Vision: Constable and Wordsworth* (Madison: University of Wisconsin Press, 1975).

Lambarde, William, *A Perambulation of Kent: Containing the Description, Hystorie, and Customes of that Shire*, 3rd edn. (London: R. Hodgkinsonne, 1640).

Lambert, R. S., *Grand Tour: A Journey in the Tracks of the Age of Aristocracy* (London: Faber & Faber, 1935).

Langbauer, Laurie, 'Dickens's Streetwalkers: Women and the Form of Romance', *ELH* 53 (1986), 411–31.

—— *Women and Romance: The Consolations of Gender in the English Novel* (Ithaca, NY and London: Cornell University Press, 1990).

Larson, Cheri, 'Dickens' Twisted Heroine: A Study of Oliver's Role as a Female', Unpublished paper delivered at *Dickens and Others*, 21–23 Feb. 1986, at the University of California–Santa Barbara.

Levinson, Marjorie, *Wordsworth's Great Period Poems: Four Essays* (Cambridge: Cambridge University Press, 1986).

LINDSEY, MAURICE, *The Eye is Delighted: Some Romantic Travellers in Scotland* (London: Frederick Muller, 1971).

LITTLEHALES, HENRY, ed., *Some Notes on the Road from London to Canterbury in the Middle Ages* (London: N. Trubner & Co., 1898).

LIU, ALAN, *Wordsworth: The Sense of History* (Stanford, Calif.: Stanford University Press, 1989).

LOW, ANTHONY, *The Georgic Revolution* (Princeton, NJ: Princeton University Press, 1985).

LUKACHER, NED, *Primal Scenes: Literature, Philosophy, Psychoanalysis* (Ithaca, NY and London: Cornell University Press, 1986).

LYON, JUDSON STANLEY, *The Excursion: A Study* (New Haven, Conn.: Yale University Press, 1950).

MACCANNELL, DEAN, *The Tourist: A New Theory of the Leisure Class* (New York: Schocken, 1976).

MCCRACKEN, DAVID, *Wordsworth and The Lake District* (Oxford and New York: Oxford University Press, 1985).

MCGANN, JEROME J., *The Romantic Ideology: A Critical Investigation* (Chicago and London: University of Chicago Press, 1983).

MACLEAN, KENNETH, *Agrarian Age: A Background for Wordsworth* (New Haven, Conn.: Yale University Press, 1950).

MAITLAND, FREDERIC WILLIAM, *The Life and Letters of Leslie Stephen* (London: Duckworth & Co., [n.d.]).

MALLET, DAVID, *The Excursion*, in *The Works of David Mallet Esq. In Three Volumes. A New Edition Corrected* (London: A. Millar & P. Vaillant, 1759).

MARPLES, MORRIS, *Shanks's Pony: A Study of Walking* (London: J. M. Dent & Sons, 1959).

MARX, LEO, *The Machine in the Garden: Technology and the Pastoral Ideal in America* (New York: Oxford University Press, 1964).

MEREDITH, GEORGE, *The Egoist*, ed. George Woodcock (Harmondsworth: Penguin, 1968).

METZGER, LORE, *One Foot in Eden: Modes of Pastoral in Romantic Poetry* (Chapel Hill and London: University of North Carolina Press, 1976).

MINGAY, G. E., *The Victorian Countryside*, 2 vols. (London and Boston, Mass.: Routledge & Kegan Paul, 1981).

MILLGATE, MICHAEL, *Thomas Hardy* (Oxford and New York: Oxford University Press, 1985).

MITCHELL, EDWIN VALENTINE, *The Pleasures of Walking* (New York: The Vanguard Press, 1979).

MOERS, ELLEN, '*Bleak House*: The Agitating Women', *The Dickensian*, 69/1 (Jan. 1973), 13–24.

—— *Literary Women* (New York: Oxford University Press, 1977).

MOLDENHAUER, JOSEPH, 'Walden and Wordsworth's Guide to the English Lake District', *Studies in the American Renaissance* (1990), 261–92.

MORITZ, CARL PHILIP, *Journeys of a German in England*, trans. Reginald Nettel (London: England, 1983).

MURDOCH, JOHN, 'The Landscape of Labor: Transformations of the Georgic', in Kenneth R. Johnston *et al.* (ed.), *Romantic Revolutions: Criticism and Theory* (Bloomington: Indiana University Press, 1990).

NEWSOM, ROBERT, *Dickens on the Romantic Side of Familiar Things* (New York: Columbia University Press, 1977).

NUGENT, THOMAS, *The Grand Tour; Or, A Journey through the Netherlands, Germany, Italy and France*, 3rd edn., 4 vols. (London: J. Rivington & Sons *et al.*, 1778).

The Observant Pedestrian; or, Traits of the Heart: In a Solitary Tour from Cærnarvon to London, in Two Volumes, By 'The Author of The Mystic Cottager' (London: William Lane, 1795).

The Observant Pedestrian Mounted; or a Donkey Tour to Brighton. A Comic Sentimental Novel in Three Volumes (London: W. Simpkin & R. Marshal, 1815).

OLMSTEAD, FREDERICK LAW, *Walks and Talks of an American Farmer in England* (New York: George P. Putnam, 1852).

The Oxford English Dictionary, 2nd edn. (Oxford: Oxford University Press, 1989).

PATTERSON, ANNABEL, *Pastoral and Ideology: Virgil to Valéry* (Berkeley and Los Angeles: University of California Press, 1987).

—— 'Wordsworth's Georgic: Genre and Structure in *The Excursion*', *Wordsworth Circle*, 9 (1978), 145–54.

PLUMPTRE, JAMES, *The Lakers: A Comic Opera in Three Acts* (London: n.p., 1798).

POGGIOLI, RENATO, *The Oaten Flute: Essays on Pastoral Poetry and the Pastoral Ideal* (Cambridge, Mass.: Harvard University Press, 1975).

ROBINSON, JEFFREY, *The Walk: Notes on a Romantic Image* (Norman: University of Oklahoma Press, 1989).

ROPPEN, GEORG, and SOMMER, RICHARD, *Strangers and Pilgrims: An Essay on the Metaphor of Journey* (New York: Humanities Press, 1964).

ROSENMEYER, THOMAS G., *The Green Cabinet: Theocritus and the European Pastoral Lyric* (Berkeley: University of California Press, 1969).

RØSTVIG, MAREN-SOFIE, *The Happy Man: Studies in the Metamorphoses of a Classical Ideal*, Oslo Studies in English, 27 (Oslo: Akademisk Forlag, 1954–8).

ROUSSEAU, JEAN-JACQUES, *The Reveries of the Solitary Walker*, trans. Charles E. Butterworth (New York: Harper Colophon, 1979).

RUBINSTEIN, DAVID, and SPEAKMAN, COLIN, *Leisure, Transport and the*

Countryside, Fabian Research Series, 277 (London: Fabian Society, 1969).

RUSKIN, JOHN, *Modern Painters* (Chicago and New York: Belford Clarke & Co., [n.d.]).

SAVAGE, RICHARD, *The Wanderer,* in *The Poetical Works of Richard Savage,* ed. Clarence Tracy (Cambridge: Cambridge University Press, 1962).

SIDGWICK, A. H., *Walking Essays* (London: Edward Arnold, 1912).

SIMPSON, DAVID, *Wordsworth and the Figurings of the Real* (Atlantic Highlands: Humanities Press, 1982).

—— *Wordsworth's Historical Imagination: The Poetry of Displacement* (New York and London: Methuen, 1987).

SMITH, CHARLOTTE TURNER, *Rambles Farther: A Continuation of Rural Walks: In Dialogues. Intended for the Use of Young Persons* (Dublin: P. Wogan *et al.,* 1796).

SMITH, LORRIE, ' "Walking" from England to America: Re-Viewing Thoreau's Romanticism', *New England Quarterly,* 59/2 (1985), 221–41.

STEPHEN, LESLIE, 'In Praise of Walking', in *Studies of a Biographer* (2nd ser.), vol. iii (London: Duckworth & Co., 1902), 254–85.

—— *Life of Henry Fawcett,* 3rd edn. (London: Smith, Elder, & Co., 1886).

—— *Some Early Impressions* (London: Hogarth Press, 1924).

STEVENSON, ROBERT LOUIS, 'Roads', in *Essays of Travel and in the Art of Writing,* Biographical Edition (New York: Charles Scribner's Sons, 1905), 98–107.

—— 'Walking Tours', in *Virginibus Puerisque,* Biographical Edition (New York: Charles Scribner's Sons, 1914), 232–47.

STOKSTAD, MARILYN, *Santiago de Compostela: In the Age of the Great Pilgrimages* (Norman: University of Oklahoma Press, 1978).

SUSSMAN, AARON, and GOODE, RUTH, *The Magic of Walking* (New York: Simon & Schuster, 1967).

SUTTON, MAX KEITH, 'Truth and the Pastor's Vision in George Crabbe, William Barnes and R. S. Thomas', in Richard F. Hardin (ed.), *Survivals of Pastoral* (Lawrence: University of Kansas Publications, 1979).

SWIFT, JONATHAN, *Gulliver's Travels,* ed. Robert A. Greenberg (New York: Norton, 1970).

TAPLIN, KIM, *The English Path* (Woodbridge, Suffolk: The Boydell Press, 1979).

TATE, W. E., *The English Village Community and the Enclosure Movements* (London: Victor Gollancz, 1967).

TAYLOR, JOHN, *The Pennyles Pilgrimage, or The Money-lesse Perambulation of John Taylor, Alias the Kings Majesties Water-Poet* (London, 1623).

THELWALL, JOHN, *Ode to Science; John Gilpin's Ghost; Poems; The*

Trident of Albion, introd. Donald Reiman (repr. New York and London: Garland, 1978).

—— *The Peripatetic; or, Sketches of the Heart, of Nature and Society; in a series of Politico-sentimental Journals, in verse and prose, of the Eccentric Excursions of Sylvanus Theophrastus; supposed to be written by himself,* introd. Donald Reiman (1793; repr. New York and London: Garland, 1978).

THOMSON, JAMES, *The Seasons and The Castle of Indolence,* ed. James Sambrook (Oxford: Clarendon Press, 1972).

THOMPSON, FLORA, *Lark Rise to Candleford: A Trilogy* (London and New York: Oxford University Press, 1945).

THOREAU, HENRY DAVID, 'Walking', in *The Writings of Henry David Thoreau,* vol. v (Boston, Mass. and New York: Houghton Mifflin, 1906), 205–48.

TRAHERNE, THOMAS, *Poems of Felicity,* ed. H. I. Bell (Oxford: Clarendon Press, 1910).

TRENT, GEORGE D., ed., *The Gentle Art of Walking* (New York: Arno Press/ Random House, 1971).

VAN DER KISTE, JOHN, *Queen Victoria's Children* (Gloucester: Alan Sutton, 1916).

VIRGIL, *The Georgics,* trans. L. P. Wilkinson (Harmondsworth: Penguin, 1982).

A Walk to Islington. With a Description of New Tunbridge-Wells and Sadler's Music House. By the Author of the Poet's Rambles after Riches (London, 1701).

WEBB, SIDNEY and BEATRICE, *The Story of the King's Highway* (1913; repr. London: Frank Cass & Co., 1963).

WHITTLE, TYLER, *Victoria and Albert at Home* (London: Routledge & Kegan Paul, 1980).

WILBERFORCE, WILLIAM, *Journey to the Lake District from Cambridge, 1779* (Stocksfield: Oriel Press, 1983).

WILLIAMS, RAYMOND, *The Country and the City* (London: Chatto & Windus, 1973).

—— *Culture and Society, 1780–1950* (New York: Columbia University Press, 1983).

WINCHELL, ALEXANDER, *Walks and Talks in the Geological Field* (New York: Chautauqua Press, 1886).

WORDSWORTH, DOROTHY, *Journals of Dorothy Wordsworth,* ed. Mary Moorman, 2nd edn. (Oxford: Oxford University Press, 1971).

WORDSWORTH, JONATHAN, *The Music of Humanity* (London: Thomas Nelson & Sons, 1969).

WORDSWORTH, WILLIAM, *Guide to the Lakes,* ed. Ernest de Selincourt (1906; repr. Oxford: Oxford University Press, 1970).

WORDSWORTH, WILLIAM, *The Poetical Works of William Wordsworth*, ed. Ernest de Selincourt and Helen Darbishire, vol. v (Oxford: Clarendon Press, 1949).

—— *The Prelude, 1799, 1805, 1850*, ed. Jonathan Wordsworth, M. H. Abrams, and Stephen Gill (New York and London: Norton, 1979).

—— *The Ruined Cottage and The Pedlar*, ed. James Butler (Ithaca, NY: Cornell University Press, 1979).

—— *The Salisbury Plain Poems of William Wordsworth*, ed. Stephen Gill (Ithaca, NY: Cornell University Press, 1975).

—— *William Wordsworth*, ed. Stephen Gill (Oxford and New York: Oxford University Press, 1984).

—— and Wordsworth, Dorothy, *The Letters of William and Dorothy Wordsworth: The Early Years*, ed. Ernest de Selincourt, 2nd edn. rev. Chester L. Shaver, vol. i (Oxford: Clarendon Press, 1967).

—— *The Letters of William and Dorothy Wordsworth: The Later Years. Part III. 1835–1839*, ed. Ernest de Selincourt, 2nd edn. rev. Alan G. Hill, vol. vi (Oxford: Clarendon Press, 1982).

YOUNGSON, A. J. *Beyond the Highland Line: Three Journals of Travel in Eighteenth Century Scotland* (London: Collins, 1974).

Index